The Plugged-In Profess

Chandos
Social Media Series

Series Editors: Geoff Walton and Woody Evans
(email: *g.l.walton@staffs.ac.uk* and *kdevans@gmail.com*)

This series of books is aimed at practitioners and academics involved in using social media in all its forms and in any context. This includes information professionals, academics, librarians and managers, and leaders in business. Social media can enhance services, build communication channels, and create competitive advantage. The impact of these new media and decisions that surround their use in business can no longer be ignored. The delivery of education, privacy issues, logistics, political activism and research rounds out the series' coverage. As a resource to complement the understanding of issues relating to other areas of information science, teaching and related areas, books in this series respond with practical applications. If you would like a full listing of current and forthcoming titles, please visit our website *www.chandospublishing.com* or email *wp@woodheadpublishing.com* or telephone +44 (0) 1223 499140.

New authors: we are always pleased to receive ideas for new titles; if you would like to write a book for Chandos in the area of social media, please contact Jonathan Davis, Commissioning Editor, on *jonathan.davis@chandospublishing.com* or telephone +44 (0) 1993 848726.

Bulk orders: some organisations buy a number of copies of our books. If you are interested in doing this, we would be pleased to discuss a discount. Please email *wp@woodheadpublishing.com* or telephone +44 (0) 1223 499140.

The Plugged-In Professor

Tips and techniques for teaching with social media

EDITED BY
SHARMILA P. FERRIS
AND
HILARY A. WILDER

CP
CHANDOS PUBLISHING

Oxford Cambridge New Delhi

Chandos Publishing
Hexagon House
Avenue 4
Station Lane
Witney
Oxford OX28 4BN
UK
Tel: +44(0) 1993 848726
Email: *info@chandospublishing.com*
www.chandospublishing.com
www.chandospublishingonline.com

Chandos Publishing is an imprint of Woodhead Publishing Limited

Woodhead Publishing Limited
80 High Street
Sawston
Cambridge CB22 3HJ
UK
Tel: +44(0) 1223 499140
Fax: +44(0) 1223 832819
www.woodheadpublishing.com

First published in 2013

ISBN: 978-1-84334-694-4 (print)
ISBN: 978-1-78063-342-8 (online)

Chandos Social Media Series ISSN: 2050-6813 (print) and ISSN: 2050-6821 (online)

British Library Cataloguing-in-Publication Data.
A catalogue record for this book is available from the British Library.

Project management by Neil Shuttlewood Associates, Gt Yarmouth, Norfolk, UK
Printed in the UK and USA

Printed and bound in the UK by 4edge Ltd, Hockley, Essex.

Contents

List of tables and figure

Tables

Figure

List of abbreviations

AACE	Association for the Advancement of Computing in Education
AASL	American Association of School Librarians
ACLS	Advanced Cardiac Life Support
ACMC	Asynchronous Computer Mediated Communication
ACRL	Association of College and Research Libraries
ACTFL	American Council on the Teaching of Foreign Languages
ATP	Adenosine TriPhosphate
CMC	Computer Mediated Communication
DM	Direct Message
FL	Foreign Language
GTA	Graduate Teaching Assistant
HTML	HyperText Markup Language
ICT	Information and Communication Technology
IMTE	Integrated Media and Technology Education
ISP	Internet Service Provider
ISTE	International Society for Technology in Education
LGBTQ	Lesbian, Gay, Bisexual, Transgender, and Queer/Questioning
LMS	Learning Management System
RT	ReTweet
SALG	Student Assessment of Learning Gains
SLO	Student Learning Outcome
SM	Social Media
TA	Teaching Assistant
TESL	Teachers of English as a Second Language

Acknowledgments

We'd like first and foremost to acknowledge the unwavering support and encouragement from our husbands, Brian Lubbert and Michael Merritt, who never once grumbled about the long phone calls or many takeout Indian dinners.

We are grateful for Jean M. Stewart's help with the Index. Her patience and attention to detail were invaluable.

We appreciate William Paterson University's commitment to research. The university's continued emphasis on faculty scholarship was an excellent motivator when the pressures of teaching and service threatened to shipwreck this project.

We'd like to thank Dr. Glyn Jones and our editors and support staff at Chandos, with special thanks to Jonathan Davis. Our editors at Chandos always provided prompt responses and clear guidance, as did Neil Shuttlewood, our project manager.

Last, but far from least, we appreciate the hard work and dedication to teaching of all those who submitted essays for consideration in this book. We were impressed with the range and scope used for social media in the class, and regret that there were many submissions we could not include.

Preface

We write this Preface using tools that were conjecture mere decades ago, and inconceivable just centuries ago. Reed, chalk, and quill were used for millennia; today information is routinely recorded, stored, and retrieved digitally. Although we have lived through the development of electronic media and witnessed first-hand the growth of the World Wide Web, social media were not on our radar even in the 1980s or early 1990s. As new as computer and digital technologies are, social media are even newer! (For example, MySpace and Delicious were launched in 2003, Facebook and Flickr in 2004, Twitter in 2006, and Tumblr in 2007.) Social media may be new to us, but today's classrooms are filled with a generation of students to whom social media are a way of life – and who cannot envisage a world before Internet and digital technologies. Social media usage has spread to encompass adults as well as youth – and educators are increasingly considering social media as teaching tools, both in order to more effectively reach students, and because these technologies are being used more and more in the workplaces our students will be entering. One problem that often develops with our use of social media in the classroom is that the technology, rather than the pedagogy, can become the focus of the teaching. This book puts pedagogy first, considering ways in which underlying instructional purpose can guide our use of social media.

Social media and education

Before we proceed, we should define our use of the term "social media" in this book, since it has become such a popular buzzword. Social networking is the most public face of social media; in a social network such as Facebook users deepen connections by sharing thoughts, photos, links of interest, etc., and develop relationships by creating cohorts of "friends" who can then become "friend of a friend". But in this book we do not limit our understanding of social media to social networking. With Kaplan and

Haenlein (2010), we define social media as any medium enabling connectivity and interaction among users and communities. So we include wikis, blogging. and Web conferencing in our understanding of social media. In our opinion, wikis are the oldest social media (Ward Cunningham launched his wiki in 1995, with the iconic Wikipedia introduced in 2001) and perhaps have the longest history of educational application. We also include Web conferencing and blogging as electronic media that allow users to interact easily, offer quick feedback to communication, and collaborate effortlessly.

Having defined social media, we should consider the question of whether social media have a place in education. The fundamental question indeed is whether social media are a relevant and useful tool for learning. The importance of social media in our lives is indisputable, and undeniably there is a growing interest among educators in the potentials of social media in the classroom. At the same time, social media are evolving so rapidly that it is a challenge to determine what works best to promote which specific learning goals. It is our opinion that while social media pose challenges for teaching and learning, they also offer opportunities that justify exploration of their affordances. Social media can expand opportunities across a wide range of higher order learning: communication, collaboration, research, information literacy, critical thinking, and creativity, among others. Social media have the potential to help our students learn at many levels.

This is a potential not lightly dismissed, given the importance of social media in the lives of youth today. While estimates of time spent using social media vary, estimated use is nothing less than astounding. Social media account for 22.5 percent of the time that Americans spend online, compared to just 7.6 percent for e-mail (Nielsen, 2011). An illustrative example of the importance of social media can be seen in the use of a leading social medium, Facebook. Its use has grown from 175 million active users in January 2009 to 350 million users in 2011 (Socialbakers, 2012a) to 901 million in July 2012 (Facebook's S-1 filings with SEC at *http://en.wikipedia.org/wiki/Social_media#cite_note-19*). At the same time, every minute, ten hours of content were uploaded to the video-sharing platform YouTube (Socialbakers, 2012a). Student use of social media supports this data. While it is difficult to estimate the time students spend in social networking, one recent empirical study (Junco, 2012) found that the average time American students spent on Facebook was 106 minutes per day, although many spent more. In Western Europe most countries reached over 75 percent Internet penetration "with up to 99% of a population social networking" in Portugal (Socialbakers, 2012b). Asia has lower social media penetration, varying from above 50 percent (in Hong Kong, South Korea, Singapore, and Taiwan) to 3 percent in India (Richards, 2012). But social media growth in India is one of the fastest, with 20 percent growth in the past six months (Socialbakers, 2012b). Even students in the developing world with little access to computers are mobile social media users. In Africa, for example, there is 65 percent mobile penetration and 50 percent of the population is younger than 20 (*http://www.oafrica.com/mobile/video-mobile-stats-for-africa-2012/*). Interestingly, 4.8 million people in the world (of the approximate world population of 6 billion people) own a mobile phone, while only 4.2 billion own a toothbrush (Infographics, 2012).

While the pervasiveness of social media offers significant opportunities for making learning more *attractive*, perhaps more important are the affordances offered by social media technologies for making learning more *effective*. In particular, these technologies have features that "afford" (Gibson, 1977) or support the human characteristics that facilitate learning. For example, we know that socio-collaborative instructional experiences can be used to promote deeper learning as students discuss/debate, collaborate/critique, and share with/listen to peers. Clearly, many of today's social media (e.g., wikis, virtual chats, Web conferences, or electronic discussions) can be used to afford these socio-collaborative learning experiences by providing anytime/anywhere access to shared ideas while at the same time saving participants' dialogue, affording reflection, and allowing consideration of decision-making processes. Other technologies, such as online tagging and social-bookmarking tools, afford the mental processes involved in collecting, labeling, organizing, and aggregating information and ideas found on that globally shared knowledge space we call the Web.

The educational potentials of social media, when considered in conjunction with students' attraction to social media, lead us to conclude that we should seize the opportunity and take advantage of the unique habits of our students. Careful and considered use of social media by educators becomes an important way to give larger meaning to technologies that are used primarily for social and entertainment purposes.

Instructional goals and social media

The fundamental issue regarding social media use by educators is careful and considered use. The rapid growth of technologies places them in a state of high interpretive flexibility (Brent, 2005) meaning that such tools are particularly amenable to shaping by educators. This makes a pedagogical focus to social media particularly meaningful and necessary today. We feel that clear and effective instructional purpose is essential in shaping social media technologies for educational use. We agree with Halverson (2011) that goals for learning are more important than the use of any individual technology in the classroom. Too often the technology overrides pedagogy, so we strongly endorse the use of student learning outcomes as an effective way to ensure that social media are used to *facilitate* pedagogy. Learning outcomes are formal statements that articulate the knowledge, skills, and/or understanding that students should be able to demonstrate after instruction, and why they need to achieve these competencies. Outcomes may be based on standards set by professional organizations (e.g., teaching standards) or educational consortia (e.g., American Association of Colleges and Universities, *www.aacu.org*), or governmental agencies (e.g., European Parliament's Framework for Key Competences for Lifelong Learning, *http://ec.europa.eu/dgs/education_culture/publ/pdf/ll-learning/keycomp_en.pdf*) or they may be set by the course instructor, who carefully designs educational activities to ensure that students meet overall course objectives by the end of the semester. By clearly focusing on instructional purpose before selecting and utilizing social media in the classroom, educators can ensure learning by knowing what they are doing with social media, why they are doing it, and what students are learning as a result.

Rationale for this book

This book was developed to provide a comprehensive resource for using social media and other new technologies to help college students meet discipline-specific and general education learning objectives. The book includes techniques and activities built around well-known social networking technologies like Facebook and YouTube, Delicious, Tumblr, and Twitter as well as online collaborative technologies such as Web conferencing, wikis, blogs, and some functions of LMS. With a practical focus and an easy to use format, the book shows educators how to apply techniques using social media technologies, and includes clear student learning objectives, step-by-step directions, observations and advice, and supplemental readings and resources.

We feel a book such as ours is needed because today's students are in truth a social media generation, however much of their time spent with social media is for social rather than educational purposes. As Ellaway and Tworek (2011) note, "exposure to media does not necessarily equate with generative, creative or constructive learning outcomes" (p. 325). In addition, and perhaps more importantly, utilizing social media in pedagogically thoughtful ways in our classrooms allows us to expose students to ways in which these technologies can be used to effectively develop their professional careers, further their personal goals, and empower them with lifelong skills. Thus we recommend social media to not only make student academic success more attainable to the instructor, but to also make student professional and personal success more likely.

The primary audience for this book will be educators in colleges and universities, but within education we reach a broad and inclusive audience. Because of the range and diversity of the chapters, the book is of interest to anyone wishing to develop teaching to more effectively reach students. This includes anyone in higher education, and also includes K–12 teachers, as the strategies and techniques in the book are easily adaptable to a school audience. The secondary audience for the book will be practitioners in industry, as many of the teaching activities can be modified for use in training.

This book can also prove useful to both novice and expert users of social media. Novice users will find complete directions to guide them through selection and use of social media in the classroom. More experienced users of social media can get ideas that are "transferrable" across social media technologies and can be adapted to different uses.

Other noteworthy features of the book: it is as applicable to the traditional classroom as to the online classroom; it is also both discipline specific and cross-disciplinary. Each social media technique will discuss discipline-specific applications, yet the book moves beyond traditional disciplines and boundaries. With contributions from authors from four continents and chapters addressing every academic discipline including the arts, business, education, humanities, sciences, and social sciences, this book has broad and crossover utility.

Structure and organization of the book

The book is divided into four broad parts organized around the key pedagogical competencies of writing, research, and information fluency;

communication and collaboration; critical and creative thinking; and integrative learning. Our overarching focus on pedagogy guiding the use of social media can be seen throughout the book.

Part 1 – Writing, research, and information fluency

The chapters in this section focus on pedagogical techniques which promote students' skill in locating, analyzing and evaluating, organizing and structuring information with the goal of producing a written paper or similar product.

In Chapter 1, "Writing for Wikipedia: co-constructing knowledge and writing for a public audience," Lori L. Britt discusses an assignment in which students use Wikipedia as a pedagogical tool to research topics, engage with the material, see connections, and articulate their findings in their own voice. Through these processes, students can move beyond instructor-defined knowledge and classroom-limited lecture and discussion to a recognition of knowledge as fluid, connected, and "alive". Writing and revising existing Wikipedia articles also enables students to communicate more effectively to a public audience.

In Chapter 2, "Organizing with Pinterest and Delicious," Melanie L. Buffington, describes how students can research and categorize resources (such as images, videos, or information from websites) using the social bookmarking sites Pinterest and Delicious. This allows students to create conceptual linkages, and see, refine, and share ideas. It also promotes the ability to plan and organize research, and to develop products such as papers, presentation, or art. An added benefit is the anytime/anywhere feature of such learning.

In Chapter 3, "Students' inadequate exposure to learning technology: overcoming the pedagogical challenge using wikis," Linzi J. Kemp describes how students with little exposure to learning technologies can easily be shown how to use a wiki to research and post information, evaluate and synthesize information, and write collaboratively. She uses a case study assignment (in which students report on a successful real-world leader) to encourage work in a social medium, supplemented by face-to-face group work. The resultant case study is "published" in the wiki. The project has real-world value in addition to realizing the learning potential of a wiki.

In Chapter 4, "Collecting and analyzing primary sources," Lisa M. Lane considers how social media (such as a class blog, wiki, discussion forum, or collaborative document) can provide a way for students to form their own collections of visual and textual primary sources, and to develop and hone theses. Disciplines that encourage the use of primary sources in the analysis and construction of arguments can benefit from the potential of the Web, and social media encourage interdependency and peer work in developing and refining supportable theses.

In Chapter 5, "Unraveling the research process: social bookmarking and collaborative learning," Caroline Sinkinson and Alison Hicks leverage the ability of social bookmarking to capture the social, collaborative, and participatory nature of research. They demonstrate how social bookmarking sites such as Diigo can help shift the focus from a final research product to the experience of inquiry, as well as repositioning research as active dialogue. They also enable students to work collaboratively, negotiate multiple streams of information, think critically about information, and draw connections and meaning from information to inform their contributions.

Part 2 – Communication and collaboration

Because of the importance of communication and collaboration across disciplines, this section is subdivided to allow for a more complete exploration of each of the broad instructional goals of communication and collaboration.

Part 2A – Communication, oral and written

Part 2A focuses on activities in which students select communication skills appropriate to the context, compose and revise written materials appropriate to the discipline, or compose and deliver oral messages appropriate to the intended audience. In essence they create audio, video, interactive, or text-based products based on the concepts and skills taught in the course, for use by peers or a larger audience.

In Chapter 6, "Using Wimba Voice Board to facilitate foreign language conversation courses," Silvia U. Baage shows how an asynchronous audio-based threaded discussion forum can be used to strengthen speaking and listening skills. Students can use the voice tool to create content in discussion threads. The discussion forum allows for peer-to-peer learning, as research and reflections about specific cultural topics in a target language are shared. This activity not only develops communication skills, it also promotes collaborative work and knowledge.

In Chapter 7, "Web conferencing and peer feedback," Kevin Garrison utilizes Web conferencing to facilitate the peer review and feedback process in a collaborative, virtual space. An online social medium can overcome the limitations of traditional peer workshops by allowing for greater interactivity among a larger number of students, while promoting revision, based on audience feedback. Additional benefits are the opportunities to develop digital communication skills, preparing students for success in workplaces that encourage collaboration.

In Chapter 8, "Learning through YouTube," J. Jacob Jenkins and Patrick J. Dillon use YouTube to promote exploration of an academic concept/theory through student presentation and peer critique. A popular social media site can engage students in an active learning process as they work in small groups to create an original short video that explicates or exemplifies a course concept/theory. The video is then presented to the class, and critiqued by the audience. Social media can thus be incorporated into action–inquiry pedagogy, allowing students to engage in open dialogue via collaborative knowledge construction.

In Chapter 9, "Wiki-workshopping: using Wikispaces for peer writing workshops," Hans C. Schmidt discusses the potential of Wikispaces to facilitate peer writing workshops. Wikis offer the opportunity for outside-class work for the processes of peer editing, reflection, and learning. Additional benefits of using a wiki for peer review include the freeing of in-class time, easy tracking of peer suggestions and revisions, and exposing students to the power of Web 2.0 technologies, which can help develop basic media literacy competencies.

Part 2B – Collaboration

Part 2B focuses on activities in which students work cooperatively, using collaboration, teamwork, and group presentation skills, to determine goals, develop plans, make ethical decisions, solve problems, and articulate ideas with individuals and groups, and, where appropriate, create audio, video, interactive, or text-based products based on the concepts and skills taught in the course.

In Chapter 10, "Using persistent wikis as a pedagogical resource," Evan D. Bradley avails of wikis' potential for collaborative learning. Wikis have a unique ability to build content incrementally across multiple courses, or over time periods beyond a single term. By participating in the creation, maintenance, preservation, and growth of such wikis, students can benefit from an accelerated learning curve and access to a strong content resource, instructors can benefit from evidence of student achievement, and both instructors and students can benefit from continuing contributions.

In Chapter 11, "Social media and public speaking: student-produced multimedia informative presentations," Paul E. Mabrey III and Juhong "Christie" Liu utilize social media to supplement face-to-face interactions as students create and present a group multimedia informative presentation focusing on a course concept, and teach other students an important communication concept reinforced by the production of digital exam questions. Combining face-to-face interactions with digital video develops students' ability to effectively convey course concepts in an interactive manner, as well as promote the peer review process.

In Chapter 12, "Collaborative presentations using Google Docs," Michael S. Mills discusses a project in which students produce a collaborative presentation using Google Docs. The synchronous editing capabilities of the social medium allows groups of students to create multiple parts of a presentation independently and then serve as peer reviewers and collaborate to synthesize material into a final form. Using Google Docs to create a presentation has the benefits of familiarizing students with online content creation and problem-solving tools, preparing them for writing in team-based scenarios and teaching them to harness user-friendly Web 2.0 tools and apply effective presentation design.

In Chapter 13, "Cooperative study blog," Amanda E. Waldo discusses an activity that uses student blog posts to identify and discuss key course concepts. Students individually post definitions, explanations, and analysis of a specific concept. The shared posts function not only as a resource for review and understanding, but allow students to think critically about how course material relates to larger course themes. This activity has the additional benefit that students can see the added value of a shared forum in study and exam preparation.

Part 3 – Critical thinking and creativity

Because of the importance of critical thinking across disciplines, this section is also subdivided to allow for a more complete exploration of each of the broad instructional goals.

Part 3A – Critical thinking

Part 3A focuses on activities in which students question, understand, explore, analyze, and synthesize concepts and skills taught in the course.

In Chapter 14, "Using Facebook to apply social learning theory," Michelle Kilburn describes an active learning exercise that frames social learning in a social networking medium. The activity allows students to understand and apply course theory in a real-world forum, and has the benefit of creating awareness of posting socially inappropriate materials, and of the impact of friends and other social associations in social networking sites. As students transition from the classroom to their careers, such awareness can be of real value.

In Chapter 15, "Technology as a tool to develop problem-solving skills in general chemistry," Madhu Mahalingam and Elisabeth Morlino scaffold electronic and traditional (face-to-face) learning to reinforce deeper learning. They utilize commonly available technology, such as online homework systems, online quizzes, and personal response systems in the classroom to build a knowledge base within the discipline. The level of problem solving is raised gradually to culminate in higher level learning in face-to-face group work. Scaffolding of technology and group work allows instructors to effectively develop students' problem-solving skills.

In Chapter 16, "Communicating experiential learning through an online portfolio in Tumblr," Aaron J. Moore uses Tumblr to document integrative learning by students performing experiential work (internships, co-ops, fieldwork). The social medium allows students to connect their academic coursework to their professional or field environment, while feedback from the instructor, and from other students, forms communal discourse. In requiring students to pull together their entire experiences inside and outside of the classroom and create a narrative that exhibits intellectual and professional development, this project has the benefit of serving as a resource for the student and an artifact for the instructor.

In Chapter 17, "The Biology Taboo Wiktionary: a tool for improving student comprehension of key terminology in introductory biology courses," Jeffrey T. Olimpo and Patricia A. Shields use an interactive in-class game supplemented by a course wiki to promote knowledge of terminology and understanding of foundational processes and concepts. The in-class game requires that students first define concepts in their own words, then individually upload definitions to a course wiktionary. The benefits of these activities are not only the development of a deeper understanding of connections and a foundational understanding of the discipline, but also the creation of an online study resource.

Part 3B – Creativity

Part 3B focuses on activities in which students use concepts and skills taught in the course to generate new and unique ideas, make connections, and become more comfortable with unorthodox methods.

In Chapter 18, "Mobile digital storytelling in the second language classroom," Apostolos Koutropoulos, David Hattem, and Ronda Zelezny-Green harness the power of mobile digital video technologies to help students learn about a target culture, as well as develop new vocabulary and new grammatical structures. The assignment calls for students to prepare and tell stories using audio and visuals of their choosing in a short narrated video that can be created using smartphones or pocket digital video recorders. Videos are then uploaded to YouTube for review by, and comments from, classmates. This assignment has the benefit of allowing students autonomy in learning, which not only increases their motivation to learn but also develops their ability to express ideas more articulately.

In Chapter 19, "Creating a video dialogue with streaming video clips," Sandra L. Miller describes the potential for streaming video in the classroom. Streaming video not only allows for anytime, anyplace learning but using annotations and playlists (a series of annotations or customized clips accessed through a single link) promotes active learning. Discussion and the ability to share comments with others build interactivity into the experience of watching media, which removes passivity. In these ways, streaming video can augment student learning in a social media environment.

In Chapter 20, "Remix as an educational activity," Christopher Shamburg, Kate Mazzetti-Shamburg, and John Shamburg introduce and develop the concept of remix as a tool for understanding and developing literary and communication skills. Here "creativity" is not limited to creation of new material, but also encompasses reorganizing and recombining existing work to produce a new, unique interpretation. Two projects from the humanities are described, which can easily be adapted for any discipline or source material. Learning experiences such as these foster students' imagination as well as engagement.

In Chapter 21, "Using Twitter to assist students in writing a concise nut graph," Tia C. M. Tyree harnesses the potential of microblogging to teach students how to encapsulate information using the formula of 5Ws – Who, What, When, Where, and Why. Using this formula in a Twitter nut graph (a journalistic paragraph that summarizes the news value of the story) allows students to concisely provide information to an audience with and without time constraints. Participation in live microblogging with classmates has the added benefit of sharpening students' summarization and audience engagement skills.

Part 4 – Integrative learning

The chapters in this section focus on activities in which students apply disciplinary knowledge, skills, and responsibilities to real-world contexts and complex problems, and reflect (in a real-world setting) on concepts and skills taught in the course.

In Chapter 22, "Simulation, video sharing, and discussion threads for practice-based skills," Lindsay B. Curtin and Laura A. Finn discuss how computer-based simulations, video recording, and online discussion can be used to improve practice-based skills and critical thinking. Students first experience a computer-based simulation; they are then video recorded completing a live simulation; finally they view uploaded recordings of their peer teams and assess their peers in an online discussion board. Supplementing technology with social media has the benefits of active learning, challenging students to use reflective and critical thinking skills in a comprehensive activity that assesses their abilities globally, and reinforcing skills in applying theoretical knowledge to real-world scenarios.

In Chapter 23, "Using Facebook Mobile as a tool to create a virtual learning community for pre-service teachers," Erkkie Haipinge describes how, in an environment with low Internet penetration (Africa), Facebook and mobile phones can be used to connect pre-service teachers with practicing teachers in the field. Accessible social media can be used to create a learning community in which pre-service teachers, through online discussions and postings with practicing teachers, explore ways in which educational technologies are used in the schools. This enriches both groups by improving both learning and practice, and is an innovative use of social media in a country where Internet penetration is low, but mobile phone usage is high.

In Chapter 24, "Using social software tools to facilitate peer e-mentoring and self-reflection among students on practicum," Mark J. W. Lee and Catherine McLoughlin discuss ways in which Web-based social software can facilitate peer-to-peer mentoring relationships among students undertaking practicum placements at geographically dispersed locations. Weekly blog entries and voice recordings of critical incidents allow students to assist and support one another as they post, comment, respond, and react to peers. As they learn about their professions and themselves as practitioners, they become active members of a supportive community. This activity has the benefits of developing students' self-awareness, reflective, and collaborative/communicative skills, while promoting professional skills in the use of social media.

In Chapter 25, "Using opinion leaders on Twitter to amplify PR and marketing messages," Sarah H. VanSlette explains how students can use a microblogging tool, Twitter, in a social media campaign. By engaging an opinion leader or celebrity (through a retweet, @ing them in messages, or a direct request) students can amplify the reach of their social media campaign. This activity helps students understand the power of opinion leaders within any public relations or marketing campaign. It has the benefits of teaching students how to use Twitter with consideration and propriety, how to write short (within the 140 character Twitter limit) compelling messages, and to think of ways to creatively engage their audiences.

Chapter structure

Throughout the book, every chapter follows the same structure:

- Chapters begin with "Abstract", "Key words", and "Discipline/ Academic areas addressed" sections, which are followed by the sections outlined below:
- "Instructional purpose" explains the broad purpose of the activity, assignment, or teaching technique. It covers the social media used and the reasons for using these media, and shows how pedagogical goals are achieved.
- "Student learning outcomes" (SLOs) states clear, measurable competencies that are expected of the student after successful completion of the assignment, project, or activity.
- "Prerequisite skills and knowledge" outlines how instructors can determine the adequacy of students' preparation for the activity, project, or assignment. Where appropriate, resources are recommended to help students attain the necessary skills.

- "Step-by-step directions" lead the reader through the activity, project, or assignment, using step-by-step instructions which facilitate the development of students' competencies (as specified by the SLOs) and achievement of the larger instructional goal. Also included in this section are directions for evaluation and clear guidelines for students.
- "Approximate time required" provides information on how much in-class and out-of-class time is needed to complete the activity, assignment, or project.
- "Required resources" details any technological or content resources that are necessary for the effective execution and completion of the activity, project, or assignment, as well as links to tutorials or guides for getting started with the technology.
- "Variations on the basic theme" discusses ways in which other social media can be used for this assignment or activity, and how the activities can be adapted for different disciplines or alternative learning outcomes.
- "Observations and advice" provides authors' reflections on what they have observed when their students engaged in the project, so that others can benefit from their experience.
- "Recommended reading" provides a list of resources which can be used to learn more about the social media, the theory, or the discipline.
- "Supplemental materials" provides examples of handouts and guidance used by the authors when implementing the activity or assignment. This may include instructions or guidelines given to students and/or rubrics used to assess the students' work.

As we have already noted, each teaching technique provided in the book has a clear pedagogical focus and is designed to be easily utilizable, whatever one's level of experience with social media. We hope that this book will prove a timely and valuable resource for educators. Since social media have become integral to the landscape of daily life, a careful and considered incorporation into our teaching can help prepare our students for personal and professional success.

References

Brent, D. (2005) Teaching as performance in the electronic classroom. *First Monday*, **10**(4). Available from *http://firstmonday.org/htbin/cgiwrap/bin/ojs/index.php/fm/article/view/1221/1141*

Ellaway, R., and Tworek, J. (2011) The net generation illusion: challenging conformance to social expectations. In: S. P. Ferris (Ed.), *Teaching, Learning, and the Net Generation: Concepts and Tools for Reaching Digital Learners* (pp. 324–40). Hershey, PA: IGI Global.

Gibson, J. J. (1977) The theory of affordances. In: R. Shaw and J. Bransford (Eds.), *Perceiving, Acting, and Knowing: Toward an Ecological Psychology* (pp. 67–82). Hillsdale, NJ: Erlbaum.

Halverson, E. R. (2011) Do social networking technologies have a place in formal learning environments? *On the Horizon*, **19**(1), 62–7.

Infographics (2012) Social media statistics for 2012. Available from *http://www.digitalbuzzblog.com/social-media-statistics-stats-2012-infographic/*

Junco, R. (2012) Too much face and not enough books: The relationship between multiple indices of Facebook use and academic performance. *Computers in Human Behavior*, **28**(1), 187–98, doi: 10.1016/j.chb.2011.08.026.

Kaplan, A. M., and Haenlein, M. (2010) Users of the world, unite! The challenges and opportunities of social media. *Business Horizons*, **53**(1), 59–68.

Nielsen.com (2011) The state of the media: The Social Media Report. Available from *blog.nielsen.com/nielsenwire/social/*

Richards, L. (2012, January 17) Econsultancy. Social media in Asia: Understanding the numbers. Available from *http://econsultancy.com/us/blog/8674-social-media-in-asia-understanding-the-numbers*

Socialbakers.com (2012a) Facebook statistics by country. Available from *http://www.socialbakers.com/facebook-statistics/*

Socialbakers.com (2012b) 15 most growing countries on Facebook. Available from *http://www.socialbakers.com/blog/684-facebook-statistics-2012-top-growing-countries/*

About the editors

Sharmila P. Ferris (*FerrisS@wpunj.edu*) is Professor in the Department of Communication, and Director of the Master's in Professional Communication at William Paterson University, U.S.A. She was recently Director for the university's Center for Teaching Exellence. Her research is in new technologies, bringing an interdisciplinary focus to computer-mediated communication. In this area she has published in a variety of print and electronic journals. She has also published several books: a co-authored book in faculty development, *Beyond Survival in the Academy* (2003); an edited book, *Teaching, Learning, and the Net Generation* (2011); several co-edited books: *Online Instructional Modeling* (2007), *Collaborative Teams: Theories, Process and Practice* (2005), and *Teaching and Learning with Virtual and Collaborative Teams* (2004).

Hilary A. Wilder (*WilderH@wpunj.edu*) is an Associate Professor in the Department of Educational Leadership and Professional Studies, and the coordinator for the M.Ed. Curriculum and Learning, Learning Technologies concentration at William Paterson University, U.S.A. A Fulbright and IFESH (International Foundation for Education and Self-Help) scholar, her research is in the use of Information and Communication Technologies (ICTs) in education. Most recently she has been exploring the use of online and social-networking tools to promote writing literacy. She has also been involved in research in the use of technology to facilitate international collaborations as well as the use of ICTs in teacher education programs in developing nations.

About the contributors

Silvia Baage, Ph.D. Silvia (*sbaage@mcdaniel.edu*) holds a Ph.D. in French Modern Studies from the University of Maryland, College Park, where she taught undergraduate courses in French Language, Literature, and Culture for six years. She is currently a Visiting Assistant Professor at McDaniel College. Her research focuses on the intersection between literature, film, and popular culture, including digital media, in the French-speaking world.

Evan Bradley, Ph.D. Evan (*evan@evanbradley.net*) received his Ph.D. in Linguistics and Cognitive Science at the University of Delaware and is currently a Fellow in Psychology and Creativity at Lawrence University. His research focuses on representations of sound information: how the perceptual system turns acoustic information into linguistically and musically meaningful structures, and how this process is modified by experience. As a scientist studying the mind, he finds that his role as an educator provides both insight into and an application for his scholarship.

Lori L. Britt, Ph.D. Lori (*brittll@jmu.edu*) is an Assistant Professor of Communication Studies at James Madison University. She researches and promotes collaborative forms of engagement in the classroom, the world of work, and in communities.

Melanie L. Buffington, Ph.D. Melanie (*mbuffington@vcu.edu*) is an Assistant Professor of Art Education and the Director of the Graduate Program at Virginia Commonwealth University. Her research interests include Web 2.0 technologies, multiculturalism, teacher preparation programs, museum education, and social justice. Her recent articles have been published in *Computers in the Schools*, *Distance Education*, *Art Education*, *Visual Arts Research*, and the *Journal of Cultural Research in Art Education*.

Lindsay B. Curtin, Pharm.D., B.C.P.S., C.G.P. Lindsay (*curtinl@mlhs.org*) is a critical care clinical pharmacist at Riddle Hospital in the Greater Philadelphia Area. She conducted research in the scholarship of teaching during her time as an Assistant Professor at the University of the Sciences – Philadelphia College of Pharmacy in Philadelphia, PA. She has been published in the *American Journal of Pharmacy Education* for her work with simulation of advanced cardiac life support in pharmacy education and has presented posters on scholarship of teaching and learning at the Society of Critical Care Medicine Annual Congress, Lilly East Conference on College and University Teaching, and International Society for Exploring Teaching and Learning Annual Conference.

Patrick J. Dillon (M.A., Central Michigan University, 2009). Patrick (*pdillon@mail.usf.edu*) is a doctoral candidate in the Department of Communication at the University of South Florida. His research interests include patient–provider interaction, health disparities, and research methodology. He teaches courses in family communication, health communication, and interpersonal communication.

Laura A. Finn, F.A.S.C.P., C.G.P. Laura (*l.finn@usciences.edu*) is an Adjunct Associate Professor of Pharmacy Practice at the University of the Sciences – Philadelphia College of Pharmacy in Philadelphia, PA. She has been published in the *American Journal of Pharmacy Education* and has presented posters on scholarship of teaching and learning at the Lilly East Conferences on College and University Teaching, the Teaching Professor Conference, and International Society for Exploring Teaching and Learning Annual Conference.

Kevin Garrison, Ph.D. Kevin (*Kevin.garrison@angelo.edu*) graduated from Texas Tech University in May 2009 with a Ph.D. in Technical Communication and Rhetoric. He currently works as a Tenure-Track Assistant Professor of Technical and Business Writing at Angelo State University (ASU). Also, he is a director of the ASU Usability Testing Lab, teaches a course in usability testing, and studies the intersection of technology and culture. Recent publications include articles in *Computers and Composition* and the *Bulletin of Science, Technology, and Society*.

Erkkie Haipinge. Erkkie (*ehaipinge@unam.na*) is a lecturer for Integrated Media and Technology Education at the University of Namibia in the Faculty of Education. Prior to that he has taught the same course at Windhoek College of Education (now Khomasdal Campus) before the

College merged with the University. He is currently doing his postgraduate studies at the University of Oulu in Finland. His research interests cover ICT integration in teaching and learning, use of Web 2.0 in creating learning communities and communities of practice, and use of social networks to facilitate learning and knowledge sharing. He also has a special interest in teacher continuous professional development.

David Hattem. David (*Davehattem@gmail.com*) graduated from Rutgers-Newark in 2006 with a B.A. in History and Philosophy. In January of the same year, he began working as an ESL instructor around the primarily Hispanic and Portuguese communities of Newark, becoming captivated by the culture exchange and the creative and productive use of language in the ESL setting. In 2011, David attained his M.A. in Applied Linguistics from the University of Massachusetts-Boston. Some of his primary interests in language study are computer-assisted language learning, corpus linguistics, and sociocultural theory.

Alison Hicks. Alison (*alison.hicks@colorado.edu*) is the Romance Language Librarian at the University of Colorado, Boulder. Her interests include the integration of critical information literacy into foreign language instruction.

J. Jacob Jenkins. Jacob (*jjacobjenkins@mail.usf.edu*) received his doctoral degree in the Department of Communication at the University of South Florida. He received his B.A. in Architecture from Drury University; he has studied abroad in France, Germany, Italy, and the Netherlands. His current research interests include community and community building, organizational learning, and positive organizational change. He teaches courses in organizational and interpersonal communication.

Juhong Liu "Christie", Ph.D. Christie (*liujc@jmu.edu*) is an Instructional Technologist and Assistant Professor at James Madison University. She has taught undergraduate, graduate, and adult learner classes online and workshops in classroom and online environments. She has presented at national and international conferences on instructional design, and technologies and media in online learning. Her research interests include online learning, assessment, and evaluation of the educational use of technologies.

Linzi J. Kemp, Ph.D., M.B.A., B.Ed. (Business), Diploma in Marketing. Linzi (*lkemp@aus.edu*) is Assistant Professor with the School of Business Management, American University of Sharjah, United Arab Emirates (UAE). She teachers Leadership and Organizational Behavior. Previously Faculty Associate, Empire State College, State University of New York, teaching and mentoring students in the Centers for Distance Learning and International Programs. Originally from the U.K., Linzi has worked there in private and public organizations within education (lecturer), retail (area manager), and the NHS (administrator). Previous academic and educational experience has been international, including ten years in the UAE, Saudi Arabia, and the People's Republic of China.

Michelle Kilburn, Ed.D. Michelle (*mkilburn@semo.edu*) is an Assistant Professor in the Department of Criminal Justice and Sociology. She served as the first director of online programs and interim instructional designer at Southeast Missouri State University and has a specific interest in using technology to enhance the learning environment. Her various teaching mediums for course delivery have included webinar, online, interactive television, blended, and course redesign formats.

Apostolos Koutropoulos. Apostolos (*a.koutropoulos@umb.edu*) is the Program Coordinator for the Applied Linguistics Online Program at UMass Boston. He holds a B.A. in Computer Science, an M.B.A. with a focus on Human Resources, an M.S. in Information Technology, an M.Ed. in Instructional Design, and an M.A. in Applied Linguistics from the University of Massachusetts Boston. His research interests include knowledge management, educational technology, linguistics, mLearning, MOOCs, and epistemology.

Lisa M. Lane. Lisa (*llane@miracosta.edu*) teaches history both on-site and online at MiraCosta College in Oceanside, California, and directs the Program for Online Teaching there. She began offering online classes in 1998. In 2005 she founded POT (the Program for Online Teaching), an all-volunteer faculty group which provides, in an open-access format, a broad pedagogical education to faculty teaching online, hybrid, and technology-enhanced classes. Lisa has published book chapters in both history and online teaching, and articles on the perils of learning management systems, and makes ample use of social media for her own professional development.

Mark J. W. Lee. Mark (*malee@csu.edu.au*) is an Adjunct Senior Lecturer with the School of Education at Charles Sturt University. He concurrently holds Adjunct Senior Lecturer and Honorary Research Fellow appointments with the DEHub Research Institute at the University of New England and with the School of Science, Information Technology and Engineering at the University of Ballarat, respectively. Previously, he worked in a variety of teaching, instructional design, and managerial roles at various private tertiary education institutions. Mark has published widely in the areas of educational technology, e-learning, and innovation in tertiary teaching, with close to 60 refereed papers, articles, and chapters to his name. He is the Editor of *MERLOT's Journal of Online Learning and Teaching* as well as an Associate Editor of both the *IEEE Transactions on Education* and the *International Journal of Games and Computer-Mediated Simulations*. In addition, he serves on the editorial boards of 15 other international journals.

Paul E. Mabrey III. Paul (*mabreype@jmu.edu*) is a Lecturer of Communication Studies and Assistant Director of Debate at James Madison University. He has received university funding and attended workshops for incorporating social media and other technologies in his communication courses. His classes have integrated the use of YouTube, Twitter, WordPress, and other social media technologies. His research interests include rhetorical theory and criticism, argumentation, food communication, and sustainability in higher education.

Madhu Mahalingam. Madhu (*m.mahali@usciences.edu*) is an Associate Professor in the Department of Chemistry & Biochemistry at University of the Sciences, Philadelphia. She is a Physical Chemist by training. Her current research interest is in the area of chemical education specifically teaching methodologies that improve students' problem-solving ability, student learning, and retention of learning. Her most recent publication in this area was in the *Journal of Chemical Education*. She was invited to be a co-facilitator for a POGIL (Process Oriented Guided Inquity Learning) problem-solving workshop at the Mid-Atlantic Regional Meeting of the American Chemical Society in 2008. She has presented her work at several national and regional conferences.

Kate Mazzetti-Shamburg. Kate (*kmazzetti1@email.phoenix.edu*) is an instructor at the University of Phoenix. She was previously a high-school drama and English teacher and has won several awards for her teaching. She has her B.A. from Loyola and her M.A. in Shakespeare Studies from the Shakespeare Institute in Stratford-upon-Avon.

Catherine McLoughlin. Catherine (*catherine.mcloughlin@acu.edu.au*) is an Associate Professor in the School of Education at the Australian Catholic University, Canberra, where she formerly served as Head of School. She also is the coordinator of the Australian Capital Territory branch of the Research Centre for Science, Information Technology and Mathematics Education for Rural and Regional Australia (SiMERR). With 30 years' higher education experience in Europe, Southeast Asia, the Middle East, and Australia, Catherine has gained exposure to a wide variety of learning and teaching settings throughout her career, working with students across a diverse range of cultural contexts. She currently teaches undergraduate courses in Educational Psychology and postgraduate courses in Educational Research Methods. She is the Editor of the *Australasian Journal of Educational Technology* and an editorial board member of several leading journals. Together with Mark Lee, she co-edited *Web 2.0–based E-learning: Applying Social Informatics for Tertiary Teaching* (2010, Information Science Reference).

Sandra L. Miller, Ed.D. Sandie (*millers@wpunj.edu*) provides leadership and vision for the Student Technology Consultant program, and the Departments of Academic Technology, Media Services, and Broadcast, Production and Support for Cable, Satellite, and Videoconferencing at William Paterson University. She was recently the PI for NJVid, New Jersey's statewide digital video repository, and an IMLS National Leadership Grant winner (2007–11). Her recent conference presentations have included: EDUCAUSE National Conference in 2010 on "NJVid: A Collaborative Portal for Statewide Video Access" and "Streaming Video: Soup to Nuts" at CCUMC. Sandie published "Student response systems: Are they for large classes only?" in the *College and University Media Review 2009–10*, "Video as process and product" in *EDUCAUSE Quarterly*, 2005, and numerous other technology articles on online tutoring. She received her doctorate in Educational Technology from Pepperdine University, which was both online and f2f.

Michael Mills, Ed.D. Michael (*mmills@uca.edu* or *michaelsmills@gmail.com*) is an Assistant Professor of Teaching and Learning at the University of Central Arkansas in Conway, Arkansas. He specializes in integrating technology into K–12 classrooms, particularly through collaborative-based applications of the iPad and interactive whiteboards. He has taught secondary language arts for 10 years and served as a secondary literacy and technology specialist for 7 years. In addition, he has taught multiple online courses in composition and literature. He teaches workshops across the state in technology integration methods, including Web design, photo/video editing, Google tool application, iPad implementation, advanced SMART Board interactivity techniques, multimedia-infused lesson design, information management, and incorporation of social media.

Aaron Moore. Aaron (*amoore@rider.edu*) is an Assistant Professor of Public Relations at Rider University. He teaches classes in public relations and event planning, and is the Internship Coordinator for the Department of Communication and Journalism. Aaron's main area of specialty and scholarship is sports public relations. He created "Who Owns What", a database of media ownership for the *Columbia Journalism Review*. He is also a member of the United States Basketball Writer's Association.

Elisabeth Morlino. Elisabeth (*e.morlino@usciences.edu*) is an Assistant Professor in the Department of Chemistry & Biochemistry at University of the Sciences, Philadelphia. While she is an experimental physical chemist by training, she is also interested in understanding how people learn to problem-solve at a high level. Her teaching methodologies to improve problem-solving skills can be found in the *Journal of Chemical Education* as well as presentations given at regional and national meetings.

Jeffrey T. Olimpo, M.S., M.A. Jeffrey (*jeolimpo@umd.edu*) is an instructor in the Department of Cell Biology & Molecular Genetics at the University of Maryland, College Park. During his time at the university, he has had the pleasure of teaching a variety of courses on Genetics, Epidemiology & Public Health, and Biology Education. His research interests lie in visualization in the sciences, curriculum development, and professional development for undergraduate teaching assistants.

Hans C. Schmidt, PhD. Hans (*hcs10@psu.edu*) is an Assistant Professor of Communications at the Pennsylvania State University, Brandywine. His research focuses on media education, instructional media, journalism education, and media literacy.

Christopher Shamburg. Chris (*cshamburg@njcu.edu*) is a Graduate Professor of Educational Technology at New Jersey City University. His professional interests focus on the pedagogical applications of new literacies and digital technologies.

John Shamburg. John (*jshamburg@hccc.edu*) is a teacher of English and ESL Education, currently teaching College Composition at Hudson County Community College. He has taught literature, writing, speaking, and performing at high-school and college levels throughout northern New Jersey. His professional interests focus on the synthesis of student-centered literacy skills with contemporary culture.

Patricia A. Shields, Ph.D. Patricia (*pshields@umd.edu*) is a lecturer in the Department of Cell Biology & Molecular Genetics at the University of Maryland, College Park. She has primarily been responsible for teaching courses in the introductory biology series at her university, as well as Genetics and teaching practicum courses for biology majors. Her research interests lie in curriculum development for majors and non-majors courses that promote active and engaged learning in the classroom.

Caroline Sinkinson. Caroline (*caroline.sinkinson@colorado.edu*) is an Assistant Professor, Instruction Coordinator, and Undergraduate Services Librarian at the University of Colorado, Boulder. She coordinates the campus information literacy initiatives and instructional programming.

Tia C. M. Tyree. Tia (*ttyree@howard.edu*) is an Assistant Professor in the Department of Journalism at Howard University. She is the public relations sequence coordinator and teaches various public relations courses, including Public Relations Writing I & II, Introduction to Public Relations, and SR: Friends, Followers & Social Media. Her research interests include African American and female representations in the mass media, hip hop, rap, reality television, film, and social media. She has published articles in several journals including *Women and Language*, *Howard Journal of Communications*, *Journalism: Theory, Practice & Criticism*, and *Journal of Black Studies*.

Sarah VanSlette, Ph.D. Sarah (*sarahvanslette@gmail.com*) earned her M.A. and Ph.D. in Public Relations from Purdue University. She teaches Public Relations, Research Methods, Public Speaking, and Social Media for Strategic Communication in the Department of Speech Communication at Southern Illinois University Edwardsville. Her research focuses primarily on public relations and organizational discourse. Her interest in social media was originally inspired by her students and their natural use of the tools, and has grown into an important element of her public relations curriculum. She looks forward to tracking the development of new social media tools and integrating them into the assignments of her PR and Strategic Communication courses. You can follow her on Twitter @sarahvanslette.

Amanda Waldo. Amanda (*awaldo@ucla.edu*) is a graduate student in English at the University of California, Los Angeles, where she currently works as an instructional technology consultant at the Center for Digital Humanities. Her dissertation topic is ethical consumption in contemporary American literature.

Ronda Zelezny-Green. Ronda (*rondazg3@gmail.com*) is a language educator and learner who has lived and taught on four continents and visited more than 30 countries. She has been an ESL/EFL educator for more than six years and is now a postgraduate student in ICT4D and Sustainable Development at Royal Holloway, University of London. In June 2011, she completed an M.A. in Applied Linguistics with a foreign language pedagogy concentration at the University of Massachusetts at Boston. During her studies she specialized in the use of technology for educational purposes, with a focus on mobile-assisted language learning and e-Learning design. She has published and presented on ICT4D, race and ethnicity in higher education, and the use of mobile devices for development. Ronda enjoys reading, experiencing new cultures, and learning languages. Her head and her heart are still in Africa.

Part 1
Writing, research, and information fluency

Writing for Wikipedia: co-constructing knowledge and writing for a public audience

Lori L. Britt

Abstract: This assignment allows students to research topics in depth and become skilled at communicating academic knowledge for a public audience. The assignment draws attention to the collaborative construction of knowledge and the forces that shape what counts as knowledge and what gets disseminated. It also encourages students to consider how to organize information to be useful and illuminating to others, and how to consider connections between topics and concepts. The assignment engages students in critique, as they are more willing to critique and revise their writing when that writing will be accessible to the public. The assignment also exposes students to a social media information-sharing medium, Wikipedia, and encourages their critical consideration of the strengths and limitations of this online encyclopedic resource.

Key words: bridging classrooms and society, online writing, public audience, research, Wikipedia.

Discipline/Academic areas addressed

Communication studies (but applicable to almost any discipline), epistemology (the study of knowledge), and expository writing skills.

Instructional purpose

The purpose behind using Wikipedia as a pedagogical tool is twofold: Students often engage with topics/content in courses as discrete ideas to be learned, filed, and discussed in the same terms that they were taught. They are hesitant to risk trying to reshape knowledge in their own voice and to see connections between topics that instructors do not explicitly articulate. Having students write and revise Wikipedia articles helps move students beyond just discussing information with the instructor and their peers where knowledge is confined within the walls of the classroom, to a recognition of knowledge as fluid, connected, and "alive".

Second, writing for Wikipedia helps students integrate theoretical knowledge, and "own" it in such a way as to be able to re-present it, contextualize it, and make it meaningful and useful for others.

By understanding theories and ideas well enough to write and communicate them for a public audience on Wikipedia, students more actively engage in the material, explore connections, and participate in the collaborative construction of knowledge for public consumption.

Student learning outcomes

Students will write a Wikipedia article or offer substantial revision to an existing Wikipedia article on that topic. In doing so students will:

1. Translate academic knowledge of topics and concepts for a public audience.
2. Expand their research skills in multiple arenas: academic literatures, encyclopedia sources, and new sources.
3. Concisely describe a topic and communicate why it is important and relevant.
4. Distill information about a topic down to its most salient points.
5. Situate knowledge in social and historical contexts.
6. Recognize and reflect different perspectives on topics and concepts.

Prerequisite skills and knowledge

Prerequisite skills and knowledge for students

Students should have general research skills, an understanding of primary and secondary sources of research, and a familiarity with search functions in academic databases, both discipline specific and more general. Students should also be exposed to encyclopedia sources of information that are often not part of more general databases. Instructors may need to devote some time before the start of the activity to ensuring the appropriate skills.

Recommended prerequisites for instructors

Explore the Wikipedia Education Program information site

http://outreach.wikimedia.org/wiki/Wikipedia_Education_Program

to get a feel for the global initiative, then explore the U.S. Education Program site at

http://en.wikipedia.org/wiki/Wikipedia:USEDU

to see how to get involved. See what types of courses people are infusing with Wikipedia projects, explore a variety of assignments, and see what universities and colleges are currently involved in the project.

While the Wikipedia Education Program is an invaluable resource and working through this program has many benefits, certainly any instructor could incorporate a project using Wikipedia without officially linking to the Wikipedia U.S. Education Program (WP:USEDU). However, there are a number of invaluable resources that are a part of this program (see "Supplemental materials").

Step-by-step directions

The steps below are directed towards faculty.

Decide on how to incorporate a Wikipedia project into your course

1. Write your Wikipedia assignment (students create new Wikipedia pages, revise and edit existing pages, do technical editing) and consider how it is best integrated into the course. In the case of this project, it was one of several different types that students worked on throughout the semester, in stages. Wikipedia projects can last a few weeks, or the length of the term, and can be designed to be conducted during class time or primarily out of class, by individuals or teams.

2. Decide on the level of orientation to Wikipedia and technical training that will be needed for your students to be successful. Work such training into your course plans. If you are working with a Campus Ambassador (see Appendix A in "Supplemental materials"), this is a great time to meet with them to find out what they recommend based on the type of project you are having students do.

Explore content and conventions of Wikipedia

3. Have students explore content related to the course on Wikipedia to begin to understand how information is presented in the online site. One way to do this is to provide students with a list of terms, ideas, concepts, or seminal people related to the course and have them look to see how many of these are covered by Wikipedia. (SLO 1)

4. Ask students to identify patterns in formatting, tone, and source referencing across the pages. What are common features of Wikipedia entries, what purpose do these serve? (SLO 3 and 6)

5. Have students consider whether the content on Wikipedia is written in such a way to give the user a broad, concise, useful overview of the concept/idea/person and whether the article encourages further exploration of related knowledge through appropriate in-text links (SLO 5).

Expose students to the vision, values, and standards of Wikipedia

6. Have students create Wikipedia accounts and provide you with their user names. (Note that, as a security measure, Wikipedia limits the number of user accounts that can be created in a short time frame from one IP address – in this case a campus network, so encourage students to create their accounts before class time. These user names allow you to track the edits that each student makes.)

7. Ask students to read several short informational pieces about Wikipedia: the five pillars of Wikipedia, what constitutes a good article, Wikipedia editing basics, and *Manual of Style* (see "Recommended reading").

Launch students in actual Wikipedia work

8. Engage students in critical evaluation of Wikipedia pages to build their comfort level and their understanding of the process of collaborative knowledge-building. Show students the features of an article's "talk page" which is the subtext page that shows any discussion related to concerns or ideas for the page by collaborators. Also show students an article's "history" page so that they can see how an article is both created and edited by many individuals. (SLO 2)

9. Have students begin to work in a Wikipedia "sandbox" to begin to develop their articles or edits. Show students the sandbox feature on Wikipedia which is basically a "private" space where students can begin work on an article and give it shape before it "goes live" on the Wikipedia site. Although these are thought of as private spaces, student sandboxes are accessible through their user page and, if using the WP:USEDU project, linked to the course page so instructors and campus ambassadors can view, edit, and make suggestions on work in progress. The sandbox acts just like a wiki, a collaboratively developed page (similar in nature to a Google doc). It requires the same type of basic coding and markup language as Wikipedia so it is a great place for students to practice simple coding. (SLO 1)

10. If possible, schedule a work day in a computer lab where students can each make edits to an existing page for practice. Wikipedia has a list of pages that need simple copyediting. Simply type WP:Open Tasks in the Wikipedia search box.

11. Have students move their developing work out of their sandboxes and "live" on Wikipedia to begin to gain feedback from the Wikipedia community. This is a scary step for students as they are not used to others being able to read and/or change their work. (SLO 1)

Feedback and evaluation

12. Engage students, once their work is developing, in a peer-to-peer workshop. If students are working in groups on a page, have them read each other's pages in advance and have them provide constructive criticism on each other's pages (see "Peer Feedback Form" in Appendix B). (SLO 6)

13. Have students continue to edit and revise their pages based on peer, instructor, and Wikipedia community feedback on the article's talk page. (SLO 3 and 4)

14. Grade student or team work and reflection on the process. Students were graded in this course on how they improved the page or how well their new page was constructed to meet Wikipedia standards and be useful, engaging, and adequately represent the breadth of content. Instructors can visit the article's "history" page to see the edits done by students. Assure students they are being graded on their contributions to the page and not to the final page which may have been subsequently edited by other Wikipedians. A part of the student grade can also be based on a reflective response about how they attended to the feedback of their peers, the instructor, and other Wikipedians to make the page more informative, better supported by credible sources, and balanced in its treatment of the subject matter. (SLO 6)

Here is a recommendation for grading a Wikipedia project although there are many other options that you can explore on the WP:USEDU course sites:

- 10%: Participation grade for meeting milestones of project (Wikipedia account, sandbox, in-class page-editing practice, quiz on Wikipedia standards and conventions).
- 10%: Peer reviews and collaboration with classmates.
- 10%: Group process/teamwork (if applicable).
- 10%: Research (incorporating appropriate class and database research into article to provide breadth, balance, historical and social contexts, and when possible a global focus on the topic).
- 50%: Quality of Wikipedia contributions (meets Wikipedia quality standards, is written to be accessible and informative, reflects "deep learning" of course content by broadening understanding of concepts beyond course texts, written in a way that is accessible and useful to a public audience).
- 10%: Reflection on collaborative knowledge construction process and how they addressed feedback from multiple parties (peers, campus and online ambassadors, instructor, and the Wikipedia community).

Approximate time required

Projects can vary from a few weeks to a semester-long project. In this course, this was one of several projects that students needed to work on simultaneously to give them practice at prioritizing, delegating, and planning. Overall, three full course days were dedicated to instruction: Introduction to the basics of Wikipedia and the specifics of the class project, a lab day for practice editing of Wikipedia pages, and a team peer review workshop. In addition, as this was an engaged learning class, almost every Friday was used for project work.

Required resources

- Access to Wikipedia.
- Students will need to create accounts so that you can track their work/ input.
- Although you do not need to work through the Wikimedia Educational Foundation, the support is exemplary and it is recommended that you do so while you are becoming familiar with the Wikipedia process.
- Helpful although not required, access to a computer lab for at least one class session where students can practice editing on Wikipedia with guidance.
- The Wikipedia community's portal

  http://en.wikipedia.org/wiki/Wikipedia:Community_portal

  offers excellent online and print versions of tutorials for things such as: starting an account, getting help, article standards, working with others, and ways to communicate with other Wikipedians.
- Working in Wikipedia is possible on both MAC and PC platforms, and through many different browsers.

Variations on the basic theme

Wikipedia projects have been integrated into a wide array of courses in many disciplines and areas such as psychology, business, media studies, information science, social media, economics, trade policy, political science, gender, justice, history, anthropology, and law. All of the projects have a common thread of assessing and improving how socially and historically situated knowledge related to an academic discipline or area is accessible on Wikipedia. This also covers the common thread of writing appropriately within the discipline (knowing the audience, writing concisely yet comprehensively, etc.).

Observations and advice

Students enjoy working with new technological tools, although many are hesitant at first and need reassurance that they will have support. The day that my class groups went "live" with their information on Wikipedia, they were nervous, but they were proud. In addition, what they originally dreaded, having others edit their work and make changes, was something they wanted by the end of the semester. Students whose pages were not edited by other Wikipedians were disappointed. Students gained a great deal by attending to the suggestions, comments, and edits of those reading their work.

Students were challenged by, but subsequently saw the value in, situating knowledge in social and historical contexts and exploring how ideas are related to other ideas and making these connections explicit through building in-text links in their Wikipedia articles, something that cannot easily be replicated in more traditional writing assignments.

Recommended reading

Ayers, P., Matthews, C., and Yates, B. (2008) *How Wikipedia Works: And How You Can Be A Part of It*. San Francisco, CA: No Starch Press.

Bruns, A. (2008) Blogs, *Wikipedia, Second Life and Beyond (Digital Formations): From Production to Produsage*. New York, NY: Peter Lang.

Kissling, M. (2011) A call for Wikipedia in the classroom. *Social Education*, **75**(2), 60–4.

Kittle, P., and Hicks, T. (2009) Transforming the group paper with collaborative online writing. *Pedagogy*, **9**(3), 525–38.

Konieczny, P. (2007) Wikis and Wikipedia as a teaching tool. *International Journal of Instructional Technology and Distance Learning*, **4**(1), 15–34.

Miller, M. (2010) *Teach Yourself Wikipedia in 10 Minutes*. Indianapolis, IN: SAMS Publishing.

Petronio, S. (1999) Translating scholarship into practice: An alternative metaphor. *Journal of Applied Communication Research*, **27**, 87–91.

Reilly, C. A. (2011) Teaching Wikipedia as a mirrored technology. *First Monday: Peer Reviewed Journal on the Internet*, **16**(1).

Rush, E. K., and Tracy, S. J. (2010) Wikipedia as public scholarship: Communicating our impact online. *Journal of Applied Communication Research*, **38**, 309–15, doi: 10.1080/00909882.2010.490846

Tardy, C. M. (2010) Writing for the world: Wikipedia as an introduction to academic writing. *English Teaching Forum*, **1**, 12–27.

Wikipedia Five Pillars. Available from *http://en.wikipedia.org/wiki/Wikipedia:Five_pillars*

Supplemental materials

Appendix A Wikipedia Education Program resources for instructors and courses

The Wikipedia Education Program, an initiative led by the Wikimedia Foundation, the nonprofit organization behind Wikipedia, was launched in 2010–2011. The goal is to help instructors use Wikipedia as a teaching tool. Interested instructors can read more at

outreach.wikimedia.org/wiki/Wikipedia_Education_Program

or

wikimediafoundation.org

Making your course part of this program offers free resources to instructors wanting to get started but needing a support team of their own to pilot a project. Here are a few specific ways that instructors can receive direct support.

Campus ambassadors

One invaluable resource for a first-time instructor engaging in Wikipedia are campus ambassadors, volunteer students with Wikipedia expertise and training who will serve as a resource for you and your students. They can come and visit your class and handle technical training and support. Here is a link to all of the universities that currently have trained campus ambassadors in their midst:

http://en.wikipedia.org/wiki/Wikipedia:United_States_Education_Program/Campus_Ambassadors

Wikipedia can often find campus ambassadors at other campuses as well.

If your campus does not have trained campus ambassadors, there are many brief online training resources on the WP:USEDU site that will allow an instructor to be comfortable helping students navigate Wikipedia. All it takes is a commitment to explore.

Online ambassadors

WP:USEDU courses will be assigned one or more online ambassadors for online assistance. These people are highly skilled Wikipedians who have a great deal of experience with the style, conventions, and technical issues associated with the site. They are available online to answer questions from the instructor and students for how to do formatting, where to find information, etc. They can help instructors navigate the many community sections of Wikipedia to find resources and even identify gaps in Wikipedia content areas. Online ambassadors also can periodically look at the work your students are doing with a "wikipedian" eye to let you know how well student pages and/or edits are conforming to Wikipedia conventions and standards.

Appendix B Wikipedia Article Peer Review Form

Peer review of Wikipedia articles being developed and/or revised

Please review the Wikipedia page you have been assigned and complete the review form *before* class. In class you will meet with your partners, review the feedback, and brainstorm ways to strengthen and improve the articles. Each person should complete a review sheet. Project teams should keep this feedback and turn it in with their final reflection that discusses how feedback from various parties was addressed.

Rank and comment on how the article adheres to or represents the following characteristics and traits. Rank on a Likert scale:

1 Needs major improvement

2 Needs minor improvement

3 Unsure

4 Good

5 Excellent

Table 1.1 Wiki Article Review Form

Wikipedia values		
Characteristic	**Rank**	**Comments**
Verifiable information	1 2 3 4 5	
Written from a neutral point of view	1 2 3 4 5	
Speaks to a global audience (or acknowledges a U.S. focus)	1 2 3 4 5	
Wikipedia conventions (standards)		
Characteristic	**Rank**	**Comments**
Lead section summarizes key points covered in the article and articulates why the topic is important	1 2 3 4 5	
Characteristic	**Rank**	**Comments**
The body of the article follows the lead section and includes specific headers and subheaders	1 2 3 4 5	
The organization of the article is logical and flows well	1 2 3 4 5	
Appendices and footnotes appear after the body of the article. These may include bibliographies, links to other Wikipedia articles, notes and references, relevant publications, and websites	1 2 3 4 5	
There are enough sources to support the information and make it credible	1 2 3 4 5	
General writing		
Characteristic	**Rank**	**Comments**
Overall quality of writing (accessible, clear, concise, descriptive, free of errors)	1 2 3 4 5	
All information is well integrated and it is clear how the information "fits" together	1 2 3 4 5	
Writing fits the Wikipedia style	1 2 3 4 5	

If you were in an introductory class and researched this topic, which the professor mentioned in lecture to gain information, would this page be helpful? (Why or why not?)

If you were in a research class and were researching this topic, would this page provide you with a basic understanding and some solid places to start your research? Would it alert you to some key ideas to find out more about?

Please note any specific sections that need improvement.

2

Organizing with Pinterest and Delicious

Melanie L. Buffington

Abstract: In this project, students find and organize images, videos, or websites into categories, using the social bookmarking sites Pinterest and Delicious. The act of categorizing resources helps students see connections, develop new ideas, and refine their ideas. This enables students to carefully plan and organize their thoughts as they approach a written assignment, a presentation, or an art-making assignment. The goals of this project are to teach students ways to use Internet technologies and social media to organize and plan for their assignments, and to create opportunities for them to share their ideas. This enables students to consciously think about their use of Web 2.0 tools. In these ways, students can start the planning and organization process that leads to the development of high-quality written work, artwork, and presentations.

Key words: concept organization strategies, Delicious, social bookmarking, information literacy, Pinterest, Web 2.0.

Discipline/Academic areas addressed

Adaptable to all disciplines employing writing and visual presentations, and particularly useful for art and art education.

Instructional purpose

This activity helps students be more organized, keep track of their sources, recognize where the ideas for their work emanates, and develop visuals that relate to their written work. It also allows students to recognize that learning can be anytime/anywhere. Students today spend a great deal of time online on social media and the Internet, and frequently come across useful information when not intentionally looking for it, or when working on other school-related assignments. Thus, having easy access to the "pin" and "tag" features available through Pinterest and Delicious (formerly del.icio.us) allows them to seamlessly move between leisure consumption of media and class assignments. Further, students who embrace social bookmarking technologies are frequently able to create higher quality work and give better presentations. By taking the often invisible thought processes of organizing parts of an assignment or presentation and making them visible through the use of pins and boards in Pinterest or tags in Delicious, students can become more attentive to their decision making and can clarify the hows and whys of their organizational choices.

Student learning outcomes

1. Students will be able to pin or tag websites, images, and videos.
2. Students will be able to assign meaningful categories to their tagged sites and images.
3. Students will be able to utilize Pinterest boards as presentation tools to organize various images and video.
4. Students will learn ways to use Web 2.0 tools to assist them in their assignments

Prerequisite skills and knowledge

Basic Internet searching skills, such as those possessed by the average college student today. No sophisticated skills are required, but simply the ability to input search terms into search engines on the Internet, and to follow sources thus located.

Organizational and goal-setting skills (detailed information on prerequisite skills is provided in "Required resources").

Step-by-step directions

1. This project starts with a 60-minute class in the computer lab and I engage students in a discussion of how they currently find resources and organize their ideas for multiple assignments simultaneously. Students freely share ideas about ways they have been successful and unsuccessful at organizing their ideas and resources. Through open discussion, all students get to hear the ideas and practices of their peers. I also offer suggestions of ways that I organize ideas. Since many people are successful utilizing different organizational strategies, the goal of this initial class session is to share as many different ones as possible, rather than to have students all utilize one strategy.

2. After we discuss several ways they currently keep themselves organized, I show them my Delicious and Pinterest pages

   http://delicious.com/mbuffington
   http://pinterest.com/melanie914/

   Because I frequently use these sites to organize my teaching and ideas related to what we are studying, the students can see a connection between what we are talking about in class and what I have been tagging and pinning. Additionally, I use these sites to organize other aspects of my life and frequently tag recipes and decorating ideas. I explain to my students how these sites help me organize the different aspects of my life and that, like them, I can get distracted when searching online. Using the pin and tag features allows me to capture something of personal interest and then put it aside so that I can focus on my work. Then, when I have the work accomplished, I can return to the item of personal interest.

3. This leads to a short demonstration where I teach students the basics of using Pinterest. I show them how to request an invitation (the invitation usually takes a minute or so to reach an email account), create a user name and password, create boards, and start pinning (for details, see Pinterest in "Supplemental materials"). Then, we quickly generate a class topic and each student practices pinning related images to the board they created around that topic. If it is possible with the configuration of the lab, I show students how to download and add the "pin it" button to their bookmarks bar.

4. After using Pinterest, I demonstrate ways that I use Delicious (formerly del.icio.us). Again, I start by showing them my personal page

   http://delicious.com/mbungton

   and point out tags that are relevant to what we have been doing in class. Then I ask students to create a user name and begin to tag some sites relevant to an upcoming assignment for our class.

5. At this point, I give students about 30 minutes to practice with both of these sites and to explore and experiment.

6. At the end of the class, I ask a few students to share their thoughts and I let students know that we will revisit these technologies in a few weeks.

7. When we revisit Pinterest and Delicious about two weeks later, I ask student volunteers to show the class what they have been doing with the sites and what they have pinned and tagged. This leads to a class discussion of many ideas for how these sites could be useful for students to help them organize the information that they find online.

8. As we discuss how the students can use these sites to organize information, I show them how I use tags and pins to assist me in organizing ideas as I am writing articles and papers. I explain to students that, like them, I also write papers on a regular basis and need to juggle multiple projects simultaneously. Then I ask students to share their current processes for organizing ideas and turning them into a strong paper. Following this, I share how I start with an initial outline that allows me to plan the basic sections of the article that I am writing and think about the transitions between sections. I tell students that I have learned that I can either write well or write quickly. Thus, the time that I take in planning and organizing my writing process pays off for me in terms of a higher quality finished product. This initial outline helps me develop the flow of the article before I start the actual writing process. As I work to finalize the outline, I then use the main categories of the outline as tags in Delicious. Typically, I take several days or up to a few weeks to do this. During this time, I actively tag different articles related to the main topics that I plan to address. Thus, when I sit down to write, I have my sources organized by tag and am easily able to access what I need. This pre-organization with Delicious or Pinterest helps the actual writing process proceed smoothly.

9. When students see how I create a hierarchy with the tags that I use, it helps them to understand how these tools can be used to organize ideas, and they frequently find more ways to use these sites themselves. Though I do not require that students use Delicious or Pinterest to organize their assignments for class, I do require that they practice with them and many students find them to be useful tools. While some students prefer to work with more traditional paper or note card organizing tools, many students become avid users when they see how the tools may be useful to them, and also relate to their lives and their ubiquitous computing.

Approximate time required

One 60-minute session is sufficient to show the basics of both sites and to allow students to practice. About two weeks later I follow this up with a 30–60-minute discussion and showcasing of student ideas. Thus, two class sessions are sufficient to get students started with these tools. In some cases when students have been enthusiastic users, we have devoted additional class time every few weeks to have different students demonstrate ways they use the sites.

Required resources

Delicious

1. *www.delicious.com*

2. Delicious tutorial
http://www.youtube.com/watch?v=QZRr6tJy3y4

Pinterest

1. *www.pinterest.com*

2. *http://edudemic.com/2012/02/5-tips-for-using-pinterest-in-your-classroom/*

3. Pinterest tutorials
http://www.youtube.com/watch?v=QtmmGA0M_yk
http://edudemic.com/2012/02/pinterest-how-to/

Organizational/Goal resources

1. *http://www.lifeorganizers.com/cm_articles/45_help_students_get_organized_335.html*
2. *http://www.nlight.com/Success/Study/3organize.html*
3. *http://lifeorganizers.com/Schooling-and-Education/The-Organized-College-Student/College-Organization.html*
4. *http://breitlinks.com/community/goal_setting.htm*
5. *http://www.studygs.net/shared/mgmnt.htm*

Technology needed

1. Internet-enabled computer, iPad, or other mobile device.
2. Access to Pinterest and Delicious.
3. "Pin" and "tag" buttons downloaded into the Web browser toolbars.

Variations on the basic theme

The underlying characteristic of the idea of using Pinterest and Delicious relates to ubiquitous computing. Now that many people spend much of their lives in places with Internet access and with devices that are frequently connected to the Internet, we can almost always utilize the hyperlinking capacity of the Internet that leads from one page to another to another. Thus, what we start looking for online may lead us in another direction and we may, unexpectedly, encounter information that seems useful in another context. Having the ability to pin or tag this useful information whenever we encounter it allows us to work efficiently and continuously organize our thoughts and resources.

In addition, I have used Delicious to share information among all the students in a particular class. Through Delicious, when we add the user names of others, we are able to easily share a variety of tagged sites. As a class, we can create meaningful tags and create a class repository of websites related to tags that we selected as a group. I have found it successful to generate a list of topics about which the students want information, create a list of tagged topics in class, and assign each student to find and tag ten related sites. Then all students in class have access to all the sites tagged by the other students. This results in a communal body of knowledge, specific to the class that is jointly created.

When preparing for a presentation on a particular artist, I also recommend that students try Pinterest. Because they can pin images as well as videos to a "board" (with proper citation), it can work well as a presentation tool. Also, because the Pinterest pages are on the Web, it is far easier to share their visuals from their presentations than if they were created in a traditional software program.

That Pinterest and Delicious are useful tools for research is evident in my own research and writing. I use Pinterest and Delicious to organize information and articles for my long-term research and writing goals. For instance, when I become interested in a new topic for potential research, I create a tag for it on Delicious and start tagging relevant articles and Web pages. Thus, as the ideas percolate in my head, I can simultaneously tag resources that are useful. As I move on to formulate a writing plan and time frame, I develop sub-tags and further categorize the resources as I locate them. Then, I am able to use the tagged and pinned items to develop the organizational structure for the article I am writing. Also, as I prepare for conference presentations, I use the same basic idea of locating a wide variety of resources and tagging them in Delicious. Then, when I create the presentation I already have an organized structure of resources in place. Modeling the research process for students is a useful way to demonstrate research and writing skills.

Observations and advice

Using these technologies resonates with and works for many students, but not all. I have learned that it is better to introduce these tools to the entire class in a computer lab and give them an in-class opportunity to practice for at least 30 minutes. During this practice session, I tell them that we will revisit Pinterest and Delicious in about two weeks and I encourage the students to try them on their own time in the interim. When we revisit the technologies in class, I ask students to show all of us the ways they are using Pinterest and Delicious. Many students become enthusiastic users and find ways to use the tools that I had not imagined. Students are very receptive to hearing and seeing ideas from their peers and it enables me to learn alongside my students and build a student-centered learning community.

While most students find some ways to use these technologies, a few students prefer not to use Pinterest and Delicious. Like many Web 2.0

technology tools, I have learned that Delicious and Pinterest are useful tools for some students, but not for others. I find that giving students an in-class opportunity to try these tools, requesting that they practice on their own, and allowing them to learn ideas from instructor and peers empowers them to think about what works for them and to make their own decisions about their learning preferences.

Recommended reading

Blankenship, M. (2011) How social media can and should impact higher education. *Education Digest*, **76**(7), 39–42.

Buffington, M. L. (2008) What is Web 2.0 and how can it further art education? *Art Education*, **61**(3), 36–41.

Gorra, A., Finlay, J., Devlin, M., Lavery, J., Neagle, R. et al. (2010, July) Learning with technology: What do students want? Paper presented at the *Fifth International Conference on e-Learning*. Abstract available from *http://www.ncl.ac.uk/computing/research/publication/159946*

Hemmi, A., Bayne, S., and Land, R. (2009) The appropriation and repurposing of social technologies in higher education. *Journal of Computer Assisted Learning*, **25**(1), 19–30.

Hung, H-T., and Yuen, S. C-Y. (2010) Educational use of social networking technology in higher education. *Teaching in Higher Education*, **15**(6), 703–14.

Huwe, T. K. (2011) How to craft social media for graduate study. *Computers in Libraries*, **31**(5), 25–7.

Junco, R., and Chickering, A. W. (2010) Civil discourse in the age of social media. *About Campus*, **15**(4), 12–18.

Lenhart, A., Purcell, K., Smith, A., and Zickuhr, K. (2010) *Social Media and Young Adults*. Available from *http://www.pewinternet.org/Reports/2010/Social-Media-and-Young-Adults.aspx* (the Pew Internet and American Life Project website).

New Media Consortium, and Educause Learning Initiative (2010) *Horizon Report*. Available from *http://www.educause.edu/ELI/2010HorizonReport/195400*

Rheingold, H. (2008) Using social media to teach social media. *New England Journal of Higher Education*, **23**(1), 25–6.

Schaffhauser, D. (2010) The super-secret, never-before-revealed guide to Web 2.0 in the classroom. *Campus Technology*, **24**(2), 26–35.

Silius, K., Kailanto, M., and Tervakari, A-M. (2011) Evaluating the quality of social media in an educational context. *International Journal of Emerging Technologies in Learning*, **6**(3), 21–7.

Wecker, M. (2011, June 8) *College Students Can't Go Long without Checking Their Smartphones, Laptops* (Web log comment). Available from *http://www.socialmediahighered.com/*

Supplemental materials

Pinterest tutorial

1. Go to pinterest.com.
2. Click "Request an Invite" at the top of the page.
3. An invitation will be sent to the email that you enter – usually this takes 60 seconds or less.
4. Log in to your email and follow the directions to start your Pinterest account. You can upload a photo of yourself or add as much or as little personal information as you wish.
5. Scroll over the word "Everything" at the top of the main Pinterest page to see the main categories that people use to categorize their pins.
6. Pick one that interests you and take a look at what others have pinned to the category.
7. After exploring a bit, start thinking of the "boards" that you would like to create. It can be helpful to pick a somewhat general category and then refine it further by making additional boards. I suggest that you start with a hobby or a topic of personal interest.
8. Pinterest makes some default boards with preset titles for you when you create an account, but you can easily add more or change the titles.
9. To add a new board, click on the word "Add" in the upper right-hand corner and select "Create a Board". Choose the appropriate category and add anyone else who you would like to be able to pin to your board.
10. It is helpful to download the "Pin it" button to your browser. The directions for this and several other helpful tools are available at

    http://pinterest.com/about/goodies/
11. Experiment by doing some Internet searches on topics related to the boards you created and start pinning the images that you find.
12. Also, take a look at what others have pinned by searching on Pinterest and you can "repin" their pins to your boards.
13. Now, think about an upcoming assignment you have. Do some Internet searches or search through Pinterest for your topic.

14. Create a board for your topic and start pinning what you find.
15. Experiment with different ways of organizing what you pin. For instance, if you are doing a presentation for class, you could pin all the images that you will use to a board.

Recommended Pinterest pages

1. Art and design
   http://pinterest.com/rachelmj/art-design/
2. Artists
   http://pinterest.com/jodikushins/artists/
3. Crafts
   http://pinterest.com/bjfr/crafts/
   http://pinterest.com/rachelmj/diy-crafts/
4. Higher education
   http://pinterest.com/kpatschke5/student-affairs-higher-education/
5. Info graphics
   http://pinterest.com/hetery/infografias-infographics/
6. Informal learning
   http://pinterest.com/juandoming/informal-learning/

3

Students' inadequate exposure to learning technology: overcoming the pedagogical challenge using wikis

Linzi J. Kemp

Abstract: This activity was designed to help international students overcome the challenge of using social media as a learning tool. Many of these students had little exposure to learning technologies. In this collaborative case study project students work in groups on a wiki, utilizing a blended pedagogical approach (face-to-face and online). Students are shown how to use a wiki, with the goals of encouraging research, writing, and collaborative work. Students then conduct research for the case study, utilizing the wiki as a medium to share and collaborate. The collaborative writing and editing features of the wiki prove a useful tool for both collection of information and publication of the completed case study. Through completion of the case study project, students progress from an initial state of inadequate exposure to learning technology to a state of competency in the use and understanding of social media as a learning tool.

Key words: case study, collaboration, communication, group work, international students, wiki.

Discipline/Academic areas addressed

Adaptable for all academic disciplines. In particular, this project is aimed at the disciplines of organizational behavior, management, leadership, and cross-cultural management.

Instructional purpose

The case study/wiki project encourages students with inadequate knowledge of learning technology to work successfully in a learning environment that blends face-to-face collaboration with the tools and advantages of social media. The project was piloted with international students who are members of the Net Generation, so they are familiar with social media but they have been less exposed to social media technologies in teaching and learning. Wikis offer an easily mastered technology that enables students to work collaboratively on research and writing. In developing their online skills, students are better prepared for careers in a global, digital marketplace.

This project was conducted with international students and can be particularly useful for those in less developed countries where computer technologies are not universally available. The activity is also of utility in the developed world, where students' sophistication with social media does not always transfer to educational uses of social media.

The activity has real-world value as students collaboratively research and write case studies about real-world leaders. In using a wiki to research and post information, evaluate and synthesize information, and write collaboratively, the project accomplishes dual goals of promoting collaboration and helping overcome the challenges of underexposure to learning technology. As an outcome of the original project, the case studies were published on the World Wide Web for others to read and comment upon, giving the case studies a larger audience. For the professor, a benefit is the developing of pedagogical skills through a timely and relevant project.

Student learning outcomes

1. Students will be able to research information and submit it to a wiki.
2. Students will be able to edit written work on a wiki.
3. Students will be able to publish the results as a case study.
4. Students will be able to access the online case study.

Prerequisite skills and knowledge

The only prerequisite is basic skill in the use of computers, to the extent of having the ability to wordprocess, and navigate a learning management system (LMS) such as "Blackboard". Prior knowledge of wikis is unnecessary. Knowledge of basic Internet searching, and some research skills are helpful as students must be able to locate sources online or through the library.

Step-by-step directions

1. Students will work in a team of 3–4 students to research about leaders and their leadership traits. Students are informed that their findings will be presented as a case study in written format using a wiki. The case studies will be published online.

2. An overview of leadership traits is presented by the professor to elicit student discussion about leaders and their leadership traits (see Appendix A in "Supplemental materials").

3. Students form groups (three to four students is optimal). Group members can be self-assigned or the instructor may want to assign.

   a. Students are assigned to groups or choose a team of three to four students to work with. You will need to plan how the group will work on this project. For example, assign roles (who does what?), assign coordination (how does the project all come together), assign time keeper (when are the deadlines?), assign proofreading (check all the work is to a high quality).

   b. Each group chooses a living business leader to study.

   c. Each group chooses a leadership trait to study (see Appendix A in "Supplemental materials"). For source information about the leader and her/his leadership trait, use online library and Web sources.

4. The instructor should assess student research skills in searching for and referencing online sources relating to leaders and leadership traits. Library and/or writing center staff can be involved at this step, and, depending on the level of student, a separate research workshop may be helpful.

5. The benefits of using a wiki are explained to students. A wiki is a document that groups of students form and edit together. A wiki is accessible "anytime, anyplace", and facilitates written communication amongst the groups of students.

6. Group wikis are created by the professor within the LMS, or in a commercial wiki such as Wikispaces. The advantage of LMS is that it is generally linked to the course, while the advantage of sites like Wikispaces is user-friendliness

   www.wikispaces.com/content/wiki-tour

   Once the wiki site has been selected, the instructor demonstrates how to use a wiki: submitting written work, editing, saving, and publishing. If the instructor is unfamiliar with the technology, it's recommended that IT staff be brought in to help with the creation of the wikis. The instructor may find useful resources for wiki use on their LMS, or, for example, in such sites as Educause

   www.educause.edu

   Competency should be achieved fairly quickly as the environment is similar to the functionality of word-processing software.

7. Each group ensures that all members are able to use the wiki by practicing posting and editing on the group wiki. The professor can also check students' competency.
8. Each group of students conducts research on their leader and leadership traits using an online library and/or high-quality Web sources.
9. Groups submit their research findings to the group wiki.
10. Following the project criteria (see Appendix B in "Supplemental materials"), students edit the wikis to collaboratively form a case study of their chosen leader and her/his traits.
11. Students complete and save the wiki. In preparation for posting to the World Wide Web students convert the case studies to PDF (copy and paste to a word document, save as PDF).
12. Either the students or the professor post case studies to an external website such as wikispaces.com or a blog such as

    www.blogger. com

    or a university website. Examples of such "published" blogs can be seen at

    http://facultydevelopment.wetpaint.com/page/Leadership

13. Reflection. A peer review enables students to give feedback on group members' performance (see Appendix C in "Supplemental materials").

Each student completes a peer review to facilitate individual and group reflection on the project. The peer review may also help with the professor's grading of the project.

14. Grading. The project can be graded as a group project based on the criteria. An example of grading that has been used is: "Below expectations" – the majority of the project criteria were not achieved; "Meets expectations" – substantial project criteria were achieved; "Exceeds expectations" – students achieved beyond project criteria. The project can also be graded for each student, based on their individual achievement of the SLOs. In the latter case, the professor will need to gather evidence of the individual competencies through student demonstration.

Approximate time required

Allow 50 minutes for each of the six sessions:

Week 1

Steps 1–3	Session (i). Explanation of project. Input on leadership traits.
Steps 4–5	Session (ii). Review of research skills. Overview of wiki benefits.
Steps 6–7	Session (iii). Wiki demonstration and practice.

Week 2

Steps 8–10	Session (i). Research work – students can complete outside classroom.
Steps 11–12	Session (ii). Complete case studies posted online.
Steps 13–14	Session (iii). Peer review/reflection. Grading.

Required resources

The outcome of this student wiki project has been made available on the World Wide Web:

http://facultydevelopment.wetpaint.com/page/Leadership

Here examples of case studies by students can be seen. Professors and students may wish to access the URL to see examples of outcomes. The technology needed includes a computer, LMS, wiki, and Internet access.

Variations on the basic theme

Technology used: Wiki, accessed through a learning management system (e.g., Blackboard, Angel, WebCT).

Other social media that can be used for this assignment: Students can be encouraged to use Twitter or text messaging for communication between group members. A blog could be kept by each group on the progress of the project. The facility of a blog is also often available through an LMS.

Access to an external website or blog site is necessary to post the final case studies for others to read. This may be university-provided or personal to the professor or sourced via blogger.com.

The assignment can be adapted to use in areas of the world where students have inadequate exposure to learning technology. The basic directions can be varied for other disciplines depending on a topic that involves research, critical thinking, and group work. Any discipline where students can research a "theme" can make good use of this project. For instance, in international businesses, students could research a particular business across a range of sectors. Or in English literature, students could create case studies of authors and their works.

Observations and advice

The use of social media has, as yet, been given little attention in the teaching and learning of the international Net Generation, therefore the project was a new idea within the context of international students. At the same time it was recognized that this project was important for students who had not previously been exposed to learning technology. The project is also a powerful idea; it gives practice and enables competency with social media, in preparation for students' employment.

What was observed in using wikis was that students were able to use the technology without much instruction. The professor encouraged students to help each other (those students with more exposure and comfort with learning technology taught others). The use of wikis therefore overcame a pedagogical challenge because students helped their team members to learn the technology.

Students were at first reticent to edit each other's work, as they expected the professor to do that. However, reinforcement of group responsibility for quality of outcome helped students to understand the need to peer review. Students soon recognized who was or was/not contributing by reviewing the edits in the wiki, and they followed up with each other on the progress of work.

A challenge was the amount of time necessary to review how to find sources and to reference. However, input to students from library and writing center staff helped with the review of research skills.

Recommended reading

Dobbins, K. W. (2005) Getting ready for the Net Generation learner. *Educause Review*, **40**(5), 8–9.

Feiertag, J., and Berge, Z. L. (2008) Training Generation N: How educators should approach the Net Generation. *Education & Training*, **50**(6), 457–64.

Norton, J. (2010) Interview with Don Tapscott, author of "Grown Up Digital". *Strategic Direction*, **26**(5), 29–31.

Leon, L., Przasnyski, Z., and Seal, K. (2008) Teaching Or/Ms to Net-Gens: A paradigm gap? *Or/Ms Today*, **35**(5), 10.

Lindorff, M. (2010) The personal values of tomorrow's workforce: Similarities and differences across sex and nationality. *Journal of Management and Organization*,**16**(3), 353–68

Kemp, L. J. (2011) A community of learning in graduate management education; Collaboration and creativity through social media. In: A. Mendez-Vilas (Ed.), *Education in a Technological World: Communicating Current and Emerging Research and Technological Efforts*. Badajoz, Spain: Formatex Research Center.

Monitor (2010, March 4) The net generation, unplugged technology and society: Is it really helpful to talk about a new generation of "digital natives" who have grown up with the Internet? *The Economist*. Available from *http://www.economist.com/node/15582279?story_id=15582279*

Motteram, G., and Sharma, P. (2009) Blending learning in a Web 2.0 world. *International Journal of Emerging Technologies and Society*, 7(2), 83–96.

Postman, N. (1993) *Technopoly: The Surrender of Culture to Technology*. New York: First Vintage.

Weyant, L., and Gardner, C. (2009) Wikis: An application in undergraduate management education: Allied Academies International Conference. *Academy of Educational Leadership Proceedings*, **14**(2), 52–6.

Williams, J., and Chinn, S. (2009) Using Web 2.0 to support the active learning experience. *Journal of Information Systems Education*, **20**(2), 165–74.

Xiaoqing, Y., and Hongxin, Z. (2007) Online learning community building: A case study in China. *Canadian Social Science*, 3(5), 102–13.

Supplemental materials

Appendix A Leadership traits

Traits are characteristics that distinguish one person from another. Examples are given below of traits associated with leadership. Professor/students may also add to the list after discussion.

Table 3.1 Leadership traits

Personal characteristics	**Social characteristics**	**Work-related characteristics**	**Social background**
Energy	Sociability, interpersonal skills	Drive, desire to excel	Education
Physical stamina	Cooperativeness	Responsibility in pursuit of goals	Mobility
Intelligence and ability	Ability to enlist cooperation	Persistence against obstacles, tenacity	
Intelligence, cognitive ability	Tact, diplomacy		
Knowledge			
Judgment, decisiveness			
Personality			
Self-confidence			
Honesty and integrity			
Enthusiasm			
Desire to lead			
Independence			

Adapted from Daft (2008).

Appendix B Criteria for case study

1. Cover page – group members' names, name of leader, traits studied.
   a. An image to represent the leader (not necessarily a photograph of the leader, could be a flag to represent the country, or a company logo).
2. Summary – justify the leader's importance.
   a. What he/she has achieved.
   b. Why did the group choose this leader?
3. Body – critically analyze the traits that the leader exhibits.
   a. Refer to examples as evidence of these traits.
   b. Show your understanding of the importance of the leadership trait.
4. References – cite sources. Include at least four quality references for each case
   a. Use online library/quality Web sources.
5. Publish – final version to be available in the wiki by a deadline as set by your professor.
   a. Copy and paste the wiki to a word document and save in PDF for uploading to the WWW as directed by the professor.
   b. See previous examples of this project at *http://facultydevelopment.wetpaint.com/page/Leadership*

Reflection

1. Complete a peer review on each team member.
   a. Include narrative comments.
   b. Submit a hard copy of the peer review to the professor.

Appendix C Peer Review Sheet

Table 3.2 Peer Review Sheet

Name of team member reviewed __________ ______________________

Name of reviewer __________ ______________________

Please assign a value to each item according to the following scale:

Grading scale

4	Excellent or exceeds expectations	(A)
3	Commendable or meets expectations	(B)
2	Acceptable	(C)
1	Poor or does not meet expectations	(D)

Demonstrated realistic understanding of role within the team	( )
Worked well with other team members	( )
Contributed actively to team work	( )
Completed individual research on time	( )
Turned in research to the wiki in usable form	( )
Was able to edit wiki	( )
Was able to save wiki	( )
Was able to publish wiki	( )
Shared information, perceptions, and feedback	( )
Demonstrated commitment to quality of final work	( )
Total points assigned	( )

Qualitative comments to be shared with reviewed student

Adapted from American University of Sharjah (2011).

Collecting and analyzing primary sources

Lisa M. Lane

Abstract: History, social science, and the humanities commonly utilize the examination of primary sources and the creation of theses in the development of disciplinary knowledge. Social media such as a class blog, wiki, discussion forum, or collaborative document can provide a way for students to form their own collections of visual and textual primary sources, and develop arguable theses, both collaboratively and individually. Social media sites allow students to post their sources during a specific period, after which they can create and post an individual thesis using some of the items from the source collection as support. For a fully online class, this approach is most effective as a pattern for the entire term, with tasks increasing in detail and complexity. For the face-to-face classroom, a version of the technique may be used for individual class sessions.

Key words: blogs, collaborative learning, constructivist pedagogy, forums, information literacy, World Wide Web.

Discipline/Academic areas addressed

While this activity was developed for humanities or social sciences, it is appropriate for any discipline where visual and textual works are used as primary sources, and analysis is expected.

Instructional purpose

Historians, social scientists, and humanities scholars routinely use primary sources in their work, analyzing and constructing arguments supported by the sources. The Web provides the ability for students to easily discover a wide variety of such sources, both visual and textual. Such discovery, when guided by a topic or purpose (determined by the instructor), can offer the opportunity to practice search skills and critically evaluate online sources. In working collaboratively to create a collection, students experience the interdependency involved in research. Because the collection is then used as a foundation for writing and supporting individual theses and papers, students are motivated to post sources of interest to them. The summative assessment (in the case of history, the construction of a historical thesis supported by a set of sources) is based on creating and proving a cogent argument, a skill that is valuable in many areas. Peer ratings can then hone these arguments.

Student learning outcomes

Students will demonstrate the ability to:

1. locate primary sources and share them in an online forum
2. think critically about the appropriateness and usefulness of sources
3. correctly cite each source posted with author/artist, title, date and a live link to the source
4. collaborate with others to create a collection of sources around a common topic
5. use several of the posted sources to support and explain a cogent thesis
6. critically comment on other students' work
7. work in a way that expresses digital literacy, using skills such as search, hyperlinking, attribution, collaboration, and embedding digital media.

Prerequisite skills and knowledge

The instructor should be skilled in administering whatever software is used (i.e., a learning management system, blog, wiki, collaborative document, or discussion forum) and implementing a setup for students to submit work that includes the posting of multimedia, both uploaded and linked from the Web, preferably with a user-friendly toolbar.

Students need access and posting privileges in the LMS forum, open forum, wiki, document or on the blog (commenting privileges may be sufficient for the blog), and should have some knowledge of how to post multimedia there (this may be assisted through instructor modeling and/or tutorials).

Step-by-step directions

For full-semester application

1. Use the technology selected (blog, LMS, wiki, website) and create a site for posting images and theses.

2. Develop the activity as a weekly required task with one forum or thread per week, and determine grading weight, deadlines, and how the instructor will provide feedback.

3. Create guidance (in the form of handouts, tutorials, or class discussions) about selecting databases and primary sources, and citing these sources in the preferred format. Provide websites or bookmarks to limit selection. Model an appropriate search, selection, posting, and analysis in class or in a video tutorial.

4. Provide feedback to students collectively regarding the quality of the collection, and individually regarding their work on the thesis and/or essay.

For single-class application

1. Use a computer lab for class, or require laptops and smartphones for a "lab day".

2. Model an appropriate search, selection, posting, and analysis in class.

3. Assign groups of four to six students to work on creating a collection related to a specific topic.

4. Visit each group during class to help with citations and identifying which sources are primary.

5. After a sufficient period of time (at first this may be about 40 minutes, but will decrease if you do the exercise frequently):

    a. If there is little time left, have each group use their own collection of three sources to create a thesis.

    b. If there is more time, have each group examine the entire collection as the foundation of their thesis.

6. Have each group report their theses and sources.

Instructions for students – sample for class with a single blog

Primary source collection and analysis

In this class, you will be working collaboratively to create collections of primary sources to be used as the basis for writing your essays.

Primary sources are evidence, works written or made during the time frame being studied. We will be collecting mostly visual primary sources, although written sources are accepted also.

Each week, you will:

1. work together in your group to find appropriate primary sources and embed them in a comment response to that week's blog post

2. cite each source inside the comment with artist/author, title, date and a live link to the source itself

3. select several of the sources from the week's collection to write about, and create a historical thesis supported by these sources

4. post your essay to the blog for peer review

5. rate at least one other student's essay using a rubric (you may only select an essay that has less than two ratings already).

Finding sources

This class has many Web-based sources listed at the Diigo website at

http://www.diigo.com/user/lisamlane/hist111resources

This website contains sources that have been collected by the instructor and previous students. Some are individual sources, and others are collections or databases.

1. Select sources that are of interest to you, have full citation information (see #2 above), and fit into the time frame we're studying for that week.
2. Then you can either right-click and save the image to your desktop, or copy the URL from your browser. This will be demonstrated in class.

Posting sources

Each group has its own area on the blog. Click on your group, and click "Leave a Comment". Then leave your response. To add your image, select "Add Media". You can use either the upload tab or the URL tab to add your image (a sample post can be found in "Supplemental materials").

Constructing and posting your essay

The development of essays will be discussed in class. Essays are posted under the topic for that week. First, write your essay in a separate text program, so it doesn't get lost and you have a backup. Select the topic of the week and choose "Leave a Comment". Copy and paste the text of your essay into the posting area. This will be demonstrated in class.

Peer rating

The last step is peer rating. Use the following criteria and select the appropriate choice from the following choices (note: these choices are provided in a drop-down menu online):

- an excellent interpretive thesis using cited sources
- a good interpretive thesis using cited sources
- a thesis but not enough sources or not properly cited
- not a full thesis
- good ideas but cited sources not explained
- good ideas but English/writing problems

- no thesis evident
- evidence doesn't all work.

Getting help

Making sure the technology works, and that things are going well, can be tricky. Although you can always contact the instructor for assistance, you may find it faster to post in the student Facebook group. Joining and participating in the group will be demonstrated in class (sample FAQs are provided in "Supplemental materials").

Approximate time required

There are two options:

1. Use the technique throughout the term as a basis for activity in the class. In this case, students may spend 2–3 hours a week for a three-unit semester class discovering, posting, and writing their theses and support.
2. Use the technique for one or more in-class sessions, where students have access to computers, laptops, or smartphones. Working quickly together in small groups, students can create a collection and present a group-developed thesis and brief analysis to the class in 1–2 hours.

Required resources

Instructors may either have students use the World Wide Web to search for sources, or choose to limit the resources available to students. The instructor could link to appropriate websites to assure that certain sources are used, or could create social bookmarks (in a system such as Diigo) to create a continually updated list. When using social bookmarking, one could also encourage students to add the websites they discover to the list, adding a further element of social media. The instructor or the whole class may post resource websites using a tag, to be available for students working on forming their collection.

The choice among formats (wiki, forum, blog, etc.) is complex, particularly if the forum is located in a learning management system. In a classroom setting, it is sometimes difficult for several students to log in at the same time in certain technologies (such as an LMS or wiki), which will restrict the activity. Similarly, an LMS is closed and private—the social media aspect is weakened. An open forum, collaborative document, or open blog may provide public access for commenting, and students who are concerned about privacy should be allowed to participate under a pseudonym. Possible open forums may include websites like Ning or Facebook.

Technological requirements

For the full-term application, students may use whatever technology the instructor is using for the rest of the class. Where class materials are posted in an LMS such as Blackboard or Moodle, and a closed environment is desired, a simple forum can be used for posting both source collections and theses. If the class environment is a blog, then blog comments can be configured to accept media and be used for posting. Course wikis can provide a similar environment. For classroom application, students will need access to the Internet via computer or smartphone.

Variations on the basic theme

The basic idea could be adapted for a variety of disciplines where analyzing a collection of sources would be appropriate. History is the most obvious, since the collection and evaluation of primary sources is the main skill in the discipline. The artistic disciplines fit easily, as students can create collections of artworks from various periods or styles. Many courses in the humanities and social sciences rely on primary sources of some kind, including literary works, political speeches, propaganda posters, editorial cartoons, scanned letters, or film.

What makes this method of using primary sources effective is that social media provides affordances for working together in an instant, visible way that is much more efficient than having students collect print resources and bring them to class, or do their research on their own. The immediacy provided by the social media environment (even when done asynchronously, as in a full-term online class) encourages collaboration and participation.

Observations and advice

Having the class create its own collection provides a sense of ownership and influence in the class, and moves the emphasis from "content" to skills. The success of the technique depends on the comfort level of the instructor in having students find their own resources—some are content with the open Web, while others want source choices more restricted. Students will get lost sometimes finding sources, and this is to be expected, so feedback from the instructor is important regardless of whether the technique is used in a classroom or online as a pedagogical pathway. As students continue to post more resources and construct more theses, they begin to realize that the quality of the sources is important because they'll need to use them later. Students begin to go back and add sources so that they can develop better essays. Instructors should keep all previous units open and allow students to add more to the collection, particularly if they want theses and essays to expand in terms of the time frame being studied. Instructors should also be aware that some students will have trouble with the idea of citing a source, and may need to be reminded to always provide artist/ author, title, date, and a link back to the source. When having students write essays, is a good idea not to allow the use of any source that is not properly cited.

Recommended reading

Barr, R. (1995) From teaching to learning: A new paradigm for undergraduate education. *Change*, **27**(6).

Booth, A. (2003) *Teaching History at University: Enhancing Learning and Understanding*. Philadelphia, PA: Psychology Press.

Henry, M. (2002) Constructivism in the community college classroom. *The History Teacher*, **36**(1).

Hoagland, M. (2000) Utilizing constructivism in the history classroom. Dissertation. Retrieved from *http://www.eric.ed.gov/PDFS/ED482436.pdf*

Instruction & Research Services Committee of the Reference & User Services Association (History Section) in the American Library Association (2003) *Using Primary Sources on the Web*. Chicago, IL: Reference & User Services Association (History Section). Available from *http://www.ala.org/ala/mgrps/divs/rusa/sections/history/resources/pubs/usingprimarysources/index.cfm*

Gwaltney, M. (2011, January 2) *History Education in a World of Information Surplus* (Web log post). Available from *http://mikegwaltney.net/blog/?p=255*

Kumar, S., and Deese, R. (2010) Teaching history with blogs for student engagement and critical use of digital media. *Revista de Informática Aplicada*, **6**(2).

Lane, L. (2011, September 19) *Lab Day!* (Web log post). Available from *http://lisahistory.net/wordpress/2011/09/lab-day/*

Mak, S., Williams, R., and Mackness, J. (2010) Blogs and forums as communication tools in a MOOC. *Proceedings of the Seventh International Conference on Networked Learning*. Available from *http://lancs.ac.uk/fss/organisations/netlc/past/nlc2010/abstracts/PDFs/Mak.pdf*

Malkmus, D. (2010) "Old stuff" for new teaching methods: Outreach to history faculty teaching with primary sources. *Libraries and the Academy*, **10**(4).

Roy Rosenzweig Center for History and New Media (n.d.) *Primary Source Activities: Foundations of U.S. History*. Available from *http://chnm.gmu.edu/loudountah/resources.php*

Townsend, R. (2010) How is new media reshaping the work of historians? *Perspectives in History*. American Historical Association. Available from *http://www.historians.org/Perspectives/issues/2010/1011/1011pro2.cfm*

Supplemental materials

Appendix A FAQs for students

Discussion forums

- **How often do I have to post in the forums?**

  Three times per week, once to post a primary source, once to post your thesis essay, and once to help someone.

- **When do I have to post?**

  The first post is always due by Wednesday midnight, the second by Sunday night.

- **How do I know what we're supposed to post?**

  We will be using the forums for creating collections of primary sources, then using them as a foundation for writing and commenting.

  - Each "Post sources and writing" forum has a prompt at the top – these have instructions in the first week. Each student posts a primary source for that week's era by Wednesday midnight. On Thursday or Friday morning, Lisa will post (titled "Take discussion from here, please") with instructions on creating a thesis and mini-essay that uses the sources posted that week.

- So each student posts twice a week: a primary source by Wednesday night, and a thesis/mini-essay using some of those sources by Sunday night.

- **But I lost my whole forum post!**

  At any time, there could be a power failure or your ISP could knock you off the Internet. Always write anything extensive in a text program first, then copy and paste it into Moodle.

- **Why are we rating forum posts?**

  In some classes, you are asked to rate the discussion posts. This helps give the author an understanding of how the post is being perceived. It also gives me an understanding of how students are perceiving each other's work, and provides a sense of responsibility.

- **How are my forum posts graded?**

  Posts are not graded individually, but collectively, to allow maximum opportunity for practice and improvement. Discussion, posting, and writing is part of the Contribution Assessment, which happens twice, at midterm and near the end of the semester. Each time, 10% of the grade is assigned, so participation in the course and in the forums especially is worth 20% of the grade.

- **The forum is a mess! How can I see things more easily?**

  At the top of each forum, there is a drop-down menu. I set the default at nested form, which I like because each reply is indented and you can see the whole discussion on one screen. If that's not for you, try one of the other views. For a Blackboard-style experience where you click separately on every post, try "Display replies in threaded form".

Primary sources

- **How do I add an image, video clip, or link to a website to my forum post?**

  See these tutorial pages:

  Add an image – *http://lisahistory.net/pages/uploadimage.htm*

  Add a video clip – *http://lisahistory.net/pages/uploadvideo.htm*

  Add a link to a website – *http://lisahistory.net/pages/addlink.htm*

- **It says my image is too big to upload?**

  The default upload size is set pretty darn small in Moodle. If you get this message, let me know right away so I can change the upload allowance for that forum. Be sure to say which class and section you're in.

- **The instructor says to use "primary sources". What is a primary source?**

  A primary source is created during the time period we're studying. An example would be a letter, diary, artwork, or document produced during that era. A secondary source is something about that time, but created later. Examples of primary sources might be a book by Mark Twain, a political cartoon from the nineteenth century, or an ancient Greek statue. Examples of secondary sources might include your textbook, Wikipedia, or a website about Mark Twain.

  There's one more complication! A clip from a film made during the 1930s would be a primary source if we were studying the 1930s. But if that 1930s' film were about something that happened in 1870, that same film would be a secondary source if we were studying the 1870s.

- **How can I find good primary sources, with good citations?**

  Most students start with an image search, or look at websites about a particular era. But often, people who use images on websites do not cite author/artist, title, and date. What to do?

  There are two options. The first is to use Advanced Search to limit the results to particular domains, such as .edu, that are more likely to cite sources than a blog or fan page. In Google, you can add site:.edu to your search, or use Advanced Search.

  Another option is a reverse image search. Sites like TinEye.com let you search for an image by the appearance of that image, showing you other sites where that image may appear. This lets you track it down to a museum or university that might cite the source properly.

  Where you start the search can have an impact too. Google Images will take you longer to track something down than using museum collections, university pages, and historical sites.

  So another option is to start with a list of websites. I am starting a collection of these at Diigo

  http://www.diigo.com

  using the class name as a tag.

I've tagged them for History 104

http://www.diigo.com/user/lisamlane/hist104resources

History 105

http://www.diigo.com/user/lisamlane/hist105resources

and History 111

http://www.diigo.com/user/lisamlane/hist111resources).

- **Can you show me?**

  Yes. See my video tutorial on finding and posting your sources at

  http://www.screenr.com/yMs8

- **Do I have to use only the sources posted in the forum?**

  No. You should use at least one, two if you can, of the sources posted by yourself or your colleagues. Remember, you control what's on the board, and can always add another source yourself! If you need a third source for a thesis or test question, you may add one from anywhere you wish, so long as you cite it properly.

Appendix B Instructions for students – sample for class with a single WordPress blog

Primary source collection and analysis

In this class, you will be working collaboratively to create collections of primary sources to be used as the basis for writing your essays.

Primary sources are evidence, works written or made during the time frame being studied. We will be collecting mostly visual primary sources, although written sources are accepted also.

Each week, you will

1. work together in your group to find appropriate primary sources and embed them in a comment response to that week's blog post
2. cite each source inside the comment with artist/author, title, date and a live link to the source itself
3. select several of the sources from the week's collection to write about, and create a historical thesis supported by these sources
4. post your essay to the blog for peer review

5. rate at least one other student's essay using a rubric (you may only select an essay that has fewer than two ratings already).

Getting into the website

Go to the class website – the URL will be given to you in class. You will see a link that says "New User? Register Here!" Click this and register with the email account you would like used for the class. After this, you can use Log In to post each time.

Finding sources

This class has many Web-based sources listed at the Diigo website at

http://www.diigo.com/user/lisamlane/hist111resources

These have been collected by the instructor and previous students. Some are individual sources, and others are collections or databases. Select sources that are of interest to you, have full citation information (see #2 above), and fit into the time frame we're studying for that week.

Some examples of sources include paintings, images from original books or manuscripts, photographs of architecture, sculptures, speeches, etc. Do not worry too much whether your source is exactly right—just make sure it was created during the era we're studying that week, and that you have the following information for it: artist/author, title, and date.

Then you can either right-click and save the image to your desktop, or copy the URL from your browser. This will be demonstrated in class.

Appendix C Sample source post

A sample source explanation post

My source this week for the seventeenth century is Charles I of England, painted by Anthony van Dyck circa 1635. It is now in the Louvre. I found the image at

http://en.wikipedia.org/wiki/Anthony_van_Dyck

Charles I was king of England until the English Civil War, when he was executed. Anthony van Dyck painted many portraits of him.

A sample thesis post

The portrait of Charles I by Anthony van Dyck (c. 1635), the portrait of Louis XIV by Hyacinthe Rigaud (1701), and the portrait of Marie Antoinette by Elisabeth Vigee-Lebrun (1779) all show that monarchs used portrait painting to portray their power and wealth.

5

Unraveling the research process: social bookmarking and collaborative learning

Caroline Sinkinson and Alison Hicks

Abstract: This assignment is designed to leverage the social bookmarking site, Diigo, to capture the social, collaborative, and participatory nature of research. Over the course of the semester students collaboratively bookmark a variety of research sources (experts, organizations, reports, and other formal/informal sources) in the class library before critically analyzing and evaluating connections between sources and their contribution to the academic conversation. This allows students to develop a sense of the dynamic and collaborative nature of inquiry, while also training students to negotiate multiple streams of information, to think critically about information, and to draw connections and meaning from information to inform personal contributions. Regular reflective prompts develop student ability to self-assess personal growth, an essential element of learning in the twenty-first century academic environment as well as civic, personal, and work settings.

Key words: Diigo, information literacy, research assignments, reflection, personal learning environment.

Discipline/Academic areas addressed

The assignment may be applied to any discipline in which research and inquiry are core. The assignment was originally designed for a first year writing course focused on sustainability.

Instructional purpose

The research paper is a common rite of passage in the academic world. While students are typically successful at amassing information sources, many grapple with new conventions of academic discourse and the synthesis of these foreign concepts into their own writing. Furthermore, research assignment guidelines that focus on the number or type of sources can lead students to view information as an object, and to conceive of research as a bounded, static product rather than grasping the dynamic and collaborative nature of inquiry.

Social bookmarking sites such as Diigo can help shift the focus from a final product to the experience of inquiry, as well as repositioning research as active dialog. First, Diigo enables the quick and easy bookmarking of the various informal conversations that lead to formal scholarship. Students' exposure to conversation in context (blogs, tweets, discussion) breaks down academic barriers by helping their understanding of research as an active conversation. This focus on the context also means that students can provide much more purposeful critical evaluation of sources rather than following teacher-imposed criteria. Second, the participatory nature of social bookmarking in the class Diigo library mimics the interconnected nature of research and the social construction of knowledge. By enabling students to work collaboratively and draw on other students' work and expertise, research becomes more active and meaningful. Finally, the social nature of Diigo means that students are curating a set of topical resources within a community as one would in civic, social, or academic environments. This provides an audience beyond the teacher, making research activities more authentic.

Student learning outcomes

1. As a result of exploring multiple information sources, students will be able to identify formal and informal modes of knowledge creation.
2. As a result of evaluation, students will be able to interpret the strengths and weaknesses of their information sources.
3. As a result of contributions to the class Diigo library, students will be able to categorize, combine, and compile information sources for collaborative knowledge sharing.
4. As a result of reflective writing, students will be able to appraise their information-seeking processes.
5. As a result of Web research, students will be able to summarize their research topic.

Prerequisite skills and knowledge

The only skills necessary are the Web-browsing skills commonly possessed by college students.

Step-by-step directions

Directions are mapped to American Association of School Librarians (AASL) standards (AASL, 2007).

http://www.ala.org/aasl/files/guidelinesandstandards/learningstandards/AASL_Learning_Standards_2007.pdf

First class session

a. Goals and directions for the first class period

- Students will pursue an inquiry project in order to expand their course content knowledge. (AASL Standard 1.1.1)
- Students will draw from prior background knowledge in order to pose new questions to frame inquiry. (AASL Standard 1.1.2)
- Students will monitor their information-seeking habits in order to adjust as needed and to seek help when needed. (AASL Standard 1.4.4)

b. Class activity

- Class will choose a research interest within the broad course topic.
- Teacher will facilitate a discussion about information origins, discovery, and evaluation. The teacher will invite students to recall prior information-seeking experiences, such as choosing a college or university to attend. The class will discuss where students gathered information: parents, friends, advisors, counselors, online, guidebooks, university information, orientations, etc. Students will discuss distinctions among information source types (during this experience): people, online materials, print materials, experience.
- Students will be introduced to the project stages and the reflection exercises attached to each stage. Students will create a Google document for reflective essays.

c. Out-of-class activity

- Students will use their own knowledge and search strategies to start gathering background information on the research topic.
- Students will compose the first reflective essay, using the guidelines in Appendix A in "Supplemental materials". Essays can be evaluated using the rubric in Appendix B.

Second class session

a. Goals

- Students will pursue an inquiry.
- Students will execute Web searches on the topic in order to demonstrate independence while choosing information sources. (AASL Standard 1.2.2)
- Students will explore a range of resources, including social media, in order to investigate a range of perspectives and information about their topic. (AASL Standard 1.2.3)
- Students will add resources to the class Diigo library in order to participate in knowledge sharing and to demonstrate productivity in group work. (AASL Standards 3.1.2, 3.2.3)

b. Class activity

- The teacher will guide students through a sample search in Google Scholar. The teacher will model identifying a core article, tracking author affiliations, related sources, and online conversations. The teacher will collect resources in Diigo. The teacher will emphasize how collaborative collection will help the class to extend their knowledge and to draw connections between materials.
- Students will search the community library in Diigo to see example sites, tags, and group interaction on their topic.
- Students will join the class Diigo group and download the Diigolet button to their Web browsers.
- Students will then work in groups to bookmark and tag some sample sources in the class Diigo group. (Tags can be evaluated using the rubric in Appendix B in "Supplemental materials".)

c. Out-of-class activity

- Students will bookmark at least three experts on their topic, three article sources, three informal sources (blogs, tweets, forums) and one organization or community interested in the topic prior to the next class session.

- Students will add tags appropriate to the type of source as defined in the class session (people_topic, articles_topic, organizations_topic, blogs_topic, microblogs_topic). Students may also choose to add their own tags.

- Students will compose the second reflective essay, using the guidelines in Appendix A in "Supplemental materials". Essays can be evaluated using the rubric in Appendix B.

Third class session

a. Goals

- Students will generate evaluation criteria in order to maintain a critical approach to information sources. (AASL Standard 1.2.4)

- Students will collaborate with peers in order to extend their own inquiry process. (AASL Standards 3.2.2, 3.2.3)

b. Class activity

- Students explore the links and tags of peers in the class Diigo library.

- The teacher will prompt students to discuss information-seeking experiences and strategies and the different sources collected.

- Students will work in groups to discuss how they evaluate sources and what criteria they apply. Groups will present their recommendations to the class. The class will consolidate all recommendations and develop a final list of criteria to be applied to the group library of sources. The criteria list can be evaluated using the rubric in Appendix B

c. Out-of-class activity

- Each student is assigned to evaluate and annotate three of the group library sources (must not be one she/he collected) using class-defined criteria.

- Students will add evaluation text and responses to the Diigo group bookmark in the description field. Students will receive additional credit for adding notes and annotations directly to the online source.
- Students will compose the third reflective essay using the guidelines in Appendix A in "Supplemental materials". Essays can be evaluated using the rubric in Appendix B.

Fourth class session

a. Goals

- Students will present an information source in order to demonstrate the application of evaluation criteria. (AASL Standard 3.2.1)
- Students will assess their information-seeking process in order to revise strategies for future learning expeditions. (AASL Standards 1.2.5–1.2.7)

b. Class activity

- Students will present one of the evaluated sources (3–5 minutes).
- The class will discuss how the sources informed their knowledge about the topic as well as how the sources interacted with the others (supported, contradicted, extended).
- Students will create mindmaps (online or paper) in order to illustrate the connections or contradictions between sources.
- The class will discuss expectations for the final assignment.

Final assignment

a. Goals

- Students will enter into authentic conversation with information sources.
- Students will demonstrate confidence in presenting their learning.

b. Activity

- Students may choose to write an in-depth analysis of two sources, *or* contribute to the online discussion by responding to two blog posts or online articles, *or* interview two specialists in the field (in person or virtually) and create a profile of the individual and analysis of the interview transcript.

Approximate time required

The assignment uses four class periods (each lasting 90 minutes) with additional student time out of class. The classes do not need to be scheduled sequentially; in fact the authors suggest integrating the assignment deeply into the course and using the process to inform the broader course content. Activities could also be condensed into three periods, depending on the level/prior experience of the class.

Required resources

Personal technology tools

- Diigo *http://www.diigo.com/*
- Google docs *http://docs.google.com/*

Documents

- Reflection template (see Appendix A in "Supplemental materials")
- Rubrics (see Appendix B in "Supplemental materials")

Technology

- Laptop/Device
- Internet

Diigo education account: *http://www.diigo.com/education*

Google docs account: *https://docs.google.com*

Variations on the basic theme

Discipline variations

The assignment could be adjusted for any field of study or discipline which would benefit from collaborative aggregation and evaluation of sources. The types of sources collected could be adjusted to fit the area of study, for example: data sources, multimedia sources, interviews, conference proceedings, market reports, etc. Students could be encouraged to investigate, join, and contribute to Diigo groups through the tagging and discussion features of Diigo.

Technology variations

Diigo was chosen as the social bookmarking tool for this assignment but there are a number of alternative technology options, including Evernote, Symbaloo, or Netvibes. Google Docs was chosen for the assignment because of the perceived utility of this tool beyond the class assignment. However, there are a number of other online document-sharing technologies available.

Final assignment

The culminating assignment could also be changed to capture the course objectives.

Observations and advice

The stages of the assignment are intentionally structured to slow the process of inquiry in order to invite student reflection on the nature of research. Specifically, we hope that students will discover the elements of conversation between sources, whether they are formal publications or informal online discussions. The assignment also aims to demonstrate research as a mode of learning and discovery; therefore, greater emphasis is placed on exploring, drawing connections, and reflecting than on a final statement or conclusion.

The assignment provides the opportunity for students to explore tools and methods of investigation that work to support their learning. If students discover a new tool or a new connection, teachers are encouraged to remain flexible and open.

The assignment requires time devoted to instruction on Diigo and Google Docs as well as individual student troubleshooting. However, exposure to these tools will serve students in future academic, work, and personal situations. When choosing tools for the assignment, teachers should consider the applicability to other situations as well as the stability of the technology and any privacy implications.

We suggest assigning approximately 25% of the course grade to the assignment. Students should be graded on their contribution and engagement with the process (see Appendix B) in addition to the culminating assignment.

Recommended reading

AASL (American Association of School Librarians) (2007) *Standards for the 21st-Century Learner*. Available from *http://www.ala.org/aasl/files/guidelinesandstandards/learningstandards/AASL_Learning_Standards_2007.pdf*

Bloom, B. S. (Ed.). (1956) *Taxonomy of Educational Objectives: The Classification of Educational Goals* (First Edition). New York: Longmans, Green & Co.

Blackwell-Starnes, A. (2011) Academic research, professional discourse: Social bookmarking as a catalyst for rhetorical research pedagogies. Unpublished doctoral dissertation. Denton, TX: Texas Woman's University.

Deitering, A-M., and Gronemyer, K. (2011) Beyond peer-reviewed articles: Using blogs to enrich students' understanding of scholarly work. *Libraries and the Academy*, **11**(1), 489–503.

Drexler, W. (2010) The networked student model for construction of personal learning environments: Balancing teacher control and student autonomy. *Australasian Journal of Educational Technology*, **26**(3).

Dunaway, M. K. (2011) Connectivism: Learning theory and pedagogical practice for networked information landscapes. *Reference Services Review*, **39**(4), 675–85.

Elmborg, J. (2006) Critical information literacy: Implications for instructional practice. *The Journal of Academic Librarianship*, **32**(2), 192–9.

Hamilton, B. J. (2012) Embedded librarianship: A high school case study. In: S. Polanka (Ed.), *E-Reference Context and Discoverability in Libraries: Issues and Concepts* (pp. 237–54). Hershey, PA: IGI Global.

Hamilton, B. (2011) Creating conversations for learning: School libraries as sites of participatory culture. *School Library Monthly*, **27**(8), 41–3.

Lankes, R. D. (2011). *The Atlas of New Librarianship*. Cambridge, MA: MIT Press.

McElvaney, J., and Berge, Z. (2010) Weaving a personal web: Using online technologies to create customized, connected, and dynamic learning environments. *Canadian Journal of Learning and Technology/La revue canadienne de l'apprentissage et de la technologie*, **35**(2). Available from *http://www.cjlt.ca/index.php/cjlt/article/view/524/257*

McLoughlin, C., and Lee, M. J. W. (2010) Personalised and self regulated learning in the Web 2.0 era: International exemplars of innovative pedagogy using social software. *Australasian Journal of Educational Technology*, **26**(1), 28–43.

Educause. (2009) *Seven Things You Should Know about Personal Learning Environments* (Educause Learning Initiative, Eds.) Scenario, 2. Educause. Available from *http://net.educause.edu/ir/library/pdf/ELI7049.pdf*

Supplemental materials

Appendix A Reflective template

Essay 1

- How have you sought information for research previously?
- What habits will you change for this project?
- When might you need help? Where will you seek assistance?
- What do you already know about your research topic?
- What questions do you have about your topic?
- What more do you need to know?
- Where might you discover this information? Who might be engaged in the conversation?

Essay 2

- Where did you begin searching?
- What changes did you make to your initial search in order to improve results?
- What prompted you to make that change?
- Did you learn new search strategies from your teammates?
- What do you still need to learn about your topic?
- What are the gaps/weaknesses in the sources you have collected?

Essay 3:

- What surprised you the most about your peer suggestions for evaluation criteria?
- What was your most significant contribution to the evaluation criteria discussion?
- What difficulties did you encounter while applying evaluation criteria?
- How did your opinion of the sources change during evaluation?
- How might you change the evaluation criteria for future use?

- While evaluating, what connections between sources or ideas did you discover?

Appendix B Class rubrics

Diigo social-bookmarking network

Table 5.1 Creating and using the Diigo social-bookmarking network

	Exemplary (4)	**Accomplished (3)**	**Developing (2)**	**Beginning (1)**
Content added (Class 2)	Adds appropriate sources in a variety of formats to the group	Adds mostly appropriate sources in a variety of formats to the group	Adds a few appropriate sources to the group but with little attempt to provide variety	Does not add any appropriate sources that relate to the topic
Tags added (Class 2)	Adds group tags appropriately to information sources	Adds tags appropriately to majority of information sources	Add tags to information sources, but not always appropriately	Does not add tags appropriately to information sources
Content evaluation (Class 3)	Adds evaluation criteria and annotations to three links in Diigo library; all criteria were applied to sources	Adds evaluation criteria to two to three links in Diigo library; evaluation criteria not fully or appropriately completed	Adds evaluation criteria to one to two links in Diigo library; evaluation criteria not fully or appropriately completed	Does not add complete or appropriate evaluation criteria for links

Reflection on research process

Table 5.2 Reflection on research process

	Exemplary (4)	**Accomplished (3)**	**Developing (2)**	**Beginning (1)**
Reflective essays (×3)	Coherent, focused reflection that develops thoughtful connections between class, homework, and self-analysis. Shows in-depth engagement with the topic	Fairly focused reflection where connections are made between class, homework, and self-analysis yet may remain undeveloped. Shows moderate engagement with the topic	Descriptive reflection that displays some connection between class, homework, and self-analysis. Shows passing engagement with the topic	Unfocused reflection that displays no connection between class, homework, and self-analysis. Shows little engagement with the topic

Part 2
Communication and collaboration

2A Communication, oral and written

Using Wimba Voice Board to facilitate foreign language conversation courses

Silvia U. Baage

Abstract: This project is geared towards strengthening speaking and listening skills in intermediate and advanced foreign language (FL) students. Students record mini-presentations of numerous topics on Wimba Voice Board periodically throughout the semester. Each recording is between 2–3 minutes of length in which the presenter (1) introduces the topic, (2) summarizes findings and uses specific examples to illustrate arguments, (3) talks about his or her motivation and how the information relates to the content of the course. Following each round of mini-presentations, each student listens to two of his or her peers' recordings and records two critiques of 30–60 seconds each in which the student comments on (1) a minimum of two specific pieces of information gleaned from listening to the mini-presentation and (2) the usefulness of and opinion about the information presented.

Key words: asynchronous computer-mediated communication (ACMC), audio-based threaded discussions, online voice tool, interactive technologies, peer-to-peer learning, self-assessment, Wimba Voice Board

Discipline/Academic areas addressed

Any foreign language course – including ESL (English as a second language) – with a primary focus on aural and oral skills. This assignment could also be implemented in any other discipline with a presentational component.

Instructional purpose

Wimba Voice Board is an easy-to-use asynchronous audio-based threaded discussion forum. Unlike task-based interactions in asynchronous computer-mediated communication (CMC), the voice tool allows for students to create the content of their discussion threads. Students use peer-to-peer learning to discover, learn, and share their research and reflections about specific cultural topics of their target language in preparation for their end-of-semester oral exam with the instructor.

This project keeps students engaged in the learning process on several levels. First of all, it implements all levels of Bloom's taxonomy of learning for research, mini-presentation, and critiques – knowledge, comprehension, application, analysis, synthesis, and evaluation; see

http://www.edpsycinteractive.org/topics/cognition/bloom.html

Moreover, the structure of this assignment ensures that students become exposed to different aspects of learning a foreign language through communication, cultures, connections, comparisons, and communities (the 5 C's) as outlined by the American Council on the Teaching of Foreign Languages (ACTFL) *Standards of Foreign Language Learning* – see

http://www.actfl.org/files/public/StandardsforFLLexecsumm_rev.pdf

What is most compelling about Wimba Voice Board assignments is that recording short presentations increases repetition of, and engagement with, the target language over a prolonged period of time. This helps students stay motivated because they present their work to more than one audience (i.e., their peers and their instructor).

When communicating in an asynchronous discussion there is also less anxiety than in the traditional face-to-face classroom. Presenters and critics have time to practice and reflect before recording themselves, listen to the recordings multiple times, self-assess their own work before submitting it, and engage in critical thinking to critique their peers' recordings. The scaffolding technique thus fosters deep learning due to increased exposure, repetition, and interaction with the material during research, drafting 2–3-minute mini-presentations or short (30–60-second) critiques, repetitive practice prior to recording on Wimba Voice Board, and feedback from peers (critiques) and the instructor (formative assessment).

Each recording is evaluated by the instructor based on the quality of content and language skills. Students will not be expected to comment on the erroneous use of vocabulary, grammar, or pronunciation (but some advanced students might do it anyway).

Student learning outcomes

1. Students will define topics and identify topic-specific vocabulary in the target language to prepare an audio portfolio.
2. Students will gain competency and confidence in their overall ability to create and synthesize with the target language by moving from short-sentence-level language – see the ACTFL *Proficiency Guidelines* for the skill sets of speakers at the intermediate level – towards paragraph-length discourses with proper time frames and topic-specific vocabulary – see the ACTFL *Proficiency Guidelines 2012* for the skill sets of speakers at the advanced level

   http://www.actfl.org/files/public/ACTFLProficiencyGuidelines2012_FINAL.pdf
3. Students will develop their listening skills.
4. Students will refine their interpersonal communication skills in the target language.
5. Students will strengthen critical thinking skills (complexity of ideas) and learn to make interdisciplinary connections through language learning (variety of topics).
6. Students will be able to appreciate the use of technology as a way to interact with the target language and culture while being actively engaged in a learning community outside the classroom through voice-based discussion threads on Wimba Voice Board.

Prerequisite skills and knowledge

An ability to demonstrate competency in basic structures, generic vocabulary, pronunciation, and major time frames (past, present, future) at the sentence level (intermediate) on a variety of topics is strongly desirable for this assignment to be successful (in other words, a minimum of three semesters of language courses). Students must be able to produce more than isolated words on everyday life. While mistakes and errors are to be expected, they should not impede comprehensibility for other speakers of the target language who listen to the recordings.

For more detail, see the ACTFL *Proficiency Guidelines 2012*

http://www.actfl.org/files/public/ACTFLProficiency Guidelines2012_FINAL.pdf

Step-by-step directions

1. Throughout the semester, have students identify topics of interest that relate to the covered course material but explored it from a different perspective. Since the focus of our class was cinema, I asked students to generate ideas about movies with similar topics, French actors or film makers, or the reception of a particular foreign movie (e.g., *Amélie*) abroad (see "Supplemental materials").

2. As part of the research process, students are to acquire topic-specific vocabulary to express their ideas through more elaborate narration, description, and argumentation (e.g., vocabulary to explain the complexity of a plot or character or the biography of an actor).

3. Students prepare a short talk to present their research and ideas in short and coherent paragraphs.

4. They then record their mini-presentation #1 on Wimba Voice Board (2–3 minutes) by [*date 1*].

5. The instructor gives each student individual feedback (written) on their talk and points out areas of improvement (e.g., language-specific feedback such as vocabulary and idiomatic expressions, grammatical accuracy, phonetic accuracy and comprehensibility; and content-specific feedback such as the organization of ideas and arguments, ability to contribute sophisticated ideas and to provide examples to support arguments, specific connection to course material and other disciplines). If you use a grading rubric (distinguished to novice, see ACTFL *Proficiency Guidelines*), include comments with specific examples for every section (see "Supplemental materials" for an example of grading guidelines).

6. Students listen to the mini-presentations of two peers. They are to identify (1) at least two pieces of information they gathered, and react to the information presented by (2) providing constructive

criticism. Some students need time to draft responses, consisting of a short paragraph, prior to recording it.

7. Every student records two critiques (30–60 seconds per critique) with two examples and constructive criticism on Wimba Voice Board by [*date* 2] (see "Supplemental materials" for an example of peer critique assessment guidelines).

8. The instructor gives each student individual feedback on their critiques and points out areas of improvement (e.g., vocabulary, grammatical and phonetic accuracy, formal vs. informal address between peers, how to make polite requests and how to express an opinion, idiomatic expressions). If you use a grading rubric (distinguished to novice, see ACTFL *Proficiency Guidelines*), include comments with specific examples for every section (as noted above, an example of grading guidelines is provided in "Supplemental materials").

9. For each topic, repeat steps 1–8. We had three rounds of mini-presentations and peer critiques throughout the semester.

10. *Optional step*: At the end of the semester, students compile their talks and all feedback they received to prepare for their oral proficiency exam for the use of Wimba Voice Board as a tool to prepare an oral proficiency portfolio.

Approximate time required

Fifteen minutes for a short introduction of, and hands-on experience with, Wimba Voice Board in a traditional face-to-face classroom setting (ideally equipped with technology for every student) while the remainder of the project takes place outside the classroom.

After about five weeks into the semester, I had one mini-presentation due every three weeks by midnight and critiques had to be posted three days later by midnight. I quickly recapped common problems after each round of mini-presentations/critiques.

Required resources

- Wimba Voice for Higher Education: *http://www.wimba.com/solutions/higher-education/wimba_voice_for_higher_education/*

- Computer with built-in speaker and microphone or an external headset with microphone (preferred)
- Internet access
- LMS (e.g., WebCT, Blackboard, Moodle, etc.)
- Current Java version and disabled Pop-up Blockers.

Variations on the basic theme

The primary focus of this project for conversation classes in foreign languages is to use the sound function only. Wimba Voice Board also has a voice email or written text function that can be implemented. VoiceThread is an interesting alternative that allows for the combination of audio sound, images, and text see

http://voicethread.com/?#q.b409.i848804

Variations of this project can also be implemented for research papers, compositions, and other graded assignments in foreign language literature and culture courses.

Observations and advice

As compliance with deadlines is essential for the scaffolding process to work, my students and I had an agreement that every recording had to be posted by midnight of the date the assignment was due. In return, I committed to providing feedback in a timely manner (as indicated in the step-by-step directions above). For the first round of mini-presentations and critiques, students were somewhat anxious about the nature of a voice-based discussion assignment (rather than the traditional text-based written discussion board). They therefore found it helpful to have a model of both a mini-presentation and a critique on Wimba Voice Board that I posted for them.

I used Wimba Voice Board assignments for two different courses and discovered that they were more successful when I required Wimba Voice Board recordings as incremental steps towards developing an oral proficiency portfolio for the end-of-semester oral exam (see "Supplemental material"). Oral proficiency portfolios represent a particularly relevant assessment tool in foreign language education for both students and instructors. While written portfolios for oral proficiency exams tend to be prepared individually for the sole purpose of one formative assessment (final exam), I was very pleased with the results of this project because it truly helped students build speaking and listening skills over the course of the semester in that they improved in their ability to create with the target language. I also noticed that strong talks were given by students who selected an overarching theme that connected all three topics (e.g., immigration, gender, etc.). Students who completed each step of the assignment tended to feel more comfortable during their final exam and were able to perform at a higher level of competency because they were able to refer to specific examples of peers' questions, comments, and suggestions that helped them think about their topic in new ways.

Last but not least, I strongly recommend not having students post transcripts of their talks because it will decrease their motivation to be engaged with the material by listening to it several times if need be. However, it might be helpful to have them turn in a written version of each recording. In some cases, there is a need to address the responsible use of digital technologies as outlined by the International Society for Technology in Education (ISTE) standards for students. See

http://www.iste.org/Libraries/PDFs/NETS-S_Standards.sflb.ashx

Recommended readings

American Council on the Teaching of Foreign Languages (ACTFL) (1996) *Standards for Foreign Language Learning: Executive Summary*. Available from *http://www.actfl.org/files/public/StandardsforFLLexecsumm_rev.pdf*

American Council on the Teaching of Foreign Languages (ACTFL) (2012) *Proficiency Guidelines 2012*. Available from *http://www.actfl.org/files/public/ACTFLProficiencyGuidelines2012_FINAL.pdf*

Baralt, M., and Gurzynski-Weiss, L. (2011, April 1) Comparing learners' state anxiety during task-based interaction in computer-mediated and face-to-face communication. *Language Teaching Research*, **15**(2), 201–29.

Barr, R. B., and Tagg, J. (1995, November 1) From teaching to learning: A new paradigm for undergraduate education. *Change*, **29**(6), 12–25.

Beauvois, M. H. (1998, January 1) Conversations in slow motion: Computer-mediated communication in the foreign language classroom. *Canadian Modern Language Review*, **54**(2), 198–217.

Blake, R. J. (2008) *Brave New Digital Classroom: Technology and Foreign Language Learning*. Washington, D.C: Georgetown University Press.

Cotos, E. (2011, February) Review of Wimba Voice 6.0 Collaborative Suite. *Language Learning and Technology*, **15**(1), 29–35.

Huitt, W. (2011) Bloom et al.'s taxonomy of the cognitive domain. *Educational Psychology Interactive*. Valdosta, GA: Valdosta State University. Available from *http://www.edpsycinteractive.org/topics/cognition/bloom.html* [accessed on June 4, 2012].

International Society for Technology in Education (ISTE/NETS) (2011) *National Educational Technology Standards for Students*. Available from *http://www.iste.org/Libraries/PDFs/NETS-S_Standards.sflb.ashx*

Kenning, M.-M. (2010, May 1) Collaborative scaffolding in online task-based voice interactions between advanced learners. *Recall*, **22**(2), 135–51.

Marriott, P. (2002) Voice vs text-based discussion forums: An implementation of Wimba Voice Boards. In: M. Driscoll and T. Reeves (Eds.), *Proceedings of World Conference on E-Learning in Corporate, Government, Healthcare, and Higher Education 2002* (pp. 640–6). Chesapeake, VA: Association for the Advancement of Computing in Education.

Poza, M. I. C. (2011) The effects of asynchronous computer voice conferencing on L2 learners' speaking anxiety. *IALLT Journal of Language Learning Technologies*, **41**(1), 33–63.

Ricardo-Osorio, J. G. (2011) The collaborative world languages department: A teamwork approach to assessing student learning outcomes. In: D. Heiland, L. Rosenthal, and C. Ching (Eds.), *Literary Study, Measurement, and the Sublime: Disciplinary Assessment*. New York: Teagle Foundation.

Stepp-Greany, J. (2002, January) Student perceptions on language learning in a technological environment: Implications for the new millenium. *Language Learning and Technology*, **6**(1), 165–80.

Tognozzi, E., and Truong, H. (2009, January 1) Proficiency and assessment using WIMBA Voice technology. *Italica: Bulletin of the American Association of Teachers of Italian*, **86**(1), 3–23.

What's a VoiceThread Anyway? (2007) Available from *http://voicethread.com/?#q.b409.i848804*

Yaneske, E., and Oates, B. (2010, January 1) Using Voice Boards: Pedagogical design, technological implementation, evaluation and reflections. *Research in Learning Technology*, **18**(3), 233–50.

Supplemental materials

Student instructions for using Wimba Voice Board to facilitate foreign language conversation courses

[*All instructions should be given in the target language*]

Your end-of-semester oral proficiency exam consists of holding a 10-minute conversation with your instructor. The purpose of this exam is to demonstrate that you mastered topic-specific vocabulary and that you are now able to maintain and stay actively involved in an elaborate conversation about the topics you prepared while sustaining proper sentence form and pronunciation.

Your conversation will revolve around three topics that relate to the course material and contribute new ideas, examples, arguments, or different perspectives. Each topic must fit into one of the following categories: (a) one cinematographic topic (e.g., an actor or filmmaker), (b) one Francophone movie not covered in class (e.g., another movie of one of the directors we discussed), and (c) one current event that can relate to cinema [*categories can vary depending on the focus of the course*].

1. In preparation for your oral exam, you will put together a selection of topics (oral proficiency portfolio) by compiling three mini-presentations throughout the semester. Each mini-presentation will be recorded on Wimba Voice Board and peer-critiqued by at least two classmates.

2. Identify your first topic of interest and gather information to draft a short talk to present your ideas. This is a good moment to work with a (mono-lingual) dictionary to learn new vocabulary and idiomatic expressions! Be sure to consult at least two sources and remember to rephrase the information in your own words.

3. Record mini-presentation #1 on Wimba Voice Board (2–3 minutes) by [*date*].

4. Listen to the mini-presentations of two peers and record your critique (30–60 seconds per critique) by [*date*].

5. For topic #2 and #3, repeat steps 2–4.

6. For your oral exam, you are allowed to prepare small index cards on which you can jot down some key words, dates, or other helpful information. You will be graded on content knowledge, fluency, and conversational ability; be sure to know your topics well enough to provide detailed information and examples, draw connections, and be ready to answer questions in complete sentences. Keep in mind the feedback given to you throughout the semester by your peers and your instructor. Remember: a conversation is a spontaneous exchange of information rather than a memorized role play. Good news: practice makes perfect!

Your *mini-presentation* will be evaluated based on:

1. the content of your talk: your choice of topic, the organization of your ideas, the quality of your research, your ability to apply topic-specific vocabulary and to contribute sophisticated ideas, connections you draw between your topic and the course material;
2. your language skills: vocabulary, grammatical accuracy, phonetic accuracy and comprehensibility.

Each *peer critique* will be evaluated based on:

1. references to specific examples (minimum of 2);
2. comments, suggestions, constructive criticism (minimum of 2);
3. language skills (e.g., vocabulary, grammatical accuracy, phonetic accuracy and comprehensibility).

[*All instructions should be given in the target language.*]

7

Web conferencing and peer feedback

Kevin Garrison

Abstract: This activity utilizes Web conferencing in a small (10–25 student) traditional face-to-face classroom to facilitate the peer review and peer feedback process. Using a Web conferencing tool, the instructor creates a virtual meeting place, invites the students to the online room, and then shares a student's rough draft of an assignment on the Web conference's whiteboard. The students then, in a chat room, offer both positive and critical feedback to the author of the document. This format allows students to share their ideas in an online social medium while learning a crucial component of writing: revision, based on audience feedback

Key words: chat rooms, netiquette, peer feedback, Web conferencing, Webinars, writing.

Discipline/Academic areas addressed

Writing intensive courses across both the sciences and humanities.

Instructional purpose

Early student drafts tend to be written from the student's own perspective and with less regard for how an audience perceives and interacts with a text (Flower, 1998). Peer feedback attempts to overcome this limitation by revealing how an audience might understand the text; however, traditional peer workshops (Bean, 1996) are limited because only one to four peers are able to offer feedback during a class period, effectively minimizing the quantity and quality of the feedback. This activity allows students to collectively offer peer feedback, providing the authors with insights into diverse perspectives on a piece of writing, and encouraging revision.

Using Web conferencing as a way to encourage peer feedback also serves numerous other practical functions, such as (1) providing opportunities for students to participate in nontraditional ways, (2) allowing students who are more "shy" an opportunity to share their ideas, (3) learning digital literacy skills, such as chat room netiquette and chat room interfaces, (4) preparing students for the potential of taking online training sessions and synchronous online courses, (5) allowing students to be more marketable and more familiar with a contemporary way of collectively sharing ideas, and (6) encouraging group discussion.

Student learning outcomes

1. Students will provide feedback on peers' drafts, including positive feedback and constructive criticism.
2. Students will suggest ways in which the draft could be revised.
3. Students will understand why feedback is a necessary component of the writing process.
4. Students will explore how the feedback impacts their own writing.
5. Students will learn "netiquette" and interact with peers in an ethical and courteous manner, thereby reinforcing the idea that the audience matters in all writing.

Prerequisite skills and knowledge

- Basic computer skills, including Internet browser knowledge.
- Basic knowledge of chat rooms and "texting" language.
- While it is a rare student today who is unfamiliar with texting or SMS and chats, the instructor should check to ensure basic knowledge before the activity begins.

Step-by-step directions

1. Require students to turn in a rough draft of a writing assignment. Some examples of writing assignments for this activity could be a set of instructions in a technical writing course, a resume in a business writing course, or any other writing sample that is approximately one page long and uses both elements of design and written text to communicate a message. Ideally, the assignment will have an audience of other students, such as a set of instructions geared toward college students. Students should submit their rough draft electronically as a PDF file to ensure that the formatting does not change and so that it can be uploaded to a Web conference. Be sure to receive students' permission to use their drafts in a peer review workshop.

2. Designate a day and a time for holding a Web conference. The meeting can be held in a computer classroom where all the students are in the same room, or the students can use campus or personal computers to attend class from a distance. These computers should have access to a high-speed Internet connection to access the Web conferencing link.

3. Prepare students and share expectations beforehand with students. For instance:

    a. Demonstrate the Web conference or require the students to log in and familiarize themselves with the Web conference's tools/layout before the day of the workshop.

    b. Require participation, such as a minimum of 10–30 chat responses per student, to ensure that students offer substantial feedback.

    c. Explain your expectations regarding technology failures; for instance, if a student is "late" or is unable to log in, then students should be aware of the consequences.

    d. Provide the students with a list of expectations about what constitutes "positive" and "critical" feedback. Be sure to clarify what types of chat room behaviors are allowed and not allowed.

4. Create a Web conference before the time class begins. A number of Web conferencing tools exist, both for free and for purchase. The following is a short list of possibilities (from Wikipedia, 2011):

   e. Elluminate Live! – a Web conferencing tool accessible in Blackboard (if purchased);

   f. OpenMeetings – an open-source, free Web conferencing website;

   g. BigMarker.com – a free Web conferencing website;

   h. Any purchased Web conferencing software, or software built into your academic Learning Management System.

5. Send the Web conference link to your students via email several minutes before the class begins to ensure that students can log in early and test browser/plug-in compatibility.

6. Upload a student's rough draft to the "whiteboard" section or the "presentations" section of the Web conference. Most Web conferencing websites have a window where a document can be uploaded for shared viewing.

7. Request that the students look at the draft and offer answers to the following questions in the following order:

   a. What has the author done well?

   b. What has the author written that is problematic?

   c. What could the author do to improve the draft?

   d. Why are these changes important or useful?

   e. What will you do to revise your own draft?

8. In the Web conferencing site, chat with your students to model the appropriate behaviors, to ensure that they stay on task, to summarize their feedback, and to prompt conversations to continue moving.

9. Complete peer review of as many documents as possible during the class time.

10. Save a transcript of the chat conversation (if the software/website can) – both to allow students to review afterwards and for the instructor to grade participation.

11. Hold a follow-up discussion with the class to talk about their learning experiences with the Web conference and to reinforce what was learned.

Approximate time required

Three class periods: one to talk about expectations and requirements, one to hold the workshop, and one to hold a follow-up discussion.

Required resources

- A Web conferencing website, tool, or software package such as
  - Elluminate Live! – a Web conferencing tool accessible in Blackboard (if purchased);
  - OpenMeetings – an open-source, free Web conferencing website;
  - BigMarker.com – a free Web conferencing website.
- A computer lab or students with access to their own computers (or campus computers).
- High-speed Internet connections to ensure chat conversations run smoothly. Readings might include
  - discussions of netiquette;
  - links to the help menus of the Web conferencing website, tool, or software package.

Variations on the basic theme

A Web conferencing tool allows students to interact with one another using a variety of different media, such as text, audio, and video. As such, a Web conference can be used as the basis for an entire online, synchronous course; as a way to conduct workshops of documents; as a mechanism for facilitating discussions about sensitive or complex topics; as a tool for collective brainstorming about topic ideas; and anything else that an instructor can creatively attempt.

Web conferencing could also be used for assignments and disciplines unrelated to writing, such as discussing a theoretical concept in a philosophy course, conducting usability tests of software in a computer science course, debating an issue in a communication course, and reviewing any other "document" or topic that is suitable for a shared, online class period.

Observations and advice

Students who are typically silent in a face-to-face class seem to "come alive" in a chat room. Oftentimes, they learn more from an online session than they do from a face-to-face session because they feel more engaged with the students and the instructor – largely because the presence of the screen mediates the conversation in different ways than a traditional classroom does. As well, students, collectively, are oftentimes better at helping each other brainstorm ideas and review each other's drafts than the instructor is, and the students in my courses frequently request more workshops than I have scheduled for the semester.

Recommended reading

Bean, J. C. (1996) *Engaging Ideas: The Professor's Guide to Integrating Writing, Critical Thinking, and Active Learning in the Classroom*. San Francisco, CA: Jossey-Bass.

Bower, M. (2011) Synchronous collaboration competencies in web-conferencing environments: Their impact on the learning process. *Distance Education*, **32**(1), 63–83.

Coffey, J. W. (2010) Web conferencing software in university-level, e-learning-based, technical courses. *Journal of Educational Technology Systems*, **38**(3), 367–81.

Cummings, J. (2002) Facilitating interactions among students and faculty via web-based conferencing systems. *Journal of Technology in Human Services*, **20**(3/4), 245–65, doi: 10.1300/J017v20n03_03

Ede, L., and Lunsford, A. (1984) Audience addressed/audience invoked: The role of audience in composition theory and pedagogy. *College Composition and Communication*, **35**(2), 155–71.

Flower, L. (1998) *Problem-solving Strategies for Writing in College and Community*. Fort Worth, TX: Harcourt Brace College.

Jenks, C. (2009) When is it appropriate to talk? Managing overlapping talk in multi-participant voice-based chat rooms. *Computer Assisted Language Learning*, **22**(1), 19–30.

Lietzau, J. A. (2009) Breaking out of the asynchronous box: Using web conferencing in distance learning. *Journal of Library and Information Services in Distance Learning*, **3**(3/4), 108–19, doi: 10.1080/15332900903375291

Mubarak, A. R., Rohde, A. A., and Pakulski, P. P. (2009) The social benefits of online chat rooms for university students: An explorative study. *Journal of Higher Education Policy and Management*, **31**(2), 161–74, doi: 10.1080/13600800802559310

Offir, B., Lev, Y., and Bezalel, R. (2008) Surface and deep learning processes in distance education: Synchronous versus asynchronous systems. *Computers and Education*, **51**(3), 1172–83.

Ong, W. J. (1975) The writer's audience is always a fiction. *PMLA (Publications of the Modern Language Association of America)*, **90**(1), 9–21.

Skylar, A. (2009) A comparison of asynchronous online text-based lectures and synchronous interactive web conferencing lectures. *Issues in Teacher Education*, **18**(2), 69–84.

Suduc, A., Bîzoi, M., and Filip, F. (2009) Exploring multimedia web conferencing. *Informatica Economica*, **13**(3), 5–17.

Stephens, K. K., and Mottet, T. P. (2008) Interactivity in a web conference training context: Effects on trainers and trainees. *Communication Education*, **57**(1), 88–104.

Wikipedia (2011) *Comparison of Web Conferencing Software*. Available from *http://en.wikipedia.org/wiki/Comparison_of_web_conferencing_software*

8

Learning through YouTube

J. Jacob Jenkins and Patrick J. Dillon

Abstract: This activity uses YouTube to explore an academic concept/theory through student presentation and peer critique. Students begin by working in small groups of two to four people to create an original video (approximately 1–4 minutes in length) that explicates or exemplifies a major concept/theory from the class. Once uploaded to YouTube, each group then presents their video to the class, explaining the concept or theory. Finally, classmates are given the opportunity to critique and comment on each video using specified guidelines. This process embodies the action–inquiry pedagogy, thus allowing students to engage in open dialogue via collaborative knowledge construction.

Key words: action–inquiry, collaborative knowledge, peer critique, presentation skills, video, YouTube.

Discipline/Academic areas addressed

This project is applicable across all academic disciplines. However, it is most applicable to the social science disciplines (e.g., anthropology, communication, political science, psychology, sociology, etc.), the humanities (e.g., history, English), and education.

Instructional purpose

This assignment engages students in an active learning process by using YouTube.com, a popular video-sharing website. YouTube is one of the most popular video-sharing websites in the world, with more than 800 million unique visitors each month (YouTube.com, 2012). Given its popularity, many students are likely to be familiar with the website and can be expected to be excited to use this technology in a class setting. Furthermore, videos can be used as an effective visual aid to engage an audience and clearly communicate ideas (Beebe and Beebe, 2011). Specifically, videos can offer students the opportunity to apply and present classroom information to their peers in a creative manner. In return, this project offers potential entry and discussion points for the audience to clarify, critique, and expand upon claims made by their peers within the videos and presentations.

Student learning outcomes

1. Identify a concept/theory in an accurate and concise manner.
2. Apply the concept/theory to a particular context in an appropriate way.
3. Create a unique video that demonstrates understanding and ability to apply the concept/theory.
4. Present a theory or concept through the vehicle of a YouTube video.
5. Offer constructive feedback to their peers regarding their presentations and videos.

Prerequisite skills and knowledge

- Basic computer skills (e.g., Internet navigation, file uploading, etc.).
- Basic video-recording skills (e.g., access to a video recorder, use of zoom, lighting, etc.). While most students can be expected to know how to do basic video recording using a video recorder, smartphone, or digital camera, instructors will need to assess a student's competency before the project begins, and, if necessary, provide basic instruction to novice students.
- *Optional* video-editing skills (e.g., training/experience with video-editing software) (see "Required resources" for online tutorials on video editing).

Step-by-step directions

1. Divide students into small groups of two to four people.
2. Instruct each group to identify a specific concept/theory of interest from the course readings. Only one group may choose a particular concept/theory; instructors can also provide a list of potential topics for students. In an interpersonal communication course, for example, a group might choose to demonstrate "the four elements of language" (i.e., verbal, nonverbal, oral, and non-oral).
3. Allow time (in or out of class) for students to meet as a group to discuss their chosen concept/theory, ensuring mutual understanding of the topic. We often ask students to outline the main tenets of their concept/theory before moving on to the next step.
4. Have students brainstorm, as a group, possible ways to explicate and exemplify their chosen concept in a 1–4-minute video. As students begin refining their ideas, it is important to remind them that while it is good for the videos to be entertaining, the main focus of the exercise is to demonstrate their understanding of the chosen concept.
5. Have students develop their video concept into a storyboard (i.e., sketches or illustrations used to pre-visualize the video sequence). Several storyboarding tutorials exist online to help in this process (see "Required resources"). It may also be helpful to review the storyboard process in class.
6. Give students time outside of class to meet as a group and record their video, using a video recorder, smartphone, or digital camera.
7. If appropriate, allow students to edit their video using iMovie, Adobe Premiere, Roxio Creator, AVS Video Editor, or a similar software program. Note that the editing and production value of this assignment is secondary to the clear presentation of academic knowledge and understanding. Therefore, unless this assignment is being used in a video production course, the editing process is completely optional (see "Required resources" for online tutorials on video editing).
8. Have students upload their group video to YouTube prior to class (see "Supplemental materials A" for instructions for uploading videos to YouTube). There are also a variety of tutorials online for how to

upload videos to YouTube (see "Required resources"). Note that the use of a unique title will help to ensure students' ability to locate the video quickly during their class presentation.

9. Set aside class time for students to present their videos. Before showing their videos, have each group introduce the concept or theory addressed, as well as explain the decision-making process and the purpose of the video. With "the four elements of language", for example, this would involve defining all four elements and describing how they are demonstrated in the video.

   The instructor should evaluate both the presentation prior to the video, and the video, in order to check their consistency with the way the concept/theory is presented in course materials (see "Supplemental materials B" for YouTube instructions and assessment).

10. After presentations, encourage other class members to critique and comment on the content of each video, using the handout provided (see "Supplemental materials C" for an audience worksheet). We recommend giving students time following each video to fill out the worksheet.

11. Encourage students to respond to questions that their video elicited from their classmates.

Approximate time required

- 20 minutes for the instructor to explain the assignment.
- 30–45 minutes for the students to form groups and decide on a concept/theory.
- 30–45 minutes for the students to brainstorm possible video concepts, storyboards, etc.
- One week for the students to complete their videos outside of class (filming, possible editing, and uploading to YouTube.)
- 20–40 minutes for each group to present and discuss their videos with the class.

Required resources

Storyboard tutorial

- *http://www.youtube.com/watch?v=MvdJq7RrSR0*

YouTube tutorials

- *http://www.youtube.com/watch?v=NlCQrSVMzfM*
- *http://www.youtube.com/watch?v=9w-gQAwS2uc*
- *http://www.youtube.com/watch?v=zPpn50yYQ14*

Editing tutorials

- iMovie: *http://www.apple.com/support/imovie/*
- Adobe Premiere: *http://tv.adobe.com/show/learn-premiere-pro-cs5/*
- Roxio Creator: *http://www.roxio.com/enu/support/emc8/tutorials/*
- AVS Video Editor: *http://videoguides.avs4you.com/index.aspx*

Technology

- Computer access
- Smartphone, digital camera, or other video-recording device
- *Optional* editing software (iMovie, Adobe Premiere, Roxio Creator, AVS Video Editor, etc.)
- Internet access (*www.youtube.com*).

Variations on the basic theme

The pedagogical focus of this assignment relies upon the twofold process of defining, and presenting, an original interpretation of an academic concept/theory. For this reason, the same twofold process can be explored in a variety of ways, such as writing and performing an original film scene that explicates a central concept/theory from the class.

Students can also forgo the creation process by simply locating an original video on YouTube, then explaining to the class how and why this video relates to their chosen concept/theory.

Observations and advice

Semester after semester, we have been pleasantly surprised by the level of excitement students bring to this assignment. As a result, students have repeatedly gone above and beyond the project's requirements, surpassing all expectations. Although we never require video editing, for instance, students commonly use editing software to add title screens, captions, transitions, music, and sound effects. Consequently, students are always eager to share their creations with their peers; the presentations typically result in a lively discussion and entertaining class period.

For your convenience, a student video from an introductory Communication course can be found online using the following link:

http://www.youtube.com/watch?v=WN1dfwPtihA

Entitled "Verbal Dimensions of Talk!" this video addresses three distinct concepts: gender communication, inclusive and respectful language, and the use of metaphor. In addition to the students' introduction and explanation of this video, understanding of the concepts is evidenced through their use of headings, captioning, and summary statements. Although far from perfect, we have often shown this video to our students as a past exemplar. Three additional examples, evidencing various levels of quality/success include:

(a) "Ambiguous Language"

http://www.youtube.com/watch?v=xSkS9nqWjqY

(b) "The Four Elements of Language"

http://www.youtube.com/watch?v=7tjgwcQ6rf0

and (c) "Respectful Language"

http://www.youtube.com/watch?v=7lrk0soelm4

Recommended reading

Beebe, S. A., and Beebe, S. J. (2011) *Public Speaking: An Audience-centered Approach* (Eighth Edition). Boston: Allyn & Bacon.

Biamonte, N. (Ed.) (2010) *Pop-culture Pedagogy in the Music Classroom: Teaching Tools from American Idol to YouTube*. Lanham, MD: Scarecrow Press.

Burgess, J. (2009) *YouTube: Online Video and Participatory Culture*. Cambridge, U.K.: Polity.

Fahs, C. (2007) *How to Do Everything with YouTube*. New York: McGraw-Hill.

Jones, J. B. (2011) *10 Easy Tips to Get Your Videos Found on YouTube* (Kindle Edition). Amazon Digital Services.

Kirkwood, J., Gutgold, N. D., and Manley, D. (2011). Hello world, it's me: Bringing the basic speech communication course into the digital age. *Communication Teacher*, **25**(3), 150–3.

Lange, P. G. (2007) Publicly private and privately public: Social networking on YouTube. *Journal of Computer-Mediated Communication*, **13**(1), 361–80.

Miller, M. (2009) *SAMS Teach Yourself YouTube in 10 Minutes*. Indianapolis, IN: SAMS Publishing.

Ng, H. Z., Maznah, R., and Hussain, R. (2009) Empowering learners as the owners of feedback while YouTube-ing. *Interactive Technology and Smart Education*, **6, 274–85**

Procopio, C. (2011) Using YouTubeTM to promote curricular awareness and persuasive skills in the basic communication course. *Communication Teacher*, **25**(1), 25–8.

Strangelove, M. (2010) *Watching YouTube: Extraordinary Videos by Ordinary People*. Toronto: University of Toronto Press.

YouTube.com (2012) *Statistics*. Available from *http://www.youtube.com/t/press_statistics*

Supplemental materials

A Instructions for uploading videos to YouTube

1. *Create Account*. In order to upload a video, at least one member of your group must have an account with *YouTube*. Create an account by visiting YouTube's homepage

   www.youtube.com

   Click on the link in the upper right hand corner termed "Create Account". The following Web pages will step you through a series of questions, asking for your name, email address, etc. The process should take 5–10 minutes. If a group member already has an account, he or she can simply click "Log In" on *YouTube*'s homepage, in the upper right hand corner.
2. *Title & Describe*. Once a member of your group has created an account and/or logged in, he or she can begin uploading your video by clicking "Upload" in the upper right corner of YouTube's homepage. The following Web page will ask you to title and describe your video using key words. Keep in mind that a unique title will help you to easily locate the video via search terms. Similarly, appropriate keywords will help others who

might be searching for a similar topic find your video. Once you have finished filling in the appropriate fields of information, click "Go Upload a File".

3. *Public or Private.* The next Web page you see will ask whether you want to make your video public (anyone can view your video) or private (only people who you invite can view your video). For the present assignment, choose "Public" to ensure your classmates and I can view your final product. Click "Upload Video".

4. *Upload Video.* To upload your video, click the "Browse" button and locate the video file on your computer. Click the "Upload Video" button. (Note: YouTube videos can be as large as 100 MB and up to 10 minutes in length, neither of which should apply to the present assignment. The amount of time required to upload a video varies, depending on your computer and Internet connection. Expect 1–5 minutes per megabyte of information).

5. *Additional Resources.* There are also a variety of tutorials online for how to upload videos to YouTube, including:

   - *http://www.youtube.com/watch?v=NlCQrSVMzfM&feature=related*
   - *http://www.youtube.com/watch?v=9w-gQAwS2uc*
   - *http://www.youtube.com/watch?v=zPpn50yYQ14&feature=related*

B YouTube presentation – instructions and assessment items

Assignment description

For this assignment, students will be divided into groups of two to four people. Each group must identify a specific concept or theory of interest from the course readings, and then brainstorm possible ways to explicate/exemplify their chosen concept in a 1–4 minute video. (Only one group may choose a particular concept/theory). Using a video recorder, smartphone, or digital camera, groups must meet outside of class to record their video. They will then upload the video to YouTube and present it to their peers during class. Prior to showing their video, each group must introduce the concept or theory addressed, as well as explain their decision-making process and the purpose of the video. After showing their video, each group will also respond to questions and comments that the video elicited from their classmates.

Grading criteria (50 points total)

1. Video fulfills the time requirement of 1–4 minutes. (5 points)
2. Video demonstrates participation by each group member. (5 points)
3. Video clearly identifies and explains one theory/concept from the course. (10 points)
4. Video presents the clear organization of ideas, evidencing a sufficient amount of preparation. (15 points)
5. Group members clearly explained the purpose and meaning of the video. (5 points)

C Audience worksheet

1. Identify the concept/theory that was addressed by this video. If you are unsure, say so in the space below.
2. Was the concept/theory clearly explained? If yes, explain the concept/theory in two to three sentences. If not, explain why it was unclear.
3. Having watched this video, how has your understanding of the video's concept/theory changed?
4. What was the strongest/most successful aspect about this video?
5. What is one constructive criticism you would offer about this video? How might the concept/theory have been explained more clearly?

9

Wiki-workshopping: using Wikispaces for peer writing workshops

Hans C. Schmidt

Abstract: This project uses the Wikispaces Web platform to facilitate peer writing workshops. Over the course of the semester, students will post drafts of their papers to Wikispaces. Then, students will use the wiki editing tools to revise and comment on peer drafts. Because Wikispaces tracks all revisions, it is possible to view a revised document and also identify which revisions were made by which students. Ultimately, revised documents can be stored as a Web page, allowing each student to use Wikispaces to create an electronic portfolio of her/his writing from the semester.

Key words: peer editing, wiki, Wikispaces, writing workshops.

Discipline/Academic areas addressed

Applicable to all disciplines incorporating writing and editing, and also useful to disciplines, such as communication and education, which emphasize media literacy

Instructional purpose

Since Moffett and Wagner (1968) first suggested the use of peer writing workshops, such activities have come to be viewed as an established and effective classroom practice (Karegianes et al., 1980; Macrorie, 1976). Such workshops provide students the opportunity to receive suggestions from their peers regarding how to improve the quality of their writing.

Additionally, the process of editing a peer's writing leads to reflection and learning on the part of the student editor. However, such processes can be very time consuming. When conducted as an in-class activity, they can use up valuable instructional time. When conducted outside of class, the logistics of printing and distributing copies of student drafts to other group members can be challenging, and incur additional, burdensome, printing costs for students and faculty.

The use of social media such as Wikispaces solves both of these problems, and offers other benefits as well. First, Wikispaces can be used outside of class, thus freeing up valuable instructional time. Second, it allows for drafts to be electronically shared and edited, thus eliminating the need for excessive printing and providing both environmental and financial benefits. Third, Wikispaces tracks the revisions made to the document, allowing the instructor to view which suggestion and edits were made by which students. This tracking feature provides a helpful summary so that the instructor can easily and accurately gauge student involvement in the editing and revising process. Finally, because this activity involves the use of a new media platform, it also has the added benefit of exposing students to the power of Web 2.0 technologies. As such, while this activity primarily serves the purpose of helping students become better writers, it also helps students to develop basic media literacy competencies which are very important to twenty-first century life (Jenkins, 2006).

Student learning outcomes

1. Students will become familiar with wiki technologies and the Wikispaces Web platform.
2. Students will be able to identify and correct grammatical and mechanical errors in their peers' essays.
3. Students will be able to identify and correct errors associated with source citation in their peers' essays.
4. Students will be able to suggest ways to improve the content development, introduction, and conclusion of their peers' essays.
5. Students will be able to integrate their peers' suggestions into later drafts of their own writing.
6. Students will be able to create a Web-based writing portfolio.

Prerequisite skills and knowledge

- Internet-browsing skills, such as are possessed by the average college student
- Word-processing skills, also possessed by most
- Familiarity with the conventions of written English.

Step-by-step directions

1. Prior to assigning a new writing assignment, divide students into peer workshop groups. The size of groups can vary, but three individuals is recommended.
2. Spend a class period demonstrating how the peer writing workshop process works, and explaining specific issues that students should address after reading their peers' papers. Students are instructed to
   a. Identify and correct misspelled and improperly used words.
   b. Identify and correct grammatical errors.
   c. Identify and correct errors associated with source citation.
   d. Provide comments regarding the quality of the introduction and conclusion.
   e. Provide comments regarding the paper's content development.
   f. Provide summary comments regarding overall impressions of the paper. (Note: The specific issues which students are instructed to address can be adjusted to meet course-specific objectives.)
3. Spend approximately half of a class period demonstrating how to access and use Wikispaces, and teaching students how to post their own paper, and revise and comment on a peer's paper (see below). While this Web platform is very easy to use, students may be intimidated by the technology and require specific instructions.
   a. *Directions for students posting their paper to Wikispaces*
      - Login to Wikispaces.
      - Click on "New Wiki".

- Click on "Edit".
- Delete the default text on the screen, as you would if editing a document in a word-processing program.
- Paste the text of your paper into the wiki. After you are finished, click "Save".

b. *Directions for students editing a peer's paper*

- Login to Wikispaces.
- From the menu, select the page of the group member whose paper you want to review.
- After opening the appropriate page, you will see the text of your peer's paper.
- In the menu bar above the text, click on "Edit". This will provide you an editable version of your peer's paper.
- Make any corrections that you consider necessary to your peer's paper, as you would if editing a document in a word-processing program.
- To include comments or suggestions, highlight the word or sentence about which you would like to comment, then click on the "Comment" icon. This will open a new box in which you can type your comment. After you are finished, click "Save" in the comment box.
- After you are finished correcting the paper and providing relevant comments, click "Save" in the menu bar. This will save a revised version of the paper, but mark all changes as highlighted text so that the author can identify areas that you have edited.
- Continue reviewing the papers of other members of your writing workshop group, and save your comments and revisions by the deadline.

c. *Directions for students reviewing their own edited paper*

- Login to Wikispaces.
- From the menu, select the page to which you posted your paper.
- After opening your page, you will see the edited text of your

paper, including all comments and revisions that your peers in your writing group have made.

- To view the changes made by each group member, click on "View Revisions".
- You will now see a menu that lists each revised version of your paper posted by other members of your writing workshop group. Click on the first revised version to begin.
- After opening the first revised version of your paper, you will notice that all changes are highlighted. Now, compare the revisions against your original draft to determine if these changes should be adopted in the final version of your paper.
- Continue reading through each revised version of your paper, reviewing the corrections made and comments provided by your peers.
- Respond to each change or correction made by your peers by highlighting the word or sentence about which you would like to comment, then clicking on the "Comment" icon. This will open a new box in which you can type your reply. After you are finished, click "Save" in the comment box.
- Respond to each of the comments posted by your peers by clicking on the "Reply" button in the comment box.
- After reviewing all edited versions, use the suggestions of your peers to create a new draft of your paper.
- Turn in a final draft of your paper by the appropriate deadline, and post the final draft to your Wikispaces page.

4. Assign students a writing assignment, and provide a date by which the first draft of the assignment must be posted to their Wikispaces page.
5. On the day that assignments are posted to Wikispaces, provide group members a deadline for posting revisions and comments online.
6. Instruct students to review and respond to their peers' revisions and comments.
7. Instruct students to edit or rewrite their own paper, and then post the final draft of their paper to their Wikispaces page.

8. Evaluate student participation in the peer writing workshop using the Peer Revising and Commenting Rubric and Response to Peer Revisions and Comments Rubric (in "Supplemental materials").

9. After the process, discuss challenges that students faced when using the technology.

10. This process can be repeated for multiple drafts and multiple assignments. In the process, students can see a final draft evolving before their eyes.

11. If this process is used for multiple assignments, the instructor can then assess the final Wikispaces website which constitutes an electronic portfolio of all completed assignments.

Approximate time required

In-class time requirements:

- One 50-minute class session will be required to explain the peer workshop process.
- One half of a 50-minute class session will be required to explain how to use Wikispaces.

Out-of-class time requirements:

- Each student should spend 30 minutes reading and commenting on each peer-writing draft.
- Each student will comment on two drafts, for a total of one hour of work outside of class.

Required resources

- *www.wikispaces.com*
- Computer and Internet connection
- Word-processing software (e.g., Microsoft Word)
- Wiki FAQs: *http://help.wikispaces.com/faq+teacher+wiki*

Variations on the basic theme

Wikispaces is a powerful, yet easy-to-use platform that allows multiple users to edit and refine a document or Web page. As such, it is an excellent tool for collaborative work, and provides an easy platform for students to access, edit, revise, or provide comments regarding peer writing. Further, because Wikispaces will track all revisions made by all users, it is possible for the instructor to have a summary of which students were most actively involved in the online workshop. Additionally, Wikispaces can be used to create an electronic writing portfolio. After the revision and rewriting process is complete, students can post a final version of their essay and save this as a separate Web page that can be accessed by either specific users or the general public.

Admittedly, Wikispaces is not the only technology that can make Web-based, out-of-class writing workshops possible. For instance, Google Docs could be used, and students could be provided with passwords to access the documents that contain their peers' writing assignments. Or, files could be distributed by email, and the "track changes" feature of Microsoft Word could be used to provide comments and suggestions.

Nevertheless, because Wikispaces is extremely easy to use, accessible from any computer with an Internet connection, does not require the sharing of documents via email or discussion boards, and can be used to create a Web-based writing portfolio, it is an ideal platform to use for out-of-class writing workshops.

Such an activity could be adapted for other writing projects as well. Because Wikispaces facilitates collaboration, it could be used to help students complete group writing assignments in a wide variety of disciplines. Or, wiki technologies could be used by student newspaper editors and faculty advisors who need to collaborate with student reporters during the writing process.

Observations and advice

Typically, students are very hesitant to provide constructive criticism to their peers, and what criticism is provided is often very superficial in nature (Beaven, 1977; Nilson, 2003; Pianko & Radzik, 1980). This is, at least in part, due to two reasons: insufficient experience, which makes it difficult to identify problems, and the fear of offending a peer. Simply moving the activity online does not instantly resolve those issues. Additionally, students are sometimes intimidated by the thought of using Web-based tools, and instinctively resist learning to use a new technology.

However, all of these challenges can be addressed by the instructor. Skillful classroom instruction can minimize or eliminate these problems. As such, a critical component of this exercise is to make sure that adequate time is spent teaching students about how the peer-writing workshop works, and explaining the type of issues to look for when reading and editing their peers' writing (Lam, 2010).

Additionally, instructing students how to use Wikispaces is also necessary. It is easy for instructors to assume that students—many of whom were born into the "Net Generation"—are digital natives, and naturally comfortable with Web-based technologies such as Wikispaces. This is not, however, the case. Research has shown that students are frequently involved in basic Web-based activities, like using email or streaming video, yet only rarely engage in more involved activities such as blogging or Web design (Kennedy et al., 2007). As such, it is important to spend class time explaining how Wikispaces works, helping students create their account, and make initial postings.

Thus, an investment of time is needed prior to initiating wiki-workshops. However, after students understand the process, wiki-workshops ultimately become a time-saver over the course of the semester. Students can effectively and efficiently engage in peer workshop activities outside of class, and the instructor can easily monitor student involvement without using valuable class time.

Recommended reading

Beaven, M. (1977) Individualized goal setting, self-evaluation, and peer evaluation. In: C. Cooper and L. Odell (Eds.), *Evaluating Writing: Describing, Measuring, Judging* (pp. 135–56). Urbana, IL: National Council for Teachers of English.

Caverly, D. C., and Ward, A. (2009) Techtalk: Wikis and collaborate knowledge construction. *Journal of Developmental Education*, **32**(2), 36–7.

Gooding, J. (2008) Web 2.0: A vehicle for transforming education. *International Journal of Information and Communication Technology*, **4**(2), 44–5.

Hargadon, S. (2009) Web site in a rush. *School Library Journal*, **55**(1), 16–17.

Jakes, D. (2006) Wild about Wikis: Tools for taking student and teacher collaboration to the next level. *Technology & Learning*, **27**(1), 6.

Jenkins, H. (2006) *Convergence Culture: Where Old and New Media Collide*. New York: New York University Press.

Karegianes, M., Pascarella, E., and Pflaum, S. (1980) The effects of peer editing on the writing proficiency of low-achieving tenth grade students. *Journal of Educational Research*, **73**, 203–7.

Kennedy, G., Krause, K., Judd, T., Churchward, A., and Gray, K. (2007) *Digital Natives + Others = First Year Students*. Boulder, CO: Educause. Available from *www.caudit.edu.au/educauseaustralasia07/authors.papers/kennedy.ppt*

Lam, R. (2010) A peer review training workshop: Coaching students to give and evaluate peer feedback. *TESL Canada Journal*, **27**(2), 114–27.

Lamb, A., and Johnson, L. (2007) An information skills workout: Wikis and collaborative writing. *Teacher Librarian*, **34**(5), 57.

Macrorie, K. (1976) *Telling Writing*. New York: Hayden.

Maltese, D., and Naughter, K. (2010) Taking down walls: An international wiki creates a community of thinkers. *Voices from the Middle*, **18**(1), 17–25.

Moffett, J., and Wagner, B. (1968) *Student-centered Language Arts and Reading, K-13*. Boston: Houghton Mifflin.

Morgan, B., and Smith, R. D. (2008) A wiki for classroom writing. *Reading Teacher*, **62**(1), 80–2.

Nielsen, L. (2009) Eight ways to use school wikis. *Teach & Learning*, **30**(1), 32.

Nilson, L. B. (2003) Improving student peer feedback. *College Teaching*, **51**(1), 34–8.

Pianko, S., and Radzik, A. (1980) The student editing method. *Theory into Practice*, **19**, 220–4.

Saovapa, W. (2010) Using wikis to develop summary writing abilities of students in an EFL class. *Journal of College Teaching & Learning*, **7**(12), 5–10.

Supplemental materials

This rubric is used to assess student participation in the process of revising and commenting on a peer's paper.

Table 9.1 Peer revising and commenting rubric

<table>
<tr><th colspan="2">Category</th><th>Points earned/ Comments</th></tr>
<tr><td colspan="2">Revisions related to misspellings and/or improperly used words</td><td rowspan="6"></td></tr>
<tr><td>0 points</td><td>Did not identify any misspellings or improperly used words</td></tr>
<tr><td>1 point</td><td>Identified some misspellings and/or improperly used words</td></tr>
<tr><td>2 points</td><td>Identified some misspellings and/or improperly used words, and provided some accurate revisions</td></tr>
<tr><td>3 points</td><td>Identified all misspellings and/or improperly used words, and provided accurate revisions</td></tr>
<tr><td>Not applicable</td><td>There were no misspellings or improperly used words in the essay</td></tr>
<tr><td colspan="2">Revisions related to grammar</td><td rowspan="6"></td></tr>
<tr><td>0 points</td><td>Did not identify grammatical errors</td></tr>
<tr><td>1 point</td><td>Identified some grammatical errors</td></tr>
<tr><td>2 points</td><td>Identified some grammatical errors, and provided some accurate revisions</td></tr>
<tr><td>3 points</td><td>Identified all grammatical errors, and provided accurate revisions</td></tr>
<tr><td>Not applicable</td><td>There were no grammatical errors in the essay</td></tr>
<tr><td colspan="2">Revisions related to source citation</td><td rowspan="6"></td></tr>
<tr><td>0 points</td><td>Did not identify any mistakes associated with source citation</td></tr>
<tr><td>1 point</td><td>Identified some errors associated with source citation</td></tr>
<tr><td>2 points</td><td>Identified some errors associated with source citation, and provided some accurate revisions</td></tr>
<tr><td>3 points</td><td>Identified all errors associated with source citations, and provided accurate revisions</td></tr>
<tr><td>Not applicable</td><td>There were no errors associated with source citation in the essay</td></tr>
</table>

<table>
<tr><th colspan="2">Category</th><th>Points earned/ Comments</th></tr>
<tr><td colspan="2">Comments related to the introduction and conclusion</td><td rowspan="4"></td></tr>
<tr><td>0 points</td><td>Did not provide comments regarding the quality of the introduction and conclusion</td></tr>
<tr><td>1 point</td><td>Provided brief comments regarding the quality of the introduction and conclusion, but did not offer any meaningful suggestions for improvement</td></tr>
<tr><td>2 points</td><td>Provided thoughtful comments regarding the quality of the introduction and conclusion which gave the author meaningful suggestions for improvement</td></tr>
<tr><td colspan="2">Comments related to content development</td><td rowspan="4"></td></tr>
<tr><td>0 points</td><td>Did not provide comments regarding the paper's content development</td></tr>
<tr><td>1 point</td><td>Provided brief comments regarding the paper's content development, but did not offer any meaningful suggestions for improvement</td></tr>
<tr><td>2 points</td><td>Provided thoughtful comments regarding the paper's content development which gave the author meaningful suggestions for improvement</td></tr>
<tr><td colspan="2">Summary comments</td><td rowspan="4"></td></tr>
<tr><td>0 points</td><td>Did not provide summary comments regarding your overall impression of the paper</td></tr>
<tr><td>1 point</td><td>Provided brief summary comments regarding your overall impression of the paper, but did not offer any specific examples from the text</td></tr>
<tr><td>2 points</td><td>Provided thoughtful summary comments regarding your overall impression of the paper, and offered specific examples from the text to explain your perspective</td></tr>
<tr><td colspan="2">Total points (out of 15)</td><td></td></tr>
</table>

This rubric is used to assess student responses to the peer revisions and comments regarding their own paper.

Table 9.2 Response to peer revisions and comments rubric

Category		Points earned/ Comments
Replies to revisions related to misspellings and/or improperly used words		
0 points	Did not reply to any revisions regarding misspellings or improperly used words	
1 point	Provided brief replies (e.g., Thanks, OK) to some revisions regarding misspellings and/or improperly used words	
2 points	Provided brief replies to most or all revisions regarding misspellings and/or improperly used words	
3 points	Replied to all revisions regarding misspellings and/or improperly used words, and explained how or why these revisions would or would not be incorporated into the final draft of the essay	
Not applicable	There were no revisions related to misspellings or improperly used words	
Replies to revisions related to grammar		
0 points	Did not reply to any revisions regarding grammatical errors	
1 point	Provided brief replies (e.g., Thanks, OK) to some revisions regarding grammatical errors	
2 points	Provided brief replies to most or all revisions regarding grammatical errors	
3 points	Replied to all revisions regarding grammatical errors, and explained how or why these revisions would or would not be incorporated into the final draft of the essay	
Not applicable	There were no revisions related to grammatical errors	

Category	Points earned/ Comments
Replies to revisions related to source citation 0 points — Did not reply to any revisions regarding source citation 1 point — Provided brief replies (e.g. Thanks, OK) to some revisions regarding source citation 2 points — Provided brief replies to most or all revisions regarding source citation 3 points — Replied to all revisions regarding source citation, and explained how or why these revisions would or would not be incorporated into the final draft of the essay Not applicable — There were no revisions related to source citation	
Replies to comments related to the introduction and conclusion 0 points — Did not reply to any comments related to the quality of the introduction and conclusion 1 point — Replied to some comments related to the quality of the introduction and conclusion 2 points — Replied to most or all comments related to the quality of the introduction and conclusion	
Replies to comments related to content development 0 points — Did not reply to any comments related to content development 1 point — Replied to some comments related to content development 2 points — Replied to most or all comments related to content development	
Replies to summary comments 0 points — Did not reply to any summary comments 1 point — Replied to some summary comments 2 points — Replied to most or all summary comments	
Total points (out of 15)	

2B Collaboration

Using persistent wikis as a pedagogical resource

Evan D. Bradley

Abstract: Wikis have become valuable tools for collaborative projects. A characteristic of wikis that has not been fully exploited in their educational applications is the ability to build content across multiple courses, or over time periods longer than a single term. This kind of wiki creates course continuity, benefiting both students and instructors. By extending the life of collaborative course wikis, students can get up to speed faster by exploring and building on previous work. This work can become a subject area resource benefiting the organization, the discipline, or the public, and instructors can use wikis to maintain a portfolio documenting student work.

Key words: wikis, collaboration, active learning, disciplinary resources, course continuity.

Discipline/Academic areas addressed

The examples presented here are drawn from courses in linguistics and psychology, but can be easily adapted to almost any discipline.

Instructional purpose

Wikis have become a valuable technological tool for active learning (see, for example, *http://educationalwikis.wikispaces.com/*). A wiki is a community website written collaboratively by users which users can change continuously. Educational wikis have been used as collaborative tools for class and group projects, increasing student interaction, and integrating Web content and multimedia into course projects that were not possible with term papers and other kinds of projects.

A characteristic of wikis that has not yet been fully exploited in educational applications is the ability to build content incrementally and preserve it over time periods longer than a single term. Here, I will suggest ways to create a wiki which continues from term to term – from one iteration of a course to the next, or within a family of related courses. Some of the benefits of this kind of wiki for students and instructors include

- *Accelerated learning curve.* I have found that one of the most common challenges facing students in completing a large-scale project is getting started. This is compounded when students are also adjusting to a new format and new technological tools. Examples of previously successful projects are helpful in this regard, and when a course- or discipline-specific wiki already exists, students can explore, update, and build on the work of previous students, rather than starting from a blank slate.
- *Content resource.* The best student work deserves to live longer than a single term; unfortunately, this is the usual life span of most projects. By virtue of its Web existence, wiki content has the potential for a longer useful existence. With a little careful overseeing, instructors can create a subject resource to be shared with other students and instructors in the discipline, or with the public. My students have often been my greatest source of inspiration for teaching materials, and their project topics and the resources compiled for them have formed the seeds for future lessons, which I would have lacked the inspiration or time to create myself. By building upon the foundation laid by previous students, subsequent projects based on these topics can be more advanced than if they were starting from scratch.
- *Continuing benefits and contributions.* Students learn a great deal through the process of completing research projects, and from feedback received from the instructor; but students rarely, if ever, will read the term papers of other students in their class. A benefit of wiki projects is that by presenting the product of their work in an engaging way, and connecting them all via a central online hub, students can be encouraged to explore and interact about their work. When this hub persists over time, students have even more chances to benefit from these resources. Students in the discipline may refer back to this wiki in their future studies, or be encouraged to remain as active contributors. I have found that students take greater

pride in their work when they know it will be viewed not only by the instructor, but by peers, future students, and the public.

- *Evidence of student achievement.* Wikis can also form an important component of instructors' teaching portfolios. In addition to the static representations of courses taught and student learning represented by syllabi and evaluations, instructors can use wikis to present a dynamic representation of the kind of active learning occurring in their classrooms, and of the depth and breadth of student work in their courses.

Various software packages available for wiki implementation allow the flexibility for instructors to customize wikis for their course objectives while managing the technical functions necessary for long-term management, such as user administration, incremental snapshots, and backup. Wiki implementations and assignments can be customized to meet student learning goals and curricular needs.

Student learning outcomes

Wiki projects address many of the learning and academic goals of traditional research projects, while helping to foster collaborations. Creating and using a persistent wiki can help students achieve additional learning goals, including

1. *Critically evaluate, revise, and improve disciplinary content.* Revision is a critical component of the research and writing process, but I have found that students often have difficulty recognizing areas for improvement in their own work. Revising content created by others, such as that which exists in a persistent wiki, allows students to practice the revision process, and causes them to view their own content with "fresh eyes". The ability to revise the wiki is assessed in two phases: first, the identification of problem areas in a body of work, and then in making changes or additions that address the identified weaknesses.

2. *Integrate, reorganize, or extend existing disciplinary content.* This outcome focuses on form, rather than content; even factually correct information can be obscured when organized poorly. Students are challenged to improve the presentation of a wiki page only through moving or removing content, without adding any additional information.

3. *Communicate advanced disciplinary content for consumption by a non-expert audience (e.g., less advanced students, the public).* At higher levels of the curriculum, it is important for students working to become experts in their fields to learn to communicate and teach about their subjects to a wider audience. Students can be assigned to create their wiki projects with different audiences in mind, including the general public, or less advanced students. Their work can be concurrently evaluated by students, or by reviewers in the target audience.

These outcomes are assessed by distinct phases of the wiki project (see below).

Prerequisite skills and knowledge

- General computer/Internet literacy, including
  - Typing/word processing.
  - Web navigation, including logging into and out of password-protected sites.
- Familiarity with wikis (optional).
  - Most students today are at least familiar with the concept of a wiki, but their experience may only include reading a wiki, and their comfort with editing them using wiki syntax may be highly variable.
  - Non-traditional students may be less familiar with wikis, although Wikipedia is now a mainstream phenomenon, so awareness is increasing.

Some of these prerequisites (e.g., ability to type papers) may be assumed across many courses. Familiarity with wikis can be assessed in a short survey at the beginning of the class, and through the first stages of the wiki assignment (see below).

Step-by-step directions

Here is a description of the basic phases of a semester-long research project in wiki form. The content of the project is a review of major theories and evidence addressing a particular question in psychology or cognitive science, but the components of the project are similar, regardless of the topic.

1. Wiki orientation
   - The first step in the project is to familiarize the students with the process of viewing the wiki, logging in, making edits, and creating new pages.
   - When content already exists in the wiki, this increases the comfort of students, because they can view and play with the syntax of existing pages.
   - Students' first assignment is to create a "profile" page, which includes a short biographical statement and a description of their topical interests. The assignment also asks them to use basic wiki elements (e.g., lists, images, links, headings) in their profile.
2. Exploration/revision of previous work (SLO 1)
   - Once groups have been formed and preliminary topics identified, students are asked to more comprehensively evaluate existing wiki content related to their topic (if available), identifying strengths and weaknesses, and opportunities for improvement.
   - The product of this assignment consists first of written feedback linked from the critiqued page(s), followed by the execution of changes to the existing wiki. It is helpful for grading purposes if the students link to their contributions from their profile page.
   - This assignment allows them to see examples of the structure and content of more and less successful projects, and to start to generate ideas about their own contributions to the wiki.
3. Outlining (SLO 2)
   - Groups outline the structure of existing wiki content related to their topic, as well as the organization of the contribution of their project.
   - At this stage, groups can be encouraged to identify and link areas of overlap with the projects of other groups, or with already existing wiki content, as appropriate, in order to avoid duplication of effort and to focus on creating new content.
   - This also provides an easy way to identify (and document) the responsibilities of each member of the group (both for group efficiency and instructor oversight).

4. Writing (SLO 1–3)
    - Groups work together to add content to their outlined framework.
    - Feedback and grades from the instructor can be given periodically for meeting certain benchmarks along the timeline to the completed project.
5. Feedback and revision (SLO 1–2)
    - Periodically during the writing process, or in conjunction with major course units, students provide feedback to other groups on both the content and organization.
    - This step can be repeated as necessary as groups address the criticism they receive.
    - If a goal of the project is to communicate with a target audience outside of the course (SLO 3), the wiki can cross multiple concurrent courses by assigning students from the target audience to complete the feedback and revision process as well.
6. Publishing (SLO 3)
    - The final wiki is available for all students to see and explore, and can be made viewable to the greater community in the university and discipline by linking from course and department websites.
    - When the wiki is reused and built upon over time, students who take several courses with the same instructor or within the same department may have the opportunity to use the wiki again, or to refer back to it for information and see how subsequent students have elaborated on their work.

Grading strategies

I try to strike a balance between assigning grades for project components based on individual and group marks, so that groups have an incentive to work well together, but students still feel a sense of individual ownership and responsibility over the work. Below, I illustrate one way in which the components can be broken down into individual and group grades.

Individually graded assignments

- Profile
- Revision of existing content
- Feedback to other groups
- Contribution to group's final product (optional; useful to enforce "fairness" of effort within the group).

Group grades

- Topical statement
- Outline
- Draft/progress check (or more)
- Final wiki.

Approximate time required

The individual assignments described here span the entire term, including the option to work on the wiki during class time, or outside of class on students' own time.

The longer term project of creating and maintaining a content-ful wiki can range over several terms, possibly over several years.

Required resources

- Information about wikis in general – Wikipedia:

  http://en.wikipedia.org/wiki/Wiki

- Students should have their own computers, or access to a computer lab on a regular basis to complete the project.
- Software implementation for running your own wiki: Dokuwiki

  http://www.dokuwiki.org/

- Online implementation of wikis, and numerous examples: educational wikis

http://educationalwikis.wikispaces.com/

Many course management systems have wiki capabilities built in, but these implementations may not persist over time, or may not be accessible to those not enrolled in the system.

Variations on the basic theme

Individual projects

Although wikis are ideally suited for collaborative projects, this format can also be used for individual projects in small classes, or when group projects are not preferred. The ability to interact, give and receive feedback, and link projects is still available for individually directed projects

Linking with other course components

The content of the wiki project can be linked to other course components, for example, an oral presentation of the project, or with laboratory exercises.

Teaching portfolio

Instructors can maintain a portfolio documenting topics their students have worked on, and to remix and present student work in an engaging way.

Curriculum resource

Wiki content builds over time, creating a resource for sharing subject area information among students and instructors, serving the future needs of the same or another course; for example:

- An instructor can build the wiki over several iterations of the same course (or a family of related courses).

- Multiple sections of a course (taught by the same or different instructors) can collaborate on a project during the same term.
- Students in an advanced course can build on content created by students in an introductory course.
- Advanced students (or graduate students) can create content for undergraduate/introductory students in their discipline.
- Departments can centralize resources used across courses.

Observations and advice

Some caveats apply to all wiki-based projects, and some particularly to a wiki that will be altered over a longer period of time. Some challenges to consider in designing and using such a wiki are:

Nonlinearity

- A wiki is not as straightforward and self-contained as a paper. When individuals and groups link their content together and alter one another's work, how should credit be assigned and disputes resolved?
- The ability to track edit histories in most wiki platforms provides a tool for creating and managing such policies.

Consistent style/format

- When many individuals create and edit content on the wiki over an extended period of time, variations in style and structure inevitably occur, making the readability of the wiki for an external audience difficult.
- The imposition of a structural template or style guide (which may be explicitly provided, or implicit from existing wiki pages) may help students organize their projects, so long as it does not interfere with the accomplishment of the project's learning goals.
- After each iteration of the wiki exercise (e.g., at the end of each term), the instructor may need to adapt or impose some reorganization on the wiki.

Preservation of student work

- The benefit of a content-ful wiki that is updated by new groups of students is that old information is updated and built upon over time; the downside of such a wiki is that the work of previous students may be altered or removed.

- Students may wish to preserve a copy of their work, and instructors may wish to have access to the graded work of previous students for future reference.

- Many wiki platforms provide a method for saving snapshots of the wiki at any point in time. These can be saved to document the state of the wiki after each stage.

Academic honesty

- When wiki-based work includes the editing and reuse of material written by previous students, how should reuse of such material be reconciled with academic honesty guidelines regarding plagiarism?

Content licensing

- Given that content on the wiki will be updated by many individuals, and possibly made available to the public, how should the content be licensed?

- Creative Commons (*creativecommons.org*) is a good resource for licensing options suitable to a wide range of academic projects.

Recommended reading

Brohée, S., Barriot, R., and Moreau, Y. (2010) Biological knowledge bases using wikis: Combining the flexibility of wikis with the structure of databases. *Bioinformatics*, **26**(17), 2210–11, doi: 10.1093/bioinformatics/btq348. Available from *http://bioinformatics.oxfordjournals.org/content/26/17/2210.abstract*

Bruns, A., and Humphreys, S. (2005) Wikis in teaching and assessment: The M/Cyclopedia project. In: *Proceedings of the 2005 International Symposium on Wikis* (pp. 25–32). New York: Association for Computing Machinery (ACM).

Cress, U., and Kimmerle, J. (2008) A systemic and cognitive view on collaborative knowledge building with wikis. *International Journal of Computer-Supported Collaborative Learning*, 3, 105–22, doi: 10.1007/s11412-007-9035-z.

Désilets, A., Paquet, S., and Vinson, N. (2005) Are wikis usable? In: *Proceedings of the 2005 International Symposium on Wikis*. New York: Association for Computing Machinery (ACM).

Grace, T. P. L. (2009) Wikis as a knowledge management tool. *Journal of Knowledge Management*, **13**, 64–74, doi: 10.1108/13673270910971833.

Kehrwald, B., and Danaher, P. A. (2010) Wikis as open educational resources in higher education: Overcoming challenges, realizing potential. In: *Cases on Digital Technologies in Higher Education: Issues and Challenges* (pp. 64–80). Hershey, PA: IGI Global.

Lai, Y. C., and Ng, E. M. (2011) Using wikis to develop student teachers' learning, teaching, and assessment capabilities. *The Internet and Higher Education*, **14**(1), 15–26, doi: 10.1016/j.iheduc.2010.06.001.

Mindel, J. L., and Verma, S. (2006) Wikis for teaching and learning. *Communications of the Association for Information Systems*, **18**(1). Available from *http://aisel.aisnet.org/cais/vol18/iss1/1*

Schaffert, S., Bry, F., Baumeister, J., and Kiesel, M. (2008) Semantic wikis. *Software, IEEE*, **25**(4), 8–11, doi: 10.1109/MS.2008.95.

Schwartz, L., Clark, S., Cossarin, M., and Rudolph, J. (2004) Educational wikis: Features and selection criteria. *The International Review of Research in Open and Distance Learning*, **5**(1). Available from *http://www.irrodl.org/index.php/irrodl/article/view/163*

Solomon, J., and Wash, R. (2012) Bootstrapping wikis: Developing critical mass in a fledgling community by seeding content. In: *Proceedings of the ACM 2012 Conference on Computer Supported Cooperative Work* (pp. 261–4). New York: Association for Computing Machinery (ACM).

Yates, D., Wagner, C., and Majchrzak, A. (2010) Factors affecting shapers of organizational wikis. *Journal of the American Society for Information Science and Technology*, **61**(3), 543–54, doi: 10.1002/asi.21266.

Supplemental materials

Sample rubric for feedback/revision (steps 2 and 5)

On a separate wiki page linked from the homepage of the page you are reviewing, provide feedback on these aspects of the wiki:

- *organization*: How well is the wiki organized? Is it easy to navigate and find the information you're looking for?
- *clarity*: Is the information presented clearly explained? Is there anything that doesn't make sense?
- *content*: Do the sources presented adequately address the question? Do you have any suggestions on how to improve the project?

Table 10.1 Sample rubric for feedback/revision

Category	Points	5	3	1
Organization	5	Feedback adequately addresses organization of wiki	Organization somewhat addressed	Comments do not address organization
Clarity	5	Feedback adequately addresses clarity of explanation	Clarity addressed somewhat	Comments do not address clarity
Content	5	Feedback adequately addresses content	Content addressed somewhat	Comments do not address content
Total	**15**			

Table 10.2 Sample rubric for final evaluation of wiki project

Category	Points	Sub-category	Points	5	3	1
Introduction	15	Significance	5	Clearly explains significance of topic to cognitive science in introductory page/section	Significance unclearly explained	Significance not explained
		Question(s)	5	Research question(s) clearly formulated	Research question(s) unclear	No research questions
		Summary	5	Clearly and concisely summarizes/ previews main findings	Findings mentioned	Project not summarized in introduction

(continued)

Table 10.2 Sample rubric for final evaluation of wiki project (*continued*)

Category	Points	Sub-category	Points	5	3	1
Theory	15	Explanation	5	Clearly explains major theories of phenomenon of study, including relevant historical background	Theories explained, but need further development	Content of theories unclear
		Comparison	5	Discusses differences between theories under discussion	Incomplete comparison of theories	No comparison of theories
		Predictions	5	Describes predictions of theories which will be addressed by research evidence	Theoretical predictions unclear	No discussion of theoretical predictions
Evidence	15	Summary	5	Cearly summarizes design, methods, and results of research discussed	Results discussed but design/ methods unclear	Research results unclear
		Explanation	5	Clearly explains how research results address research questions and theoretical predictions	Some explanation, but little integration of results	Little or no explanation of results

(*continued*)

Table 10.2 Sample rubric for final evaluation of wiki project (*continued*)

Category	Points	Sub-category	Points	5	3	1
Evidence (*continued*)		Variety	5	Several converging methods used to examine topic	More than one type of research discussed	Insufficient diversity of research presented
		Sufficient	5	Multiple sources of evidence presented	Few sources discussed	Little or no evidence presented
Mechanics	15	Organization	5	Wiki is well structured and easy to navigate	Some technical problems which interfere with navigation	Disorganized structure makes navigation difficult
		Clarity	5	Clear writing	Some errors which interfere with clarity	Reading difficult
		Citations	5	All sources cited correctly	Some incorrect/ missing citations	Few/no sources cited
Total	**65**					

11

Social media and public speaking: student-produced multimedia informative presentations

Paul E. Mabrey III and Juhong "Christie" Liu

Abstract: This project asks students to create and present a group informative speech and teach other students an important communication concept incorporating multimedia exam questions. Students will work in groups to research, identify, and select their communication concept, create an informative presentation centered on their selected concept, arrange the presentation according to one of the organizational models, create two multimedia exam questions assessing the audience's understanding of the concept, deliver the informative presentation, and constructively critique and assess the other group's informative presentations. To create and present the multimedia exam questions, students are asked to use a digital video camera and YouTube as vehicles of media production and delivery. After completing the assignment, students will have demonstrated proficiency in the key skills of informative speaking, digital literacy, and group collaboration.

Key words: Bloom's Taxonomy, collaborative learning, digital literacy, Flipcamera, Gagné's instructional events, informative or expository speaking, YouTube.

Discipline/Academic areas addressed

Designed for communication studies and general education but applicable to any discipline in which student presentations are important.

Instructional purpose

As members of the information age, students are asked on a regular basis to select, evaluate, arrange, and communicate their understanding of information. The ongoing digital revolution has complicated these informational demands. Not only are students expected to already have the skillset to research, select, organize, and deliver this re-presentation of information publicly and creatively, they are also increasingly being asked to do so in a digital and team environment. For this assignment, students are expected to work together in a group to create one informative presentation and two multimedia exam questions, as well as constructively critique and assess peer presentations. This activity assesses a student's ability to identify, select, and evaluate digital information through the design and creation of their multimedia informative presentation, production of digital exam questions, and in the peer review process utilizing YouTube and face-to-face interactions.

Student learning outcomes

1. Design an informative speech on a selected course concept, incorporating introductions and conclusions, utilizing transitions and signposts throughout the informative speech.
2. Design and present two multimedia exam questions with correct informative speech presentation among distractors.
3. Produce, present, and critically synthesize multimedia digital information through peer collaboration.
4. Evaluate peer informative presentations using a rubric.

Prerequisite skills and knowledge

- Access to a digital video device, the Internet, and a computer
- Basic Internet and computer skills.

Tutorials and resources are available for individuals who may need to refresh or learn these skills. An extensive list is provided in "Required resources".

Step-by-step directions

The instructional events for this project are designed based on a combination of the long-established and popularly applied Gagné's Theory of Instruction (Gagné, 1985) with collaborative learning principles (Bruffee, 1995).

1. Introduction activity, five weeks before the final presentation (SLO 1)

   a. The instructor will introduce the activity, define informative speaking, give examples of organizational models, and provide a list of suggested concepts for acceptable informative speech topics. The instructor can help explain the assignment and concepts by sharing recorded examples of informative speeches, multimedia clips and organizational models. All guidelines, rubrics, documents, examples, and other instructional material can be organized, housed, and shared in one place for easy access to the class. For example, one might use a local Learning Management System, blog, or cloud storage space.

   b. The instructor should also provide the students with the objectives for completing the project and rubric for assessment of this particular assignment. The Hickerson Oral Communication Behavioral Assessment tool developed by Corey Hickerson at James Madison University will be used as the main assessment tool in this project (see Appendix B). Hickerson's assessment rubric was adapted from and expanded on in The Competent Speaker Evaluation Form (Morreale et al., 2007) and was also used in a published study to understand oral communication assessment (Joe et al., 2011).

2. Activity preparation, four weeks prior to the final presentation (all SLOs)

   a. The instructor will divide students into groups and outline the expectations for the assignment in detail, including the presentation workshop. We have found that groups of five students have worked well. The instructor will also pair each group in the class with a different group, as they will later work together as peer groups for the presentation workshop. At the presentation workshop, each group will discuss and critique their peer group's informative speech outline and multimedia exam questions.

b. The presentation expectations are

  - a 10-minute informative oral presentation on the group-selected concept
  - original research on the concept, including at least one citation from the course text(s) and three qualified sources outside of the assigned classroom text, orally cited in the presentation
  - follow basic public-speaking guidelines, for example: a complete introduction, complete conclusion, transitions, and signposts
  - follow one of the basic speech organizational models; topical, chronological, spatial, casual, problem solution, problem cause solution, or Monroe's Motivated Sequence (Rothwell, 2010, pp. 366–8)
  - each group member speaks for roughly the same amount of time
  - two multimedia multiple-choice questions produced by the group must be included in the 10-minute presentation. The exam question format may have a multimedia question and four text answers or a text question and four multimedia answers
  - the presentation must utilize PowerPoint and include the two original multimedia exam questions.

c. The presentation workshop expectations are

  - a complete oral presentation outline from the group (see the Informative Presentation Outline Guideline created by one of the chapter authors in Appendix A.)
  - rough draft of two multimedia multiple-choice exam questions uploaded to YouTube by the group
  - two constructive comments (four in total) made and posted by each individual on YouTube responding to each of the other group's two YouTube multimedia exam questions
  - a one-page constructive critique written by each individual responding to the other group's outline and PowerPoint

slides – including one thing the group did well, one area for improvement, one reference to the classroom texts, and one piece of additional outside research related to the other group's topic.

d. Once the instructor has explained the assignment in detail and has divided the class into groups, presentation topics must be selected and/or assigned. The instructor may assign topics; or students can be actively involved in a ranking list or compete for the opportunity to pick their topic in the order of their choice.

e. For the multimedia multiple-choice exam questions, each group should use a digital camera to videotape themselves, creating digital material that they edit to create an exam question. There are two basic formats. First, they may act out a scenario based on their concept about which they then ask a multiple-choice question to assess knowledge of that concept. The edited video is the question a group would show and the answers are traditional text answers. Or, second, the group writes out a question based on their concept and then acts out and records four different scenarios that would serve as multiple-choice answers. Here, the question is a traditional text question and the group would show four different edited clips as potential multiple-choice answers.

For example, if a group selected the "functions of nonverbal communication" as their concept for the informative presentation; they would create an exam question to assess knowledge regarding the functions of nonverbal communication. They would create a simulated scenario about nonverbal communication and then ask a question based on the video clip. For example, please view the video clip located here,

http://youtu.be/T3i7AQ8CLkE

Based on this clip, a group could ask the following question:

In the following video clip, Paul is relying on which function of nonverbal communication?

A. Substitution

B. Contradiction

C. Regulation

D. Repetition

f. The video clip, question, and answer would be incorporated into the group's information presentation as one of the two required multimedia exam questions.

g. The student groups should now begin working on researching, outlining, and creating their oral presentation. Students will also be provided with tutorials and/or resources for generating and sharing digital multimedia presentations. Detailed procedures with associated tutorial resources are provided in "Required resources".

3. Presentation workshop preparation, two weeks prior to the presentation (SLO 2, 3, and 4)

   a. Each group should upload their two multimedia multiple-choice questions to YouTube, and send the other group their informative speech outline, YouTube links, and PowerPoint slides. Each individual group member is responsible for constructively critiquing the YouTube multimedia questions, speech outline, and PowerPoint slides of the other group.

   b. Three days prior to the presentation workshop, each individual group member should post their two constructive comments (four in total) on the other group's multimedia multiple-choice exam questions through YouTube video links and write a one-page constructive critique of the other group's informative speech outline and PowerPoint slides. Students will bring the one-page critique to the presentation workshop.

4. Presentation workshop, one week prior to the presentation (SLO 4)

   a. On the day of the workshop, each group will sit with their assigned peer group. The instructor should remind the students of the purpose of the workshop. The entire workshop is a discussion between groups of their respective presentations. The workshop is designed to talk through the strengths and weaknesses of each part of the presentation. Students should reference their own feedback that they provided on YouTube and their one-page outline critique. Students should ask each other questions about the other group's presentations and their constructive feedback and vice versa. Groups should utilize feedback to improve their final presentation. The instructor's role is to circulate among the pairs of groups to facilitate discussion and negotiate any potential conflicts.

5. Presentation, day of presentation

   a. Finally, on the day of presentations, each group presents their 10-minute presentation on the concept.

Approximate time required

Between 5–10 minutes to understand the instructions on the assignment, 4–5 weeks to complete the assignment depending on time allocated in class and other related homework students are already assigned, 1 hour for group draft/outline to prepare for the presentation critique workshop, 1 hour for the critique workshop, 1 hour for final presentations. The activity could be adapted for shorter and longer time frames.

Required resources

No readings, except for the text(s) that students have been reading over the course of the entire semester, are required for this project.

The instructor will provide the following suggested tutorials and resources to students for different components of the assignment:

Procedures and associated tutorial resources of publishing a video presentation on YouTube (related to SLOs 1, 2, and 3)

1. Practice complete introductions and conclusions, utilizing transitions and signposts throughout your informative speech with short video recordings captured with a Flipcamera or Web cam.

   - Edit the video clips with whatever video-editing software or apps are available.

   - Make use of free video editing software and tutorials such as YouTube Video Editor (free when a YouTube account is set up). For YouTube account setup, refer to the URL below

     http://www.youtube.com/create_detail/YouTubeVideoEditor

2. Create a group YouTube account, for instance, GCOM231-group1

via a group member's email address (by default, it'll be a gmail account associated with your YouTube account.

- YouTube help about creating a new YouTube account

  http://support.google.com/YouTube/bin/static.py?hl=en&page=guide.cs&guide=1646810

- VideoPad Video Editor (for Windows PC)

  http://www.nch.com.au/components/vpsetup.exe
  http://www.nchsoftware.com/videopad/index.html

- VideoPad Tutorials on the NCH Software channel on YouTube.

- About the software

  http://www.youtube.com/watch?v=nmstgNRZ9_0&feature=plcp

- Tutorial Part I

  http://www.youtube.com/watch?v=-AqYOwJVne0&feature=plcp

- Tutorial Part II

  http://www.youtube.com/watch?v=A-zRkY2spZY&feature=plcp

- Avidemux free for Windows PC and Mac OS X

  http://fixounet.free.fr/avidemux/download.html
  http://avidemux.sourceforge.net/download.html

- iMovie for Mac users (free).

- Free video editing apps on iPhone/iPod/iPad.

- Splice (free)

  http://itunes.apple.com/us/app/splice-video-editor-free/id409838725?mt=8

- Magisto (free)

  http://itunes.apple.com/us/app/magisto-magical-video-editor/id486781045?mt=8

3. Create a group presentation with PowerPoint, including presentation pictures with proper signposts if needed. Tutorials on creating and editing presentations using PowerPoint are available at

   http://oce.microsoft.com/en-us/powerpoint-help/basic-tasks-in-powerpoint-2010-HA101824346.aspx

4. Edit the group presentation with video clips of presentation/exam questions using the free video editors provided above.

5. Save the edited multimedia presentation of the exam questions as a .mov or a .mp4 file.

6. Manage and share video in YouTube.

   - Type in YouTube.com in the address bar of your selected Web browser and log in with your newly created group gmail/ YouTube account.
   - Find "Video Manager" under the group YouTube account which is located in the drop-down menu on the top right-hand corner of the YouTube screen.
   - Create a user name and channel for your group (e.g., GCOM231group2).
   - Set the "Privacy and Settings" for your group YouTube channel on the next page.
   - YouTube Privacy Settings help is avilable at

     http://support.google.com/YouTube/bin/answer.py?hl=en&answer=157177

   - Adjust Advanced Settings, but insure that comments are allowed in the Advanced Settings so that the other groups can provide feedback.
   - YouTube help about Advanced Settings is avilable at

     http://support.google.com/YouTube/bin/static.py?hl=en&page=guide.cs&guide=2467581&topic=2565764

   - Select "Videos" tab under your group channel's title.
   - Upload the saved .mov/.mp4 presentation file.

7. Save changes and share the published presentation of multimedia exam questions by making the YouTube URL available to other groups.

    - Set the Privacy Setting as Private and enter the gmail accounts of your classmates and instructor. You can locate the Privacy Settings in Video Manager, under the Basic Info tab, to the right of the movie Title and Description.

    - YouTube Help about sharing your video

        http://support.google.com/YouTube/bin/static.py?hl = en&topic=2565766&guide=2467581&page=guide.cs

    - YouTube Complete Help about uploading and publishing your video

        http://support.google.com/YouTube/bin/static.py?hl= en&guide=2467581&page=guide.cs

Variations on the basic theme

This assignment to teach informative speaking and digital literacy can be customized in many disciplinary areas. Informative speaking skills, digital literacy, collaborative/cooperative learning and constructive criticism can be incorporated into any discipline by drawing on the theories, concepts, and approaches unique to that discipline. The meaningful characteristics of YouTube and a digital video camera with basic digital video editing software is that they are user-friendly devices. With the tools and understanding of fundamental subject content, students can create and edit original digital content and re-present that content in a public forum. One may substitute any of a number of video sharing sites, such as Vimeo. One could also use Facebook, Twitter or Google+ to share the video in and outside of class.

Any digital video camera would work, including those in smartphones and tablets. Multimedia exam questions can be substituted by digital stories or assignments created by students. The key to effective learning is configuring assignments in alignment with the objectives of the class and eliciting student performance with the focus on deep thinking of the content rather than on the presentation format(s).

Observations and advice

Students have really enjoyed this assignment. They are typically ambivalent about teaching each other communication concepts but love the freedom and creativity in producing the multimedia questions.

The most significant piece of advice we would offer is that an instructor provides incentives to encourage or require students to go beyond mere definitional questions. Introduce them, if unfamiliar, to different elements of Bloom's Taxonomy and explain how they could create questions that require the exam taker to analyze, evaluate, or synthesize information to provide the best answer, using examples from students in classes of previous semesters when it is possible.

The final piece of advice is to remind students about privacy in a networked environment, respect to copyright when citing sources, and any possible Institutional Review Board implications for involving human subjects in a classroom presentation project.

Recommended reading

Bain, K. (2004) *What the Best College Teachers Do*. Cambridge, MA: Harvard University Press.

Baird Jr., J. E. (1974) The effects of speech summaries upon audience comprehension of expository speeches of varying quality and complexity. *Central States Speech Journal*, **25**(2), 119–27.

Bruffee, K. A. (1995) Sharing our toys: Cooperative learning versus collaborative learning. *Change*, **27**(1), 12–18.

Dumova, T. (2008) Using digital video assignments as a tool for active learning. *The International Journal of Learning*, **14**(12), 63–71.

Gagné, R. M. (1985) *The Conditions of Learning* (Fourth Edition). New York: Holt, Rinehart & Winston.

George-Palilonis, J., and Filak, V. (2009) Blended learning in the visual communications classroom: Student reflections on a multimedia course. *Electronic Journal of e-Learning*, **7**(3), 247–56.

Hall, K. M., Markham, J. C., and Culatta, B. (2005) The development of the Early Expository Comprehension Assessment (EECA): A look at reliability. *Communication Disorders Quarterly*, **26**(4), 195–206.

Hobbs, R. (2011) *Digital and Media Literacy: Connecting Culture and Classroom*. Thousand Oaks, CA: Corwin Press.

Hobbs, R. (2004) A review of school-based initiatives in media literacy education. *American Behavioral Scientist*, **48**(1), 42–59.

Joe, J. N., Harmes, J. C., and Hickerson, C. A. (2011) Using verbal reports to explore rater perceptual processes in scoring: A mixed methods application to

oral communication assessment. *Assessment in Education: Principles, Policy & Practice*, **18**(3), 239–58.
Mayer, R. E. (2008) Applying the science of learning: Evidence-based principles for the design of multimedia instruction. *American Psychologist*, **Nov.**, 760–9.
Morreale, S., Moore, M., Surges-Tatum, D., and Webster, L. (2007) *The Competent Speaker Speech Evaluation Form* (Second Edition). Washington, D.C.: National Communication Association.
Rothwell, J. D. (2010) *In the Company of Others: An Introduction to Communication* (Third Edition). New York: Oxford University Press.
Rowan, K. (1995) A new pedagogy for explanatory public speaking: Why arrangement should not substitute for invention. *Communication Education*, **44**(3), 236–50.
Sandars, J., and Murray, C. (2009) Digital storytelling for reflection in undergraduate medical education: A pilot study. *Education for Primary Care*, **20**(6), 441–4.
Smaldino, S. E., Lowther, D. L., and Russell, J. D. (2008) *Instructional Technology and Media for Learning* (Ninth Edition). Upper Saddle River, NJ: Pearson Education.
Thompkins, P. K., and Samovar, L. A. (1964) An experimental study of the effects of credibility on the comprehension of content. *Speech Monographs*, **31**(2), 120–3.
Turner Jr., F. H. (1970) The effects of speech summaries on audience comprehension. *Central States Speech Journal*, **21**(1), 24–9.
Yee, K., and Hargis, J. (2010) YouTube and video quizzes. *Turkish Online Journal of Distance Education*, **11**(2), 9–12.

Supplemental materials

Appendix A Informative Presentation Outline Guideline

Introduction (about 2 minutes)

A. Use an attention-getting technique to gain the interest of your audience and introduce the topic of your presentation. You might use a story, interactive audience survey, rhetorical question, shocking statistics, or something else to get the attention of your audience.

B. Establish the significance, relevance, and importance of your presentation topic.

C. Clearly communicate your purpose statement.

D. Preview and summarize the main points you will utilize to establish and support your purpose statement.

Then transition from the introduction to the body and your first main point.

Body (about 7 minutes)

A. Introduce your first main point.

1. A claim to support your first main point.

    a. Supporting material to back your claim: evidence, quotes, examples, anecdotes, or narratives are just some of your possibilities.

    b. Supporting material to back your claim: evidence, quotes, examples, anecdotes, or narratives are just some of your possibilities.

2. A different claim to support your first main point.

    a. Supporting material to back your claim: evidence, quotes, examples, anecdotes, or narratives are just some of your possibilities.

    b. Supporting material to back your claim: evidence, quotes, examples, anecdotes, or narratives are just some of your possibilities.

3. A different claim to support your first main point.

    a. Supporting material to back your claim: evidence, quotes, examples, anecdotes, or narratives are just some of your possibilities.

    b. Supporting material to back your claim: evidence, quotes, examples, anecdotes, or narratives are just some of your possibilities.

Then transition from your first main point to your second main point.

B. Introduce your second main point.

1. A claim to support your second main point.

    a. Supporting material to back your claim: evidence, quotes, examples, anecdotes, or narratives are just some of your possibilities.

b. Supporting material to back your claim: evidence, quotes, examples, anecdotes, or narratives are just some of your possibilities.

2. A different claim to support your second main point.

    a. Supporting material to back your claim: evidence, quotes, examples, anecdotes, or narratives are just some of your possibilities.

    b. Supporting material to back your claim: evidence, quotes, examples, anecdotes, or narratives are just some of your possibilities.

Then transition from your second main point to your third main point.

C. Introduce your third and final main point.

1. A claim to support your first main point.

    a. Supporting material to back your claim: evidence, quotes, examples, anecdotes, or narratives are just some of your possibilities.

    b. Supporting material to back your claim: evidence, quotes, examples, anecdotes, or narratives are just some of your possibilities.

2. A different claim to support your first main point.

    a. Supporting material to back your claim: evidence, quotes, examples, anecdotes, or narratives are just some of your possibilities.

    b. Supporting material to back your claim: evidence, quotes, examples, anecdotes, or narratives are just some of your possibilities.

3. A different claim to support your first main point.

    a. Supporting material to back your claim: evidence, quotes, examples, anecdotes, or narratives are just some of your possibilities.

    b. Supporting material to back your claim: evidence, quotes, examples, anecdotes, or narratives are just some of your possibilities.

Then transition from the body of your presentation to your conclusion.

Conclusion (about 1 minute)

A. Refer back to your introduction and attention-getting technique.

B. Summarize your main points.

C. Conclude with a memorable finish.

Appendix B Hickerson Oral Communication Behavioral Assessment

Table 11.1 Hickerson Oral Communication Behavioral Assessment (Part 1)

Student ID: ______________________ Date: ______________________

Rater: ______________________ Type of speech: ______________________

Speaking day (i.e., second day of speeches): ______________________

Competencies	**Description and evaluation elements**	**Score** Unsatisfactory Satisfactory Excellent
1. Topic	Chooses and narrows a topic appropriately for the audience and occasion *Consistency with purpose, treatment of topic within time limit, audience analysis*	
2. Thesis	Communicates the thesis in a manner appropriate for the audience and occasion *Thesis, audience adaptation, speech type*	
3. Supporting materials adequacy	Selects supporting materials that demonstrate information literacy and are appropriate to the topic, audience, and occasion *Linkage to thesis, types of sources, timeliness of sources, enhancement of credibility*	
4. Supporting materials citation	Provides supporting material citations that demonstrate information literacy and are appropriate to the topic, audience, and occasion *Citation format, adequacy of citations, integration of supporting materials*	
5. Organization	Uses an organizational pattern appropriate to the topic, audience, occasion, and purpose *Introduction (grabs attention, relevance, preview), organizational pattern, transitions, conclusion*	
6. Language	Uses language appropriate to the topic, audience, and occasion *Enhances comprehension and enthusiasm, creative, appropriate*	

Student ID: ____________	Date: ____________	
Rater: ____________	Type of speech: ____________	
Speaking day (i.e., second day of speeches): ____________		
Competencies	**Description and evaluation elements**	**Score** Unsatisfactory Satisfactory Excellent
7. Vocal behaviors	Use vocal variety in rate, pitch, and intensity (volume) to heighten and maintain interest appropriate to the topic, audience, and occasion *Vocal variety, paralanguage, volume*	
8. Pronunciation, grammar, and articulation	Uses pronunciation, grammar, and articulation appropriate to the audience and occasion *Fluency, articulation, pronunciation, grammar*	
9. Physical behaviors	Uses physical behaviors that support the verbal message and enhance credibility *Eye contact, facial expressions and gestures, posture and movement, appearance*	
10. Visual aids	Uses visual aids that heighten comprehension and interest appropriate to the topic, audience, and occasion. *Visual focus, design, appropriateness, simplicity, execution*	
Comments		

Table 11.2 Hickerson Oral Communication Behavioral Assessment (Part 2)

Competency	Unsatisfactory	Satisfactory	Excellent
1. Chooses and narrows a topic appropriately for the audience and occasion			
Consistency with purpose	Topic is inconsistent with the purpose (e.g., persuasive speech topic that does not present a problem, informative speech topic that is persuasive)	Topic is generally consistent with the purpose (e.g., persuasive speech topic that is a clear and concise problem, informative speech topic that is clearly informative)	Topic is perfectly consistent with the purpose (e.g., persuasive speech topic that is a particularly compelling or original problem, informative speech topic that is particularly enlightening, useful and instructive)
Treatment of topic within limit	Topic is too broad or narrow for adequate coverage within time limit	Topic is generally appropriate for adequate coverage within the time limit (e.g., some areas of speech are rushed, lacking in detail, or used time fillers)	Topic is perfectly appropriate for adequate coverage within the time limit (e.g., the speech is not rushed or stalled and topic is thoroughly covered)
Audience analysis	Topic is selected without audience analysis (e.g., topic is not relevant to the interests and lives of the audience, topic tailored to only a few members of the audience)	Topic is selected with consideration of audience analysis (e.g., topic is generally relevant to the interests and lives of a majority of the intended audience)	Topic is selected with particularly insightful audience analysis (e.g., topic is exceptionally relevant to the interests and lives of the intended audience)

Competency	Unsatisfactory	Satisfactory	Excellent
2. Communicates the thesis in a manner appropriate for the audience and occasion			
Thesis	Thesis is not communicated in the introduction of the speech	Thesis is communicated in the introduction of the speech	Thesis is communicated succinctly and clearly in the introduction of the speech
Audience adaptation	Thesis is adapted and communicated for few of the audience members. The thesis is evident and understandable for only a minority of the audience	Thesis is adapted for most of the audience. The thesis is evident and understandable for a majority of the audience	Thesis is adapted and communicated for the entire audience. The thesis is evident and understandable for the entire audience
Speech type communicated	The type of speech (informative or persuasive) is not communicated with the thesis. The type of speech is evident and understandable for only a minority of the audience	The type of speech (informative or persuasive) is communicated in the thesis. The type of speech is evident and understandable for a majority of the audience	The type of speech (informative or persuasive) is succinctly and clearly communicated in the thesis. The type of speech is evident and understandable for the entire audience

(*continued*)

Table 11.2 Hickerson Oral Communication Behavioral Assessment (Part 2) (*cont.*)

Competency	**Unsatisfactory**	**Satisfactory**	**Excellent**
3. Selects supporting materials that demonstrate information literacy and are appropriate to the topic, audience, and occasion			
Linkage to thesis	Supporting materials are not provided or only a few are linked to the thesis of the speech	Supporting materials are provided and most are linked to the thesis of the speech	Supporting materials are provided and all are linked to the thesis of the speech
Types of sources	No supporting materials are included or there are a limited number of types of sources (e.g., only magazines)	Supporting materials are included and come from at least two different types of sources (e.g., books and magazines)	Supporting materials are included and come from three or more types of sources (e.g., books, magazines, and journals)
Timeliness of sources	No supporting materials are included or most sources are older than 5 years	Supporting materials are included and come from recent sources (e.g., within the last 5 years)	Recent supporting materials are included and many are particularly timely (e.g., within the last 6 months)
Enhancement of speaker credibility	Supporting materials detract from or do not enhance the credibility of the speaker	Supporting materials are included and generally enhance the credibility of the speaker	Exceptional supporting materials are included and are particularly enhancing to the credibility of the speaker

Competency	Unsatisfactory	Satisfactory	Excellent
4. Provides supporting material citations that demonstrate information literacy and are appropriate to the topic, audience, and occasion			
Cited authorities	No sources/authorities are cited or authorities lack credibility, neutrality, or appropriateness	Most supporting materials are from credible, neutral, and appropriate sources/ authorities are cited	All supporting materials are from credible, neutral, and appropriate sources/ authorities are cited
Citation format	Citations are not included or are improperly stated (e.g., omitted publication date)	Citations are included and are generally stated in the proper format (e.g., a majority included the date and enough additional information to locate the source)	Citations are included and all are stated in the proper format (e.g., all included the date and enough additional information to locate the source)
Adequacy of citations	Statistics and facts that are not common knowledge are rarely or never cited	Most statistics and facts that are not common knowledge are cited (e.g., few researched facts/ opinions are not cited)	All statistics and facts that are not common knowledge are cited (e.g., all researched facts/opinions are cited)
Integration of citation	Citations are not integrated into the speech text	Citations are included and are generally integrated into the speech text	Citations are included and are particularly well integrated into the speech text

(*continued*)

Table 11.2 Hickerson Oral Communication Behavioral Assessment (Part 2) (*cont.*)

Competency	Unsatisfactory	Satisfactory	Excellent
5. Uses an organizational pattern appropriate to the topic, audience, occasion, and purpose			
Introduction: grabs attention	The introduction does not gain the attention of a majority of the audience or does so in an inappropriate manner	The introduction gains the attention of a majority of the audience in an appropriate manner	The introduction gains the attention of all the audience in an exceptionally appropriate and creative manner
Introduction: relevance	The introduction does not make clear the topic relevance to a majority of the audience	The introduction makes the topic relevance clear to a majority of the audience	The introduction makes the topic relevance clear for all the audience
Introduction: preview	The introduction does not preview the main points of the speech	The introduction previews the main points of the speech facilitating audience understanding of the speech's structure	The introduction previews the main points of the speech in an exceptionally clear manner enhancing audience understanding of the speech's structure
Organizational pattern	The speech organization lacks clarity and is not organized using an organizational pattern that is appropriate to the topic/audience	The speech is organized using a clear organizational pattern that is appropriate to the topic/audience and facilitates audience understanding and engagement	The speech is organized with superior clarity using an organizational pattern that is appropriate to the topic/audience and enhances audience understanding and engagement

Competency	Unsatisfactory	Satisfactory	Excellent
5. Uses an organizational pattern appropriate to the topic, audience, occasion and purpose (*cont.*)			
Transitions	No or few transitions are provided (e.g., speaker switched between main points without transitions)	Transitions are provided to help the audience understand the structure of the speech (e.g., all main points have transitions)	Transitions, as well as internal previews/ reviews and signposts, are provided where needed (e.g., all main points have transitions and the speaker adds internal previews/ reviews or signposts)
Conclusion	The conclusion does not provide a summary of the speech thesis or a review of the main points and fails to leave a majority of the audience with a clear message or call to action	The conclusion provides a summary of the speech thesis and reviews the main points in a manner that leaves a majority of the audience with a clear message or call to action	The conclusion provides an exceptionally clear and concise summary of the speech thesis and reviews all the main points in a manner that leaves all the audience with an undeniable message or call to action

(*continued*)

Table 11.2 Hickerson Oral Communication Behavioral Assessment (Part 2) (*cont.*)

Competency	Unsatisfactory	Satisfactory	Excellent
6. Uses language appropriate to the topic, audience, and occasion			
Enhances comprehension and enthusiasm	Language hinders audience comprehension and enthusiasm for the speech (e.g., language is confusing, wordy)	Language does not hinder audience comprehension and enthusiasm for the speech (e.g., language is clear, concise, and not distracting)	Language enhances audience comprehension and enthusiasm for the speech (e.g., language is vivid and interesting)
Creative	Language is not creative or creativity is inappropriate (e.g., language is cliché, uninventive)	Language adds creativity to the speech	Language adds creativity and displays exceptional understanding by the speaker for the nuances and poetry of meaning. (e.g., speaker successfully uses wordplay to enhance the speech)
Appropriate	Language is not appropriate for the audience (e.g., uses inappropriate jargon, is sexist, is racist, etc.)	Language is appropriate to the audience (e.g., free of inappropriate jargon, is nonsexist, is nonracist, etc.)	Language is especially appropriate and tailored to the audience's sensitivities, needs, and concerns. (e.g., the speech goes beyond being free of inappropriate language and uses language specifically selected for the audience)

Competency	Unsatisfactory	Satisfactory	Excellent
7. Use vocal variety in rate, pitch, and intensity (volume) to heighten and maintain interest appropriate to the topic, audience, and occasion			
Vocal variety	Minimal vocal variety and not in conversational mode (e.g., monotone, few or inappropriate changes in pitch, sounds read)	Vocal variety is appropriate and in a conversational mode (e.g., natural)	Exceptional use of vocal variety in a conversational mode (e.g., dynamic, energetic)
Paralanguage	Paralanguage is inappropriate or poorly paced (e.g., communicates boredom, lack of concern)	Paralanguage is appropriate to the topic, audience, and occasion	Paralanguage is exceptional, appropriate, and well paced (e.g., communicates excitement, concern for audience and topic)
Volume	Few members of the audience can hear the speech	Most of the audience can hear the speech	Easily heard by all audience members

(continued)

Table 11.2 Hickerson Oral Communication Behavioral Assessment (Part 2) (*cont.*)

Competency	**Unsatisfactory**	**Satisfactory**	**Excellent**
8. Uses pronunciation, grammar, and articulation appropriate to the audience and occasion			
Fluency	Poor fluency (e.g., many disfluencies, enough that the audience becomes distracted)	Appropriate fluency (e.g., few disfluencies, not enough that the audience becomes distracted)	Exceptional fluency (e.g., no disfluencies, helps engage the audience, and enhances comprehension)
Articulation	Poor articulation (e.g., many improperly formed sounds, many added or deleted syllables, enough that the audience becomes distracted)	Appropriate articulation (e.g., few improperly formed sounds, few added or deleted syllables, not enough that the audience becomes distracted)	Exceptional articulation (e.g., no improperly formed sounds, no added or deleted syllables, helps engage the audience and enhances comprehension)
Pronunciation	Improper pronunciation (e.g., many pronunciation errors, enough that the audience becomes distracted)	Appropriate pronunciation (e.g., few pronunciation errors, not enough that the audience becomes distracted)	Exceptional pronunciation (e.g., no pronunciation errors, helps engage the audience, and enhances comprehension)
Grammar	Improper grammar (e.g., many grammatical errors, enough that the audience becomes distracted)	Appropriate grammar (e.g., few grammatical errors, not enough that the audience becomes distracted)	Exceptional grammar (e.g., no grammatical errors, helps engage the audience, and enhances comprehension)

Competency	Unsatisfactory	Satisfactory	Excellent
9. Uses physical behaviors that support the verbal message and enhance credibility			
Eye contact	Little eye contact directed towards audience members. Most of the speech is read	Eye contact is made with the audience though there may be regular consultation of notes	Eye contact is consistent and well distributed with few to no returns to notes
Facial expressions and gestures	Few facial expressions and gestures are consistent with the verbal message and enhance credibility	Most facial expressions and gestures are consistent with the verbal message and enhance credibility	All facial expressions and gestures are consistent with the verbal message and enhance credibility
Posture and movement	Posture and movement do not support the verbal message and enhance credibility (e.g., speaker tied to podium; engages in distracting movements)	Posture and movement generally support the verbal message and enhance credibility	Posture and movement consistently support the verbal message and enhance credibility
Appearance	Attire and appearance choices do not support the verbal message and diminish credibility	Most attire and appearance choices support the verbal message and credibility	All attire and appearance choices especially support the verbal message and exceptionally enhance credibility

(*continued*)

Table 11.2 Hickerson Oral Communication Behavioral Assessment (Part 2) (*cont.*)

Competency	Unsatisfactory	Satisfactory	Excellent
10. Uses visual aids that heighten comprehension and interest appropriate to the topic, audience, and occasion			
Visual focus	Visual aids do not focus on visual content (e.g., too much text)	Visual aids focus on visual content (e.g., most content is graphical, text is minimized)	Visual aids exceptionally focus on visual content (e.g., visual examples are exceptional, high quality, expressive; text is minimal)
Design	Visual aids are not attractive, have errors, or are not the appropriate size (e.g., busy backgrounds, difficult-to-see colors, too small)	Visual aids are attractive, error free, and the appropriate size (e.g., easy to see and understand, well-chosen backgrounds)	Visual aids are not just attractive, error free, and the appropriate size, but are exceptionally tailored for the topic, audience, and occasion
Appropriateness	Few visual aids are appropriate for the audience and occasion; few add clarity, reinforce the message, gain attention, and/or maintain interest (e.g., few of the visual aids are needed)	Most visual aids are appropriate for the audience and occasion; most add clarity, reinforce the message, gain attention, and/or maintain interest (e.g., one visual aid was not needed)	All visual aids are appropriate for the audience and occasion; all add clarity, reinforce the message, gain attention, and/or maintain interest (e.g., all visual aids are needed)
Simplicity	Visual aids distract the audience from the topic/speaker and contain extraneous content (e.g., visual aids contain too much information, overuse of "bells and whistles" like sound effects and transitions)	Visual aids do not distract the audience from the topic/ speaker and most extraneous content is removed	None of the visual aids distract the audience from the topic/speaker or contain extraneous content

Competency	Unsatisfactory	Satisfactory	Excellent
10. Uses visual aids that heighten comprehension and interest appropriate to the topic, audience, and occasion (*cont.*)			
Execution	Visual aids are not integrated and executed poorly within the speech (e.g., speaker read from any visual aids, did not cover visual aids before and after discussing, did not maintain eye contact with audience while discussing all visual aids, skipped visual aids)	Most visual aids are integrated and executed well within the speech (e.g., speaker did not read from most visual aids, covered most visual aids before and after discussing, maintained eye contact with audience while discussing most visual aids, did not skip any visual aids)	All visual aids are integrated and executed well within the speech (e.g., speaker did not read from any visual aids, covered all visual aids before and after discussing, maintained eye contact with audience while discussing all visual aids)

12

Collaborative presentations using Google Docs

Michael S. Mills

Abstract: This project gives students an opportunity to produce a collaborative presentation using the synchronous editing capabilities of Google Docs. Groups of students create multiple parts of a presentation independently and then serve as peer reviewers and collaborators to synthesize the material into its aggregate final form. Incorporating the Web 2.0 technology of Google Docs allows students to create, revise, and edit from multiple platforms and facilitates the inclusion of multiple perspectives at different times or simultaneously. At the beginning of the project, students are given clear guidelines and expectations for presentation content and design, as well as strategies for effective team-building and collaboration.

Key words: collaboration, Google Docs, PowerPoint, presentation, Web 2.0.

Discipline/Academic areas addressed

Applicable to all academic areas.

Instructional purpose

The workplace of yesterday was primarily local and face to face. Today it is global and online. In order to compete in an ever-growing worldwide workplace, students must learn how to collaborate online on projects that might have several contributors separated geographically. The interdependent but geographically disconnected world that exists today necessitates a critical understanding of effective project collaboration skills that go beyond simple social interaction. Students need opportunities for practical engagement in assignments of substance that require thoughtful reflection and critical feedback. Students seem to be familiar with the social aspects of the Internet but are still struggling to become adept at content creation and problem-solving using tools available online.

Students need to be prepared for writing in team-based scenarios on a collaborative project. Students are often subjected to solitary approaches in which the teacher assigns a project and the student then completes a draft independent of outside peer assistance or perspective. This project gives students a practical framework that mimics real-world project collaboration by harnessing user-friendly Web 2.0 tools and the principles of effective presentation design.

At the beginning of the semester, students will be assigned a team-based project that requires them to synthesize multiple perspectives into a culminating presentation. Each team will be tasked with creating a unified, cohesive presentation by incorporating the separate documents that the team members have created individually. Students collaborate synchronously on the last stage of the project to foster a collective mind-set that focuses on one central message with several underlying supporting components. The aim is to have a presentation that presents several different voices but with a clear focus.

Student learning outcomes

1. Students will create presentation documents using a social sharing site, such as Google Docs.
2. Students will identify the benefits and limitations of a classroom management model.
3. Students will develop collaborative skills.
4. Students will collaborate in revision and editing.
5. Students will synthesize multiple perspectives into a unified, cohesive perspective.

Prerequisite skills and knowledge

Basic computer (word-processing, presentation-building) and Internet access (Web-browsing and interaction) skills are required. Students are assessed in this area by means of the technology competency exam administered through the university's information technology department. Students who fail to meet the basic requirements of basic computer and Internet access skills have the choice of concurrently enrolling in the basic educational technology course or completing a series of online tutorials available through the following links, which may also be of benefit for those universities who do not have a technology competency exam.

1. Basic skills (*http://www.ctdlc.org/remediation/*).
2. Internet 101 (*http://www.gcflearnfree.org/internet101*).
3. Teach Parents Tech by Google (*http://www.teachparentstech.org/*).
4. Technology Tutorials (*http://www.internet4classrooms.com/on-line.htm*).

Step-by-step directions

1. At the beginning of the semester, students will be assigned a classroom management method that will be covered in the first half of the semester. The directions given to students follow (see also Appendix A in "Supplemental materials"):
   a. Working as a team is both challenging and rewarding. Essentially, what you contribute to the team is a reflection of your dedication and your sense of collegiality, both of which are critical for teacher leaders. Please review the following guidelines so that this experience can be most beneficial to you and your teammates.
   b. You will be asked to not only create a presentation in Google Docs but also offer insightful suggestions and comments to the presentations your teammates have created as well. Respect their work by offering specific, noteworthy suggestions for improvement as well as specific comments highlighting exceptional work. Comments like "good job" or "needs work" do little to add to a professional relationship. Be specific and uplifting in your critique and praise.
   c. Develop mutually agreed upon guidelines for meeting. One suggestion is to schedule a particular time of day and treat that time as a class itself.

d. Be on time. Whether you plan to meet in person or meet online, punctuality is a sign of respect.

e. Develop common guidelines for communication and work allocation during each meeting. The more specific your guidelines are, the better your chances are of having a productive work flow.

f. Be prepared and put forth a good faith effort.

g. Be an active member of the group when collaborating; remember that this project is a team project. Although you have an individual responsibility, the team depends on each individual member to bring all aspects of the project into a cohesive whole.

h. Be patient with others and their particular work and learning styles.

i. If you have a problem with a member of the team, try to work it out in an open and forthright way. Avoiding the problem or complaining to another teammate will not solve the problem in a positive way.

2. After the students have received their topic, they will be grouped (no more than three per group) and assigned a collaborative presentation for visiting instructors from another country. Students will use Google Presentations (docs.google.com). For this reason, students will receive a training session on how to create and share presentations in Google Docs (see Appendix B in "Supplemental materials").

3. Students will create and share initial drafts of their respective sections of the presentation on Google Docs.

4. Students have one week in which to make constructive annotations, revisions, or edits to the other team members' original drafts and an additional week to subsequently implement any proposed revisions or additions to their own sections.

5. Students will schedule a mutually beneficial time to schedule their synchronous collaboration on the final revision of the presentation. Before that meeting, students will select one team member to aggregate all of the presentation sections into one document. The document will then be shared with all team members.

6. During the synchronous collaboration session, students will unify their sections into a single presentation and make final suggestions, edits, and revisions as needed. Students will be able to coordinate their revisions through the embedded chat function in Google Docs, as well as any other format they wish (phone, email, Twitter, etc.). Each revision is tracked and can be undone if so desired. The purpose of the final collaboration is to create one presentation with a singular theme by incorporating the salient aspects of the individual presentations and how they interrelate with the other sections and the overall theme.

7. Students will present with their respective group, each student presenting his or her own section and tying it into the larger theme as well as how it relates to the other sections. Students are encouraged to relate their content to the other sections as well as the overall theme.

8. After students have made their presentations, they will reflect on their collaborative experience in class and by means of a reflection instrument submitted only to the instructor. The reflection guidelines used are as follows. Provide a 50–100-word response to each of the following questions. This is to be completed online with the Google Forms link provided to you by the instructor.

    a. How well did our group complete the task to the highest standard?

    b. How well did our group use time effectively?

    c.. How well did our group coordinate planning and collaboration activities?

    d. How well did our group provide honest, critical, and detailed feedback to one another?

    e. What did we do particularly well as a team?

    f. What was my greatest strength as a team member?

    g. What should I do as an individual to better support my team in the future?

    h. How do I rate my team members and what are my major concerns or praises?

Approximate time required

- 30 minutes to discuss assignment expectations.
- 90–120 minutes explaining the Web 2.0 tool (Google Docs) as it pertains to the assignment.
- 7 weeks to draft, revise, and finalize the presentation.
- 90–180 minutes to deliver presentations (depends on class size).
- In-class time requirement is approximately 2–3 weekly class sessions; remainder of time is outside of class.

Required resources

Tech requirements:

- Computer or tablet.
- Access to the Internet (preferably broadband).
- Google Docs (docs.google.com).

Variations on the basic theme

This assignment harnesses the power of Web 2.0 technology, which allows for powerful real-time collaboration combined with a simple user interface. By creating a dynamic work flow, students create multiple drafts of their work on the fly. This process produces a higher quality document that contains better structural integrity and coherence (Goldberg et al., 2003).

The widespread availability of Google Docs on multiple PC and mobile platforms (Windows, Mac, iOS, Android) allows students unprecedented flexibility to draft and revise their projects, even if their team members are using a different operating system.

Students could use the Comment and Tracking feature in Microsoft PowerPoint but platform uniformity would have to be enforced because of accessibility issues. Many students use PowerPoint but an increasing number of them are using the Mac OS presentation software Keynote, which does not reliably import comments and tracking information from PowerPoint.

Additionally, while embedding comments and tracking revisions within Microsoft PowerPoint is possible, the advantage of a simultaneous multi-participant focus would be lost. Only one student at a time could review a document, which would result in a lost opportunity to develop a dynamic work flow that incorporates a continual influx of multiple perspectives.

Emailing comments and suggestions is another mechanism that could be employed but the lack of comment/revision specificity is an area of concern. Whereas an email can describe a suggestion or comment in general, revision-tracking and location-specific comments provide a clearer direction for revisions and feedback.

Another powerful Web 2.0 tool that is platform neutral and allows for multiple-user commenting is Crocodoc, a free service that allows users to upload a PowerPoint file (as well as a Word or PDF document) and then share that document so others can highlight and make comments. What users don't get, however, is version tracking or the ability for others to edit the document.

Observations and advice

What is particularly powerful about this approach is that it gives students free and easy access to a true collaborative framework, both synchronous and asynchronous. Students can access their team's presentation document through PCs, Macs, or even tablet devices (e.g., iPad) almost anytime.

Notably, students get particularly engaged in the project when revising synchronously and seem to develop a stronger sense of teamwork and project ownership. This may be due to the team's need to communicate externally (via texting or voice calls) when synchronously editing a document. Students seem to rely on an external means of communicating apart from the commenting and revision tools in Google Docs in order to synchronize ideas and come to a consensus.

Instructors should be cautioned about uploading complex PowerPoint presentations created off-line into Google Docs for editing. If the presentation is not converted to Google Docs format on upload, the site is likely to crash when attempting to edit the PowerPoint file. Also, the import is often a crude representation of the original document (especially if the document contains multiple images or dynamic elements), necessitating a time-intensive redesign. It is suggested that uploaded documents be stripped to their basics and then be revised within Google Docs.

Another important consideration is making sure that a suitable amount of time is given to train students on using Google Docs. Additionally, instructors may want to consider being flexible with the time requirements because studies have shown how the implementation of new technologies often has a negative effect on productivity and quality (Cerrato and Rodriguez, 2002; Levitt and Mahowald, 2002 (as cited in Passig and Schwartz, 2007)).

Recommended reading

Anderson-Inman, L., and Knox-Quinn, C. (1996) Synchronous writing environments: Real-time interaction in cyberspace. *Journal of Adolescent & Adult Literacy*, **40**(2), 134–8.

Anon. (2003) Facilitating students' collaborative writing. *Reference and Research Book News*, **18**(2).

Blase, D. W. (2000) A new sort of writing: E-mail in the E-nglish classroom. *English Journal*, **90**(2), 47–51.

Cerrato, T., and Rodriguez, H. (2002) Studies of computer supported collaborative writing: Implications for system design. In: K. Schmidt (Ed.), *Cooperative System Design* (pp. 139–54). Amsterdam: IOS Press.

Cowles, K., Strickland, D., and Rodgers, B. (2001) Collaboration for teaching innovation: Writing across the curriculum in a school of nursing. *Journal of Nursing Education*, **40**(8), 363–7.

Dishaw, M., Eierman, M., Iversen, J., and Philip, G. (2011) Wiki or word? Evaluating tools for collaborative writing and editing. *Journal of Information Systems Education*, **22**(1), 43–54.

Eapen, B. (2007) Collaborative writing: Tools and tips. *Indian Journal of Dermatology, Venereology and Leprology*, **73**(6), 439–41.

Goldberg, A., Russell, M., and Cook, A. (2003) The effect of computers on student writing: A meta-analysis of studies from 1992 to 2002. *Journal of Technology Learning and Assessment*, **2**(1), 1–52.

Kirschner, P., Jan-Willem Strijbos, Kreijns, K., and Beers, P. (2004) Designing electronic collaborative learning environments. *Educational Technology, Research and Development*, **52**(3), 47–66.

Levitt, M., and Mahowald, R. P. (2002) *There Should Be More to Collaboration than E-mail* (IDC White Paper). Hewlett Packard, Bracknell, U.K.

Mabrito, M. (2006) A study of synchronous versus asynchronous collaboration in an online business writing class. *American Journal of Distance Education*, **20**(2), 93–107, doi: 10.1207/s15389286ajde2002_4.

Passig, D., and Schwartz, G. (2007) Collaborative writing: Online versus frontal. *International Journal on ELearning*, **6**(3), 395–412.

Perkins, J. (1996) Collaboration and conflict: A contextual exploration of group writing and positive emphasis. *Journal of Business and Technical Communication*, **10**(3), 369–372.

Phegley, M., and Oxford, J. (2010) Cross-level collaboration: Students and teachers learning from each other. *English Journal*, **99**(5), 27–34.

Read, S. (2010) A model for scaffolding writing instruction: IMSCI. *The Reading Teacher*, **64**(1), 47–52.

Reither, J., and Vipond, D. (1989) Writing as collaboration. *College English*, **51**(8), 855–867.

Thompson, L., and Heng-Yu, K. (2006) A case study of online collaborative learning. *Quarterly Review of Distance Education*, **7**(4), 361–75.

Tutty, J., and Klein, J. (2008) Computer-mediated instruction: A comparison of online and face-to-face collaboration. *Educational Technology, Research and Development*, **56**(2), 101–24.

Supplemental material

Appendix A

Table 12.1 Collaborative Classroom Management Presentation Rubric

Classroom management method:				
Group member			**Section**	
			Organization	
			Parent communication	
			Behavior management	
	Lacking 0	Acceptable 3	Exemplary 5	Score
Content of presentation	The presentation lacked a clear purpose or focus. The presentation material was inaccurate	The presentation was interesting and provided useful information regarding the classroom management model	The presentation contained an exceptional amount of engaging information that sufficiently and correctly covered the classroom management model	
Organization	The presentation lacked organization and had little evidence of preparation	The presentation seemed organized but each section seemed independent of the presentation as a whole	The presentation was organized so that each section flowed well and created a sense of the whole theme throughout	
Presentation format	The presentation contained minimal variety. Presentation consisted of overly textual slides	The presentation used creativity to a degree. Slides contained appropriate multimedia that enhanced meaning	The presentation used multimedia and slide design to maximize an emotional impact with the audience	

Classroom management method:				
Group member			**Section**	
			Organization	
			Parent communication	
			Behavior management	
	Lacking 0	Acceptable 3	Exemplary 5	Score
Presentation style	The presentation seemed to be disorganized. The group members did not present themselves as a team	The presentation was organized. The members seemed to know their respective duties	The group was very organized in the presentation. Each member spoke clearly, was energetic, and created interest in the topic. The members seemed to feed off each other's energy and create a compelling presentation	

Appendix B Collaborative presentation using Google Docs – student instructions

Students, you will have an awesome opportunity this semester to develop a collaborative presentation using Google Docs. The scenario is this: a visiting instructor from another country wants more information on classroom management methods used here in the United States. You and two classmates will develop a presentation highlighting various aspects of your assigned classroom management method.

Table 12.2 Collaborative presentation using Google Docs – student instructions

Week 1	• Assignment of classroom management method and placement into groups. • Training on how to create collaborative presentations in Google Docs (creation, sharing, chat). • Discussion of assignment requirements. • Discussion of team-based collaboration guidelines.
Weeks 2–3	• Once teams have their assigned classroom management method, team members will decide who will focus on specific aspects of that style of classroom management. For the purposes of this assignment, those aspects are 1) organization, 2) parent communication, and 3) behavior management. If the team only has two members, the members will share the remaining aspect of classroom management. If pertinent to your team, please discuss the management of this last piece with the instructor. • Create a draft presentation of your classroom management topic. Remember that you are presenting this to a visiting instructor from another country. It is critical that you provide specifics and a rationale based on the assigned classroom management method. • Once you are finished with your draft presentation, enable sharing of the presentation document with your team members.
Week 4	• Students have one week in which to make constructive annotations, revisions, or edits to the other team members' presentation drafts. Provide detailed feedback and critiques!

Week 5	• Use this week to implement any proposed revisions or additions to your section. Feel free to communicate with your teammates for needed clarification. • By the end of this week, contact your teammates to decide which team member will aggregate all of the presentation sections into one document. The lead editor will then share the document with all team members.
Weeks 6–7	• Find mutually agreeable meeting times (either face to face or online) to collaborate on merging the independent sections of the recently merged presentation into a single, cohesive presentation. The key here is to maintain the salient aspects of the individual presentations and then show how each section relates to each other and the classroom management method as a whole. • Synchronous collaboration on the final revision of the presentation can be facilitated by the chat function within Google Docs. You are free to use any method you wish to communicate (email, Twitter, etc.), but it is my experience that chatting through Google Docs is the most efficient way to collaborate with more than one teammate at a time. • Students must collaborate synchronously on this last stage of the project to foster a collective mind-set that focuses on one central message with several underlying supporting components. The aim is to have a presentation that presents several different voices but with one dominant focus and theme.
Week 8	• Students will present with their respective group, each student presenting his or her own section and tying it into the larger theme as well as how it relates to the other sections. • Students will provide a reflection after the presentation that details their experience with the collaboration aspect of the project.

Cooperative study blog

Amanda Evelyn Waldo

Abstract: In this activity, students are asked to identify and discuss key course concepts in periodic posts to a shared blog. The title of each blog post identifies the concept; in the body of the post, the student explains the importance of the concept and provides relevant definitions and analysis. Once students have completed their individual contributions, the blog archive (a linked listing of the post titles) functions as an electronic flashcard deck covering each of the topics the students have identified as important. As it grows, the blog becomes a useful resource for students to review key concepts, test their understanding, and prepare for exams. For examples of actual student blogs please see

http://www.americanwomenwriters.blogspot.com/
http://english10bkeyterms.blogspot.com/
and
http://english142b.blogspot.com/

For a template see

http://cooperativestudyblogexample.blogspot.com/

Key words: blogs, cooperative learning, retrieval practice, review, self-testing, test preparation.

Discipline/Academic areas addressed

This activity is flexible enough to be applicable across all disciplines; it was originally designed for use in an English literature course.

Instructional purpose

Students sometimes feel that posting in online discussion forums or on blogs creates extra work without adding much value. With this activity the value is clear: each student contributes a few posts over the course of the term and receives in exchange an extensive resource in a format that lends itself to review and self-testing. By asking students to identify key course concepts beginning early in the term, this activity also encourages them to think critically about how material covered in the reading assignments and in lecture relates to larger course themes. Although it will work for strictly factual data and will be valuable to students in courses that require memorization, the format easily accommodates more analytical content (e.g., close reading analysis of a short passage). Students who may be uncertain about what is expected or nervous about applying a particular method of analysis on test day can practice with items that classmates have already identified as important. They will also benefit from seeing how other students approach the same material. This activity also creates a useful resource for the instructor, who can consult the blog to see which ideas and information students understand and which they need help with.

Student learning outcomes

Student learning outcomes will vary depending on the course. This section describes SLOs for this activity when used as a part of a discussion section for a large lecture course in English literature. Students in this course are expected to be able to identify important quotations from the assigned texts, place the quotations in context, and know the author, publication date, form, and themes associated with each text. Lecture, discussion sections, essay assignments, and exams all emphasize close reading analysis.

Students will demonstrate ability to

1. Organize course concepts to facilitate self-testing and review.
2. Identify and define key terms and concepts and discuss their application to examples discussed in class and identified independently in the assigned reading.

3. Given an assigned text, identify important quotations, place them in context (title, author, genre, scene, etc.) and perform close reading analysis.

4. Given a quotation from an assigned text, identify its source (including title and author) and perform close reading analysis.

5. Understand and respond to close reading analyses by fellow students and contribute by suggesting additional avenues for analysis or providing constructive criticism.

6. Receive feedback and suggestions from fellow students.

Prerequisite skills and knowledge

Students need Internet access and basic computer skills such as those possessed by the average college student.

Step-by-step directions

For instructors. Using the blogging software of your choice, create a blog for your class and add each of your students as contributing authors. Make sure that the template design you choose displays the blog archive prominently, and that the blog archive displays blog post titles without a preview of the body of the post. Think of the blog as an electronic flashcard – the post titles in the blog archive are the prompt side of the flashcard, so it's important that the blog archive display post titles in full and without a preview of the body of the post. For detailed instructions see Appendix A in "Supplemental materials".

For students. Instructions for students should emphasize that formatting blog posts correctly is essential to making it useful as a study tool. Students should think of their posts as online flashcards in which the post title is the prompt (the front of the flashcard) and the body of the post is the answer (the back of the flashcard). Instructors should also clearly indicate what kind of analysis is expected. Ideally, instructors should provide students with an example post that models the desired format, subject matter, and type and quality of analysis. Detailed instructions follow. (Note that these instructions were designed for students in an English literature course. Feel free to modify it to fit your instructional needs.)

Posting to the blog

1. *Choose a topic that has not already been covered.* Before you post, check the blog archive to make sure that another student has not already posted on your topic. To ensure that no one posts on your topic while you are working on it, make a placeholder post with your title and a message in the body to indicate that you are working on the post. Once you have finished writing your post, just edit the initial post and replace the message with your finished post.

2. *Title your post.* The title of your post should usually be either a term discussed in class, or a quotation from the assigned reading. *Important:* You and your fellow students will use your post title as a prompt for self-testing. Think of each post a part of an online flashcard deck: your post title is the front of the flashcard, and the body of your post is the back. If the title of your post is too vague or if it contains both the prompt and the answer, it won't be useful for self-testing. Choose titles like:

    - Metaphor
    - Dramatic irony vs. situational irony
    - "For sale: baby shoes, never worn"
    - "124 was spiteful. Full of a baby's venom"
    - "The thing you have always suspected about yourself the minute you become a tourist is true: A tourist is an ugly human being"
    - Haiku
    - Ecocriticism

    Avoid titles like:

    - Amanda's second post
    - A little clarification about two terms that are often confused
    - Wow, this story is so short it could have been written on a ouija board!
    - "124 was spiteful. Full of a baby's venom" (from *Beloved* by Toni Morrison)
    - This is how I think we should interpret Jamaica Kincaid's writing about tourism in *A Small Place*

- A haiku is a poem with 17 syllables split into three lines of 5, 7, and 5 syllables each
- The theoretical approach we talked about in class today.

The titles in the first group are useful for self-testing because they clearly indicate the term, concept, or quotation that the post will address without giving away the answer. The titles in the second group are not useful because they either don't clearly identify a term, concept, or quotation or they give away the answer. Your post titles don't have to look exactly like the ones in the first group, but you should always make sure that you are using a title that your fellow students will be able to use for self-testing.

3. *Write your post.*

If you are posting about a term: A term could be any literary device, genre, movement, concept, or theoretical approach that was discussed in class or in the reading and that is relevant to our discussion of the course texts. If you are posting about a term, the title of your post should be the term you are posting about. In the body of your post

i. Define the term in your own words.

ii. Give examples. Explain any examples that were provided in class, and then provide at least one example of your own.

iii. Explain how the term contributes to our discussion of a particular course text. Your post should contribute to our discussion of the course texts as well, so if you post on a term make sure that you can articulate why that term is relevant to our discussion of a specific text. If the term you post about is "metaphor" your post should comment on the role of metaphor in a particular text – what does the author's use of metaphor accomplish? If the term you post about is "industrialization" you should define industrialization but also comment on why it would be useful to think of one of the course texts in relation to this phenomenon. *What is this text's attitude toward industrialization? Is it critical or celebratory? How does the text imagine industrialization?* If the term you post about is "ecofeminism" you should define ecofeminism and then also explain how an ecofeminist approach would add to our understanding of a particular text.

iv. Cite your source. Always include a full citation of your source, including page numbers and publication information.

v. Sign your name! Always sign your name to your posts and comments – if you don't, your instructor has no way of knowing that you completed the assignment.

If you are posting about a quotation, the title of your post should be the quotation you are posting about. You'll build your analysis on your observations about this quotation, so use one with language that interests you! Unless instructed otherwise, limit the length of your quotation to two sentences at most. (Shorter quotations work better with the blog format, and will also limit any temptation to plot summary and let you focus on analyzing the language of the quotation.)

i. In the body of your post, identify the source of the quotation. Include the author, the title of the text, and the original date of publication. If the quotation is from a play, identify the act and scene. Very briefly (in no more than two sentences) give the context: who is speaking to whom, where are they, what are they talking about? Remember, your audience is familiar with the text so you don't need to go into great detail.

ii. Also, in the body of the post, write a close reading of your quotation. Do a close reading of your quotation just like you would in a paper or on an exam. Your analysis should come out of your close observation of the text, so spend some time observing before you get started. Here are a few questions to ask yourself to get the ball rolling: What made me choose this particular quotation? Is there something interesting about the language of this quotation, or the logic it uses? Who is speaking? Who is the audience? What is the tone, and how is that communicated? Are there any ambiguities or contradictions? What is the sentence structure? Is there anything unusual about the punctuation? Are there any metaphors? Read the quotation aloud – what does it sound like? Paraphrase the quotation – if the author had used your paraphrase instead, would the quotation have a different effect?

Feel free to consult any handouts provided by your instructor, or take a look at your classmates' posts to see what kinds of observations they found useful in their close reading (it's not cheating – this is what the blog is for!). You can also find resources about close reading online:

http://www.brocku.ca/english/jlye/criticalreading.php
http://www.personal.psu.edu/users/s/a/sam50/closeread.htm
http://web.cn.edu/kwheeler/reading_lit.html

iii. Cite your source. Always include a full citation of your source, including page numbers and publication information.

iv. Sign your name! Always sign your name to your posts and comments – if you don't, your instructor has no way of knowing that you completed the assignment.

See Appendix B in "Supplemental materials" for tips for students on posting to the blog. See Appendix C for studying with the blog.

Evaluation

Your post will be evaluated based on:

- accuracy and completeness
- usefulness to fellow students (make your contributions on time, make your posts relevant to the course, format your posts correctly, choose terms and quotations that other students have not already covered);
- contribution to our discussion of course texts (builds on discussions and further develops discussion topics)

Approximate time required

This is an at-home activity, but instructors should be prepared to spend at least 20–30 minutes in class explaining (and preferably demonstrating) how to post to the blog, what format to use, and how to use the blog for studying and self-testing. Instructors who are asking students to include analysis (e.g., close reading) rather than just factual information in the posts should be prepared to spend longer. It may also be helpful to make students aware of recent research suggesting the importance of retrieval practice in learning.

Required resources

Tech requirement:

- Internet access
- Web browser
- blogging software such as WordPress or Blogger.

Variations on the basic theme

This activity can be varied depending on the kinds of skills instructors want to emphasize. In a literature class that emphasizes close reading and in which students are also expected to be able to identify key passages from the texts they have read, ask students to post a line from a key passage as the title of their post. In the body of the post, have them list the source of the quotation (author, text, date) and include a short close reading.

In a language course, the title of the post might be a word that students are expected to know, with a translation and example sentence in the body of the post. In a math class, the title might be a problem the students are expected to be able to solve, and then the body of the post would contain the solution and an explanation of how it was reached. In a history course, a post title might be "causes of the American Civil War" with the body of the post exploring the causes. In a biology class, a post title might be "characteristics of vascular plants" with a listing of the characteristics and a discussion of their evolutionary role in the body of the post.

Observations and advice

- Introduce this activity on the first day of class (or in the first discussion section) and have students turn in their first round of posts well before their first midterm or exam. This will get them thinking about which ideas are important to post about early on and will keep the posts from focusing too much on material from later in the term.
- Start the blog with at least one example post. This will help to clarify your expectations in terms of level and amount of analysis in the body of the post, and will also give students a format to mimic.
- To get the ball rolling, consider suggesting a few possible post titles for students to use.
- It is very important to show students how the post titles appear in the blog archive and explain how the blog archive functions as an electronic flashcard deck. Students who don't understand how this works will deviate from the title = prompt, body = answer format, and their posts may not be useful for self-testing.
- Although you should know your students' "handle" so that you can confirm participation and address any misunderstandings, students who

prefer to post anonymously can do so by creating a pseudonym. If privacy is a concern, you can also make the blog private to only students in the course.

- Make sure that students understand what they are getting out of this activity. Do the math: in a class of 100 students in which each student is expected to contribute 3 posts, students will have 300 posts to study from.

Recommended reading

Arvan, L. (2010) Teaching with blogs. *Inside Higher Ed*. Available from *http://www.insidehighered.com/views/2010/07/27/arvan*

Belluck, P. (2011) To really learn, stop studying and take a test. *New York Times*. Available from *http://www.nytimes.com/2011/01/21/science/21memory.html*

Clark, C. (2011) Taking steps to respect student privacy in public work. Available from *http://ltlatnd.wordpress.com/2011/12/19/taking-steps-to-respect-student-privacy-in-public-work/*

Foo, P. W., Mora, J. J., and Tkacz, S. (1994) Student study techniques and the generation effect. *Journal of Educational Psychology*. **86**(4): 567–76.

Goldman, R. H., Cohen, A. P., and Sheahan, F. (2008) Using seminar blogs to enhance student participation and learning in public health school classes. *American Journal of Public Health*, **98**(9), 1658–663.

Glogoff, S. (2005) Instructional blogging: Promoting interactivity, student-centered learning, and peer input. *Innovate*, **1**(5).

Hanson, J. J. (n.d.) *Latest Study Validates Testing, Forced Retrieval and SQRRR*. Openeducation.net. Available from *http://www.openeducation.net/2011/01/25/latest-study-validates-testing-forced-retrieval-and-sqrrr/*

Hiltz, S. R. (1998) Collaborative learning in asynchronous learning networks: Building learning communities. Paper presented at *Web98, Orlando, FL.*

Karpicke, J. D., and Roediger III, H. L. (2008) The critical importance of retrieval for learning. *Science*, **319**(5865) 966–8.

Lohnes, S. (2006) Using blogs in a college classroom: What's authenticity got to do with it? Available from *http://blogsforlearning.msu.edu/articles/view.php?id=7*

Supplemental materials

Appendix A Instructions for instructors

Setting up a cooperative blog using blogger.com

1. *Create your blog:* Go to *www.blogger.com* and sign in using your Gmail account (or create a new one). Click "New Blog" and fill out

the title and address fields. Choose a template that shows your blog archive in a sidebar menu (this is very important because it is what enables your students to use the blog as an online flashcard deck).

2. *Publish an example post:* Click "Start Posting." In the title field for the first post, enter a term, concept, or quotation you want your students to learn or post a problem that you want them to solve. In the body of the post, offer a discussion of that term, concept, or quotation or give the answer to the problem and explain how you got it. The format and the type of analysis you provide in this post should be a model for what you want your students to do in their posts. Click "Publish".

3. *Check the blog format:* Click "View Blog" and confirm that your post appears in a sidebar archive (if it doesn't, you can change the settings by clicking "Design" and then "Layout") and use the Template Designer.

4. *Add your students as authors:* Click "Design" and then "Settings" to open your blog settings. Under "Permissions", add your students as authors by entering their email addresses separated by commas.

You can do this activity with any blogging software as long as it allows multiple authors and offers a sidebar archive as a navigation option. This activity could also be easily adapted for use with the Moodle forum tool.

Managing accuracy and comprehensiveness of the cooperative study blog

You have two options for managing the accuracy and comprehensiveness of the cooperative study blog: make the students responsible, or do it yourself.

Option 1 Make the students responsible (recommended)

In my experience, this activity works best when students take ownership over the study blog and understand that they are responsible for both the accuracy of the posts and the blog's comprehensiveness as a study tool for their exams. Students who see it as an assignment to complete acceptably and hand in write less helpful posts and engage with the blog less than students who see it as a communal resource over which they have control and for which they share responsibility. Although I grade student posts and watch the blog to get a general sense of what students are posting about and how well they understand the material, I do not review individual posts for accuracy before allowing students to post to the blog. I also do not check to be sure that everything that will be on an exam has been covered in the blog.

If you take this approach, it's important to be clear with your students that they need to be responsible to one another to post accurate information and alert one another immediately (by commenting on the post) when they see a mistake. Students should be aware that, like other collectively authored online resources, the blog can be a valuable resource but it is only as accurate and as complete as they make it. It should not be considered an authoritative source and it definitely should not represent students' first or only encounter with concepts covered in the course.

There are several ways to encourage accuracy in the blog posts without reviewing them individually prior to publication:

- Require students to cite sources.
- Encourage students to comment on a post if there is something they don't understand or if they find a mistake – consider making this kind of participation mandatory.
- Consider requiring students to fact-check a certain number of posts – students can comment on posts to identify errors or indicate that they have fact-checked a post and believe it is accurate.
- Consider offering extra credit to students who identify factual errors in published posts.

There are also ways to encourage posts that give a comprehensive view of the course materials:

- Require students to post to the blog regularly (if posts are due just once or twice during the course, materials covered just before deadlines will be overrepresented) – if you're only asking for a few posts from each student, consider dividing them into groups and staggering the deadlines so that posts are due from at least one group in each week of the course.
- Encourage students to post on particular topics by suggesting them in class or providing a list of suggested topics along with the study blog handout or incorporated into the course syllabus.

Option 2 Do it yourself

If you want to review each post for accuracy before it is published to the blog, you'll need to choose a blogging software like WordPress that allows you to restrict students' ability to publish their own posts. If you are using WordPress and add your students with contributor (rather than author) roles, they will be able to log on and write and manage their posts but not publish them. As an administrator of the blog, you will then be able to review each completed post and either publish it or let the student know about errors that need to be fixed.

If you decide to manage the blog this way it may also be a good idea to assign topics for posts rather than have students choose their own, as the delay in publishing will make it difficult for students to identify what topics have already been covered and to let one another know which topics they are working on.

Tips: If you are working with more than one teaching assistant and want your TAs to grade or monitor students' posts, have students tag their posts to indicate which section they are in. TAs can sort the blog and review only the posts tagged for their sections, which will make grading much easier.

Appendix B Tips for posting to the blog

- It takes time to write a thoughtful post. Consider composing your post in a program like Microsoft Word or Google Docs. This way you won't risk losing your work if your Internet connection is interrupted or if you get logged out of the blog.
- To keep other students from posting on the same topic while you are composing your post, publish a post with just a title to let your fellow students know you're working on it. When you're done writing, you can edit the original post.
- Always sign your name to your posts and comments – if you don't sign your name, your instructor has no way of knowing that you completed the assignment. If you are uncomfortable signing your real name for privacy reasons, talk to your instructor about restricting blog access to enrolled students or assigning you a handle to use when you post.

Appendix C Studying with the blog

1. Open the blog in your browser.
2. Locate the "archive" of posts (usually on the right-hand side).
3. Read one of the post titles (but don't click on it!) and answer these questions mentally, in writing, or aloud with your study partner. For longer titles, the archive may not show the whole title. If the post title in the archive listing ends with an ellipsis, go ahead and click through to

see the whole title but be careful not to read the body of the post before you have tested yourself.

If it is a key term

a. Define the term.

b. Use the term in a sentence.

c. Give one example of how this term was used in a lecture or discussion session.

d. Give an example of how this term could be used that does not come from a lecture or discussion session. If possible, use the term to say something about one of the assigned texts. If nothing comes to mind try applying the term to something from outside of class.

If it is a quotation

a. Identify the source – be as specific as you can. *What text is the quotation from? When was it written? What is the genre? Who is the author? Is a character speaking – if so, which? If a narrator is speaking, what kind of narrator is he or she?*

b. Identify the form. *Is it prose or verse? Is there a rhyme scheme?* (If you had trouble identifying the source of the quotation, thinking about the form may help to narrow it down.)

c. Decide why the quotation is important. *Does it exemplify a form that was discussed in class? Does it play a key role in the text? Is it related to an important theme? Why do you think the poster thought this was an important quotation to remember?*

d. Plan out a close reading/explication of the quotation. *Make a few observations about the language of the quotation (word choice, sentence structure, etc.) – how is the language working to create meaning?* If you have trouble, try paraphrasing the quotation. *If the author had used your paraphrase instead, would the quotation still have the same effect? Why or why not?*

4. Click on the post title and read the entry. Did you miss anything mentioned in the post? Does the post raise any points that you didn't think of? Did you think of anything that the poster didn't? (If you did, add your thoughts as a comment on the post.)

Tips: Everyone makes mistakes – if you see an error in a post you are studying with, write a comment to let the author know. This gives the post's author a chance to correct any errors and makes the study blog a better and more accurate resource for everyone.

The blog can be a valuable tool for reviewing material you are already familiar with; it should never be your first or only exposure to the course material. The blog is only as accurate or as comprehensive as you and your fellow students make it – by doing the assigned reading and attending lectures before using the study blog you protect yourself from being misled by potential errors in the published posts and also put yourself in a position to improve the blog for everyone by identifying and helping to correct any errors.

Part 3
Critical thinking and creativity

3A Critical thinking

Using Facebook to apply social learning theory

Michelle Kilburn

Abstract: Facebook, Twitter, MySpace, and many more social networking sites are becoming mainstream in the lives of numerous individuals in the United States and around the globe. Yet a notable trend is that young adults post socially unacceptable behavior, including some information used against them in a court of law. Peluchettte and Karl (2007) suggest that young people make a conscious effort to portray a particular image, sometimes posting updates describing socially unacceptable information to impress their peers. This activity utilizes a foundational framework of social learning for each student to consider the motivations behind, and purpose of, activities in the online social networking medium of Facebook.

Key words: differential association, Facebook, observational learning, reinforcement, social learning, social networking sites.

Discipline/Academic areas addressed

- Criminal justice, criminology, sociology.
- Also applicable for general education, to raise awareness of the impact of posting socially inappropriate materials on social networking sites.

Instructional purpose

In the context of social learning theory, individuals may choose to post socially unacceptable behavior in an attempt to imitate the behavior of targeted groups on Facebook. For example, negative messages about certain moral behaviors increased male profile owner's perceived physical attractiveness. Walther et al. (2008) speculate "that if greater attractiveness is perceived for males who misbehave, confirmatory and rewarding reactions by others might reinforce such behaviors or set observational learning dynamics into play encouraging others to behave in a similar manner" (p. 45).

This activity provides an active learning exercise that frames social learning in an arena in which students can relate to and tend to be very familiar. The activity allows students to not only understand, but also apply, the knowledge they have gained relating to social learning. The project also serves a public service/awareness message of the impact of friends and other social associations as they relate to social networking sites.

Student learning outcomes

After the completion of this activity students should

1. Be able to recognize the major premises of social learning theory by recognizing and providing examples of social learning exhibited in the student and/or friends' Facebook status and/or pages.
2. Observe and analyze social networking sites for socially inappropriate posts.
3. Reflect on the role of social networking sites in their own social networks through writing.

Prerequisite skills and knowledge

1. Access to Facebook. It is the rare student who does not have a Facebook account, but should it be necessary, the instructor can direct students to sign up at

   www.facebook.com/r.php

2. Basic understanding of social networking: How to post to walls, access friends' pages, read status updates (a great resource for individuals new to Facebook can be found at *http://howtousefacebook.com/*).
3. Access to the Internet.

4. Basic computer knowledge: basic keyboarding skills, knowledge of how to access websites, and read/post comments.

Step-by-step directions

1. Research and review information regarding social learning (see Appendix A in "Supplemental materials" for an overview of social learning theory). Considering Facebook is one of the most widely used social networking sites in the world (Hepburn, 2011), social interactions/communications naturally take place in this environment. Think about how social learning might influence some individuals to post inappropriate material on Facebook.

2. For two weeks, observe posts made by Facebook friends (or Twitter, Myspace, etc.). Keep notes of any socially inappropriate posts and also note if friends appear to be supporting or discouraging the behavior by posting comments in reference to the socially inappropriate post (see Appendix B in "Supplemental materials" for guidelines and instructions). For example, an underage friend might post that he/she went out drinking Friday night. Another friend may "like" that post. Similarly, also make notes of any positive comments and note if friends appear to be supporting or making fun of the positive post. For example, if a friend posts that he/she made an "A" on an exam and one friend "liked" the post while another friend commented, "Nerd". Note: All references to "friends" and their activities should be anonymous. Any identifiers or actions that would directly indicate the person's real identity should be omitted. By tracking these types of activities and applying what you have learned from your research, you will be able to recognize the role social learning can play in one's decision to either participate or refrain from socially inappropriate activities.

3. After making detailed observations, write your personal reflection piece (500–1000 words). Describe how this activity has impacted your perception of what motivates individuals to post socially unacceptable material on social networking sites. Also, discuss if this activity has influenced your current and/or future Facebook status updates, wall posts, comments, and/or notes (see Appendix C in "Supplemental materials" for assignment details and rubric).

Approximate time required

- 2–3 weeks to observe friends' status, wall post comments, and notes
- 1–2 hours to make observation notes
- 2–3 hours to compile and write a reflection piece.

Required resources

- Computer/smartphone and access to the Internet
- Required participation in website:

http://www.facebook.com

Variations on the basic theme

This activity could also utilize other social media such as the social bookmarking site MySpace (*myspace.com*), the microblogging site Twitter or any other social networking sites. This exercise could be modified to apply to a variety of disciplines including, but not limited to, criminal justice, criminology, sociology, psychology, communication, political science, marketing, and education, with students utilizing discipline-specific perspectives (as provided by the instructor) to monitor friends' posts.

Observations and advice

I have used this exercise in a number of courses the past two semesters and have received very positive feedback. Most students report that they did not realize the impact their Facebook posts and/or comments can have on other members of the networking site. The activity also provides the opportunity to discuss how employers review social networking sites when making employment decisions.

It is important to make sure the students realize that all of their "findings" should be anonymous. All "Friends" should be given aliases and any reference that might identify someone should be omitted.

After completing the activity, many students report an increased awareness of the impact of social networking on the day-to-day activities of friends/acquaintances. Other students have acknowledged posting inappropriate material to appear "cool" or more readily accepted by their peers.

Recommended reading

Akers, R. (1973) *Deviant Behavior: A Social Learning Approach*. Belmont, CA: Wadsworth.

Akers, R., and Jensen, G. (2007) *Social Learning Theory and Explanation of Crime*. New Brunswick, NJ: Transaction Publishers.

Barker, V. (2009) Older adolescents' motivations for social network site use: The influence of gender, group identity and collective self-esteem. *CyperPsychology & Behavior*, **12**(2), 209–13.

Bandura, A. (1969) *Principles of Behavior Modification*. New York: Holt, Rinehart & Winston.

Bandura, A. (1976) *Social Learning Theory*. Upper Saddle River, NJ: Prentice Hall.

Bandura, A. (2003) Observational learning. In: J. H. Byrne (Ed.), *Encyclopedia of Learning and Memory* (Second Edition, pp. 482–4). New York: Macmillan.

Citron, D. K., and Norton, H. (2011) Intermediaries and hate speech: Fostering digital citizenship for our information age. *Boston University Law Review*, **91**(1435), 1435–84.

Cole, E.R. (2006) Guess who else is reading those "Facebook" entries? Available from *http://www.black-collegian.com/news/bcwire/archives/facebook_employers_0306.htm*

Hepburn, A. (2011) *Facebook, Stats & Facts for 2011*. Available from *http://www.digitalbuzzblog.com*

Hirschi, T. (2002) *Causes of Delinquency*. New Brunswick, NJ: Transaction Publishers.

Jones, Q. (1997) Virtual communities, virtual settlements and cyber-archaeology: A theoretical outline. *Journal of Computer Mediated Communication*, **3**(3), 24.

Katz, J. (1998) The social side of information networking. *Society*, **35**(2), 403–5.

Marsico, E. M. (2010) Social networking websites: Are MySpace and Facebook the fingerprints of the 21st century? *Widener Law Journal*, **19**(3), 967–76.

Mikami, A. Y., Szwedo, D. E., Allen, J. P., Evans, M. A., and Hare, A.L. (2010) Adolescent peer relationships and behavior problems predict your adults' communication on social networking websites. *Developmental Psychology*, **46**, 46–56.

Peluchette, J. V., and Karl, K. (2007) The impact of workplace attire of employee self-perceptions. *Human Resource Development Quarterly*, **18**(3), 345–60.

Schmalleger, F. (2009) *Criminology Today: An Integrative Introduction* (Fifth Edition). Upper Saddle River, NJ: Pearson Education.

Stone, B., and Brown, R. (2006). Web of risks: Students adore social-networking sites like Facebook, but indiscreet postings can mean really big trouble. *Newsweek*, **148**(8/9), 76–7.

Sutherland, E. (1947) *Principles of Criminology* (Fourth Edition). Philadelphia, PA: J.B. Lippincott.

Walther, J., Van Der Heide, B., Kim, S., Westerman, D., and Tong, S. (2008) The role of friends' appearance and behavior on evaluations of individuals on Facebook: Are we known by the company we keep? *Human Communication Research*, **31**(1), 28–49.

Young, K. (2011). Social ties, social networks and the Facebook experience. *International Journal of Emerging Technologies and Society*, **9**(1), 20–34.

Supplemental materials

Appendix A Social learning theory

Albert Bandura (1969), a well-known psychiatrist, is considered the father of social learning theory. Bandura (1976) states: "Learning would be exceedingly laborious, not to mention hazardous, if people had to rely solely on the effects of their own actions to inform them what to do. Fortunately, most human behavior is learned observationally through modeling: from observing others one forms an idea of how new behaviors are performed, and on later occasions this coded information serves as a guide for action" (p. 22).

Ronald Akers (1973) relates *social learning theory* to criminality and suggests that individuals learn to engage in inappropriate activities through their association with others. Akers purports that there are three primary mechanisms that teach individuals to engage in inappropriate activities: *differential reinforcement*, *beliefs*, and *modeling*. Many times, the reinforcement comes from not getting caught or reported. In the context of social networking, the activity can also be reinforced/supported by other Facebook friends who comment positively or ignore inappropriate activity.

The concept of *differential reinforcement* purports that inappropriate behavior is more likely to be repeated when it is frequently reinforced and infrequently punished. Akers and Jensen (2007) suggest that both peer groups and families reinforce crime as an option if the behavior is tolerated, ignored, or rewarded.

Having a *belief system* is seen to be a very important component of social learning theory. Individuals who associate with individuals who are more tolerant of crime and inappropriate behavior learn to adopt the same belief system.

Finally, Akers (1973) suggests that individuals will imitate or *model* the behavior of others especially if they like or respect the person engaged in the activities. For example, negative messages about certain moral behaviors increased male profile owners' perceived physical attractiveness. "We might speculate that if greater attractiveness is perceived for males who misbehave, confirmatory and rewarding reactions by others might reinforce such behaviors or set observational learning dynamics into play encouraging others to behave in a similar manner" (Walther et al., 2008, p. 45).

Another important and complimentary theory relating to social learning is Sutherland's (1947) theory of differential association. Sutherland agrees that criminal acts are learned behaviors. His strongest assertion was that if an individual is exposed to more social acceptance of deviance (or inappropriate behavior), as opposed to being exposed to opposition of deviance, the individual is more apt to function defiantly.

Social networking sites make it very convenient for individuals to self-select their social groups or to weaken associations with groups who they may feel are too strict. Some of the social learning that is traditionally received from community, parents, civic, and religious groups may play a more muted role with individuals who rely heavily on social networking to form associations (Katz, 1998).

Appendix B Assignment guidelines and instruction

*Facebook observation guidelines and instruction.** For two weeks observe posts made by Facebook friends (or Twitter, MySpace, etc.). Keep detailed field notes of any socially inappropriate posts and also note if friends appear to be supporting or discouraging the behavior by posting comments in reference to the socially inappropriate post. It is also important to note if no one comments at all (ignores the post).

Social learning theory in context. When looking for examples of social learning, observe your friends' status updates, wall posts, and comments. Try to recognize examples of "inappropriate behavior" of either your friends and/or comments made in response to your friends' statements. The term inappropriate is somewhat subjective and is partially based on your own moral and social biases (as the researcher). For example, someone might post that they "sampled" the grapes at the local grocery

* Any identifiers or actions that would directly indicate the person's real identity should be omitted in your observation.

and they were overripe so they did not buy any this week. One researcher might consider this stealing, while another researcher might not see anything inappropriate at all about the activity. As you make your observations, discuss how a particular comment, post, etc., is inappropriate in your opinion and within your social context.

It is important to note, however, that there are many instances where the general population can agree on the definition of inappropriate. For example, in general, most would agree it is inappropriate

- for an 18-year-old to have a sexual relationship with a 15-year-old;
- to engage in racial slurs and/or cyber-bullying;
- for someone under 21 to discuss their binge drinking activities over the weekends;
- to post nude or semi-nude photos;
- to use profanity in an open, public forum, such as Facebook.

When you consider whether a comment or post is inappropriate think about whether society as a whole considers the activity socially acceptable or not. Any criminal activity is undoubtedly inappropriate. Other activities may not appear as black or white. Just as social learning theory purports, you have learned what is socially acceptable by your own personal associations. Your definition and my definition may not always be the same. As you complete the assignment, make sure you discuss why a particular comment is inappropriate.

The assignment requires that during your observation period you find three examples of social learning as a positive influence and three examples of social learning as a negative influence. When you discover a negative example (i.e., your friend updates their status and comments about drinking and you know they are underage), observe how many "likes" the person has on their status update. Did anyone voice their approval of the activity? Did anyone post that they did the same thing? This would be an example of social learning as a negative influence. By liking or approving the activity, your friend's activity is being reinforced. They may also be imitating the actions of the person that posted they did the same thing.

Using this same example, if someone posted disapproval of underage drinking, it would be an example of social learning as a positive influence. Your friend would be learning that their behavior is socially unacceptable and his/her inappropriate activity was not being ignored. As you make your observations, tie them back to major tenets of social learning.

Appendix C Reflection piece instructions and assignment rubric

Reflection piece instructions

After conducting your observations for 2 weeks, compile and review your field notes. Choose one of the best examples of social learning as a positive influence and one of the best examples of social learning as a negative influence. For each example, provide the following:

- Brief discussion of each observation.
- Whether your observed post is socially appropriate or inappropriate and why.
- How your observation is an example of social learning and if either your friend's post, or comments made to your friend's post, are examples of social learning as a positive or negative influence and why.

After discussing your observations in detail, reflect upon the impact of social learning in the online environment. Describe how this activity has impacted your perception (if any) of what motivates individuals to post socially unacceptable material on social networking sites. Also, discuss if this activity has influenced your current and/or future Facebook status updates, wall posts, comments, and/or notes.

Table 14.1 Assignment rubric

Submitted detailed field notes	**30**
Provided at least three observations of social learning as a positive influence	10
Provided at least three observations of social learning as a negative influence	10
Discussed why each observation was considered appropriate or inappropriate in their notes and why	10
Effectively discussed two of the best observations of social learning	**30**
Chose and described the best example of social learning as a positive influence	5
Chose and described the best example of social learning as a negative influence	5
Discussed how each example was socially appropriate or inappropriate and why	10
Discussed how each observation was an example of social learning as either a positive or negative influence	10
Effectively discussed the role social learning can play in one's decision to either participate or refrain from socially inappropriate activities	**10**
Effectively discussed how the activity has influenced personal status updates, wall posts, comments, etc. and why	**10**
Grammar	**5**
Spelling	**5**
Clarity	**5**
Overall organization and flow	**5**
Total points	***100***

15

Technology as a tool to develop problem-solving skills in general chemistry

Madhu Mahalingam and Elisabeth Morlino

Abstract: Students must have good problem-solving skills to do well in general chemistry, as in many other disciplines. We have identified three levels for our general chemistry problems based on the revised taxonomy for learning by Anderson and Krathwohl (2001). Level 1 problems require "Remembering" and involve a single concept or formula, Level 2 problems involve application of a concept or formula and require "Understanding", and Level 3 problems involve multiple concepts and/or formulas. Our strategy is to build on these levels using existing technology such as personal response systems (clickers), online homework systems, and learning management systems to develop students' problem-solving skills up to Level 2 prior to group work in recitations. In recitations, groups of four multiskilled students work on more challenging Level 3 problems. This scaffolding of electronic and traditional (face-to-face) learning reinforces deeper learning. Research conducted in our class supports the effectiveness of the scaffolding technique.

Key words: clickers, online homework, learning management system (LMS), personal response systems, problem solving.

Discipline/Academic areas addressed

General chemistry – an introductory course that is a prerequisite for all science majors. Also adaptable to any discipline in which knowledge and understanding of content is fundamental to the discipline.

Instructional purpose

Problem solving is an important part of many disciplines including chemistry. In order to do well in general chemistry students must have good problem-solving skills. General chemistry problems are classified as well-structured problems according to Jonassen (1997). Developing problem-solving ability in general chemistry requires both a sound knowledge base which includes knowledge of the various concepts involved within the field and structural knowledge which is the ability to interconnect these concepts. Since contemporary students have grown up in a digital environment, scaffolding electronic and traditional (face-to-face) learning is an excellent way to reinforce deeper learning. Scaffolding provides instructional support through social interactions with the teacher and others, facilitating the student's progression from their current understanding to a higher level (Vygotsky, 1978). The technology currently available (such as online homework systems, online quizzes, and personal response systems) in the classroom can be used to help students build their understanding and knowledge base in a scaffolded progression. Students then have an opportunity to practice the acquired skills outside of classroom in a small-group discussion format, solving more challenging problems that require collaboration. The goal of this approach is to improve students' problem-solving skills in general chemistry by scaffolding learning. The level of problem solving is raised gradually, prior to recitation, using technology, such as online homework systems, online quizzes, and personal response systems in the classroom culminating in higher level problem solving in the face-to-face recitation.

Prior to lecture students are provided a reading assignment. In lecture, personal response systems or clickers are used to actively involve the students and further develop their understanding from the readings and the concepts presented. Clickers are particularly suited to developing the knowledge base as students can compare their responses to the class responses and evaluate their knowledge in comparison to the rest of the class. When the distribution of answers displayed indicates that a majority of the students did not grasp the concept, the students are given an opportunity to discuss the question in small groups and the question is repolled. Often this results in a shift in responses towards the correct answer. This is the first step in developing the knowledge base.

After the lecture, students are assigned homework problems. Typically tutorials within the online homework system that lead students through the logic involved are used, before assigning exercises that do not provide "leading" help. This helps to build confidence in problem solving and clarify any misconceptions that may be present. These exercises are often followed by online quizzes that provide students with a self-assessment of their progress. Students then come to the recitation classes to work on the more challenging Level 3 problems. Scaffolding of clicker questions, online homework, and online quizzes works together as formative assessments that help build the necessary domain and structural knowledge for problem solving. If a discussion board on an LMS can be moderated, it can serve as a useful tool to further enable students to build the necessary knowledge and skills through peer-to-peer interactions.

A Student Assessment of Learning Gains (SALG) survey conducted at the end of each semester suggests that a majority of the students (75–81%) perceive an improvement in their problem-solving abilities. Supporting this student perception, the average percent correct on exams increased from 73.5% in 2004 to 75.2% in 2010 while the average problem level on exams increased from 1.25 to 1.31.

Student learning outcomes

1. Be able to recall or remember previously acquired knowledge such as terminology, formulas, methods, and conventions in general chemistry.
2. Be able to interconnect ideas (i.e., understand the meaning behind the knowledge), to generate solutions to problems at various levels (Level 1 through Level 3)
3. Be able to articulate the understanding to a group of peers.

Prerequisite skills and knowledge

Basic skills needed to work on the Internet such as knowledge of the Web-browsing environment, entering information as required in each environment (LMS, online homework, and clickers). Such skills are possessed by most students, but students who do not have these basic skills will need to work with instructors, or with the university Computing Center, prior to the activity. In the classes in which these activities have already been utilized, students are directed to a tutorial in the LMS system which helps students learn how to input numbers and answer possible types of questions within the system. Most universities will have such tutorials available – for example,

www.blackboard.com/quicktutorials/

The clickers are pretty self-explanatory to students and they do not often have any issues with the hardware.

Step-by-step directions

1. Provide reading assignments to students for the material to be covered in class. The reading assignment provided is specific to the sections being covered in class. This is provided through a weekly syllabus posted on the LMS where each reading assignment is tied to specific sections of the chapter and corresponding homework problems. Students can attempt the homework problems either prior to lecture or after lecture.

2. Scaffolding is developed further in the lecture classes. If possible, start the face-to-face lecture with a couple of clicker questions. This focuses students on the material at hand. The questions must evaluate students' knowledge and understanding from the reading. Based on the class responses to the questions, the lecture can be tailored to suit the students' needs. Further, if the distribution of responses is not satisfactory, the question can be repolled following a brief small group discussion among students. Having students talk through their responses in this type of social interaction improves their understanding of the material and models active problem solving. Clicker questions can also be used in the middle of lecture to evaluate understanding of the concept presented at that time, and at the end of lecture to summarize or bring out an overarching theme or idea for the students.

3. To promote the scaffolding process, homework must be assigned on a weekly basis covering topics presented in lecture for that week. Homework for the week can be set up specific to each lecture (no more than 5 problems per lecture) and the due date set such that students are prepared for the next lecture. These can also be weekly assignments with 10–15 problems per week. Homework could be made available online prior to the presentation of the material so students can start developing the necessary problem-solving skills.

This may even help them grasp the concepts better in lecture. At the very least, students should be able to attempt homework problems soon after material is discussed in the lecture.

Homework questions assigned should help students develop domain and structural knowledge as well as understand discipline-specific methodologies used for problem solving (develop problem-solving schema). If the online homework system adopted has tutorials, these should be assigned as they help develop the problem-solving schema by leading students through the problem using hints. In any case the due date must be set prior to the higher level problem-solving sessions in recitation.

4. Additional online quizzes can be provided on a weekly basis as formative assessments that provide students the ability to evaluate their own progress and understanding of the material. Online quizzes could also be end-of-chapter quizzes that bring all the concepts discussed in the chapter into focus.

5. The final and most important piece of the scaffolding is the group work in face-to-face recitation. Details follow. (Note that the rationale and implementation of group problem solving as well as the details of the nature of the problems used for the recitation have been described in detail by Mahalingam et al., 2008).

   - Each semester, students are organized in groups of four students with mixed skill ability using SAT math scores or grades from the previous semester's chemistry course.

   - Each recitation session is started with a brief question-and-answer period mainly to focus the students on the material to be covered in that week's worksheet.

   - Each group is then given a worksheet with problems to be solved and handed in at the end of the session. To ensure maximum participation of all group members during the problem-solving sessions, it is paramount to develop problem sets that promote discussion among group members. Multistep problems, problems that cannot be solved from direct application of formulas, and problems that encourage discussion of ideas (estimations, qualitative answers) are necessary to promote discussion. The problems given often do not specify a particular form for the answer; the questions can be answered quantitatively or qualitatively. The ambiguity will typically start discussion within the group. Multistep problems circumvent an approach in which the group simply divides the work. The problems generally have a higher level of difficulty than standard homework problems.

- While the groups are ultimately responsible for developing solutions to the problems, an instructor and two teaching assistants, who had previously been through the course and are familiar with the process, are present during the recitation sessions to serve as facilitators of the problem-solving process. The instructor and teaching assistants do not provide solutions to the problems but can explain the concepts involved or ask leading questions to guide the students.

  The ability to discuss the acquired knowledge, articulate understanding to peers, and construct a logical path to arrive at a solution to a problem enables students to apply the knowledge and skills acquired during the week to problem solving in recitation. The more challenging Level 3 problems require discussion among the group members that further enhances comprehension and solidifies the skills acquired.

- The problem sets are graded according to what is asked for in each problem: correct or incorrect, work shown, logic. We acknowledge that there are often several different ways to solve a problem and do not penalize for working a problem one way as opposed to another way as long as the group can show a logical progression of work/thought/argument and a correct answer. We have used aggregate student performance on exams (all multiple choice) before and after implementation of the group work to assess the impact of the group work model in recitation.

The idea behind the scaffolding strategy is to gradually increase the level of problem solving by using technology to schedule the activity appropriately until students are ready to attempt problems that require higher order thinking skills. The technology helps provide a structure for the time spent on the material increasing the quality time and reducing the level of frustration as students navigate through the concepts.

Approximate time required

- Clicker questions take approximately 10–15 minutes of class time.
- Both online quizzes and online homework are done outside of class.

- Students meet once a week in small groups for recitation for 12 weeks in a semester.
- Prior to use of online homework the first 10–15 minutes are devoted to questions with the rest of the time used for group problem solving.
- Currently, with the use of online homework, students start working on the problem sets immediately, spending between 45 and 50 minutes.

This works out at 9–10 hours total time per semester.

Required resources

- An Internet-enabled computer.
- There are several online homework systems available. Some are through textbook publishers – for example, MasteringChemistry®:

  http://www.masteringchemistry.com

  and others are solely online homework providers – for example, Webassign®:

  http://www.webassign.net

  Students need an access code for all the online homework systems. The access code can be bundled with the textbook if through a publisher or can be purchased online through the homework system's website.
- Students must purchase personal response devices – for example:

  www.turningtechnologies.com)

  or a mobile device such as a tablet, smartphone, etc. that can use the software needed for the personal response system.
- Computer with a receiver for the personal response system.
- A/V-equipped classroom with projection.
- Relevant websites for teaching and learning aids:

  http://www.salgsite.org

  (for student feedback on methodology) or

  http://web.missouri.edu/jonassend/problems.htm

  (for research on problem solving).

Variations on the basic theme

The strategy is to scaffold electronic and traditional (face-to-face) learning to reinforce deeper learning. Scaffolding can be successfully achieved by various combinations of in-class and out-of-class technology as appropriate, gradually raising the level of problem solving and building the necessary foundation including the knowledge base and interconnections between the concepts involved.

The strategy can be applied in conjunction with any of the available technologies including mobile technologies. It can also be adapted not just for use in the sciences, but for any discipline in which knowledge of basic terms and concepts is necessary.

Observations and advice

Use of technology engages students both inside and outside of the classroom ensuring that the time spent on the activity is quality time. The technology enables "deliberate" practice outside of the class, and engages students. Use of due dates, and deadlines after which an assignment becomes unavailable online, provides structure for students to manage their time and forces students to adopt better study habits rather than just cramming right before a test. All of the assignments that use technology – clicker questions, online homework, and online quizzes – are used as formative assessments rather than summative assessments and provide feedback to students on a regular basis with minimal impact on their overall grade. Students who do not submit their online assignments on time soon realize that they are unable to contribute effectively to the problem solving in recitation. They also see that their group members who did complete assignments on time seem to understand the problems in recitation better and can contribute more effectively. This serves to motivate these students to complete their assignments on time so they are better prepared for recitation. The scaffolding of both online assignments with tutorial help followed by in-class activity (group work in recitation) that tests their skills enables students to build on their skills and gain confidence in problem solving.

Recommended reading

Anderson, L. W., and Krathwohl, D. R. (2001) *A Taxonomy for Learning, Teaching, and Assessing: A Revision of Bloom's Taxonomy of Educational Objectives*. Boston, MA: Allyn & Bacon.

Asirvatham, M. R. (2009) *Clickers in Action: Increasing Student Participation in General Chemistry*. New York, NY: W.W. Norton & Co.

Cole, R. S., and Todd, J. B. (2003) Effects of web-based multimedia homework with immediate rich feedback on student learning in general chemistry. *Journal of Chemical Education*, **80**(11), 1338.

Deslauriers, L., Schelew, E., and Wieman, C. (2011, May 13) Improved learning in a large-enrollment physics class. *Science*, **332**(6031), 862–4.

Duncan, D. (2005) *Clickers in the Classroom: How to Enhance Science Teaching Using Classroom Response Systems*. San Francisco, CA: Pearson.

Leinhardt, G., Cuadros, J., and Yaron, D. (2007) "One firm spot": The role of homework as lever in acquiring conceptual and performance competence in college chemistry. *Journal of Chemical Education*, **84**(6), 1047.

Jonassen D. (1997) Instructional design models for well-structured and ill-structured problem-solving learning outcomes. *Educational Technology Research and Development (ETR&D)*, **45**(1), 65–94.

Mahalingam, M., Schaefer, F., and Morlino, E. (2008) Promoting student learning through group problem solving in general chemistry recitations. *Journal of Chemical Education*, **85**, 1577.

Morgan, J., and Williams, B. (2007) *Overview of Problem Solving: Faculty Guidebook* (Fourth Edition, pp. 181–4). Lisle, IL: Pacific Crest Publications.

Nygren, K. (2007) *Elevating Knowledge from Level 1 to Level 3: Faculty Guidebook* (Fourth Edition, pp. 165–8). Lisle, IL: Pacific Crest Publications.

Vygotsky, L. S. (1978) Mind in society. In: M. Cole, V. John-Steiner, S. Scribner, and E. Souberman (Eds.), *The Development of Higher Psychological Processes*. Cambridge, MA: Harvard University Press.

Communicating experiential learning through an online portfolio in Tumblr

Aaron J. Moore

Abstract: This semester-long project uses an online or e-portfolio for students performing experiential work (internships, co-ops, fieldwork). Students use Tumblr as their online portfolio and connect their academic course work to what they are currently learning in a professional or field environment. The project calls for students to regularly update their portfolios with information and insight about the tasks assigned to them by their workplace supervisors. Along with posting relevant pictures and videos, students also write concise narratives and articulate how fieldwork is associated with the ideas and theories learned in other courses. Using Tumblr as an online portfolio allows instructors to regularly provide feedback and guidance to students during the semester. The feedback from the instructor and from other students forms communal discourse. This is useful in a class where students are geographically separated while engaged in field experience and don't physically encounter their peers on a regular basis.

Key words: blogging, e-portfolios, experiential learning, integrative learning, internships, Tumblr.

Discipline/Academic areas addressed

Applicable across all academic disciplines, including education, that incorporate experiential learning through internships, co-ops, and fieldwork. In the social sciences and humanities, the online portfolio works particularly well for English, communication, journalism, art, history, and psychology.

Instructional purpose

This project serves as a method to initiate and document integrative learning that occurs during an experiential course. Integrated or connected learning has both academic and professional relevancies. Criticism is levied by both academics and professionals regarding the mind-set of the millennial college student. Academicians have been critical when they contend students do not properly connect or synthesize material from one course to another, especially across disciplines (Arum and Roksa, 2011; Graf, 2009). Many employers have voiced similar displeasure regarding how poorly millennials connect different sources of materials in one final project, saying that younger employees have trouble "seeing the big picture".

An online or e-portfolio for experiential work provides a platform for students to form connections between various subject areas and disciplines based on what they encounter in the field. Experiential courses serve as excellent opportunities for students to engage in and elaborate on integrative learning. Updating the online portfolio throughout the semester requires students to pull together their entire experiences inside and outside of the classroom and create a narrative that exhibits their intellectual and professional development. The final product becomes an effective tool that can be utilized for overall student assessment conducted by either an academic department or college wide.

As more schools encourage their students to take internships and co-ops, it is essential for instructors to make sure these experiences satisfy academic requirements and goals. Assignments must be cultivated that ensure both rewarding academic and professional experiences. An online portfolio as a semester-long project requires students to consistently make connections between class work and professional work in an effort to help them see the "big picture". Also, an online portfolio allows instructors to regularly monitor student performance and provide expeditious feedback. It remedies a common situation in fieldwork courses where students hand in all of their academic work at the end of the semester, and there is little interaction between the student and the instructor over the course of the semester. The online portfolio facilitates a learning environment where students do consistent academic work alongside their professional responsibilities over the course of the semester.

This assignment also allows instructors to model proper social media communication. Using the concept of backwards design, the instructor creates his or her own online portfolio (a Tumblr page that students can model). This teaches students best practices for social media and lays the scaffolding for a positive professional image. Before academicians can demand their students use social media in a beneficial manner, they need to review proper examples (Cunnane, 2010).

Student learning outcomes

1. Students will use text and images to explain their work/duties at the field site.
2. Students will effectively communicate via social media by using clear and concise prose, properly citing any sources, and adhering to the rules of fair use of any copyrighted material.
3. Students will demonstrate integrated learning by composing a narrative with text and images that synthesizes connections among experiences outside of the traditional classroom with their scholarly work.
4. Students will demonstrate their self-reflection by making a progression of posts throughout the semester that build upon past experiences that have occurred across multiple and diverse contexts.

Prerequisite skills and knowledge

Digital natives are versed in communicating with peers via social media but for this project their main focus should be writing in concise paragraphs that serve as individual thoughts and ideas. Each post should have a consistent look and appearance.

For those students unfamiliar with blogging or writing for social media, instructors should direct them to the numerous online sites that provide such tips. Tumblr and Zemanta provide step-by-step instructions and a video tutorial on how to upload images and videos with proper attribution. Students should be at least second-semester sophomores in good standing (in order to have enough classroom experience to make connections).

Step-by-step directions

1. Get approval from the internship supervisor to create an online portfolio documenting your fieldwork. If this conflicts with the organization's confidentiality requirements, contact the instructor to make alternative plans. Do not create a Tumblr page without consent from a supervisor. Also, get approval from coworkers before posting their names/images. In order to privatize a Tumblr portfolio for only the professor to view, the student must make a secondary blog by clicking on the plus (+) button located in the right corner of the Tumblr home page and select "password protect the blog".
2. Go to the discussion board on Blackboard (WebCT, etc.) and list the location of your internship (fieldwork), duties, and URL to your Tumblr page.
3. Follow each classmate on Tumblr.
4. Design your Tumblr page so it clearly identifies you by name, the place where, and the industry in which, you are working. Download the free plug-in Zemanta

   http://www.zemanta.com

   This provides attribution for borrowed Web-based content.
5. Post your biography and resume.
6. Go to Tumblr

   http://cmaintern.tumblr.com/
   http://leonyolanda.tumblr.com/
   http://internscott.tumblr.com/

   to see the proper way to create and work with a Tumblr e-portfolio for the class. The following video gives an overall Tumblr tutorial:

   http://www.youtube.com/watch?v=vTRGPKU8SlQ
7. Two to three times per week you will make Tumblr posts that recap and explain the assignments you did during the week. You will upload visual (stills or videos) examples of your work (projects, assignments, reports) done in the field along with a written recap of the fieldwork. Explain with a brief narrative of what the experiential assignment is and *how* it relates to your academic work. Examples of your fieldwork can be press releases, promos, designs, videos, professional emails,

advertising copy, field reports, pictures, etc. Also, you can upload previous examples of your academic work conducted in class and write a narrative on how it relates to work done in the field. Find a way to explain how the work you did in the field connects to previous academic work.

8. When documenting your experiences (both positive and negative), don't use common informal social media abbreviations – keep in mind you are writing this for a professional audience. Communicate as a professional in terms of tone, content, and style. Social media writing is based on concise sentences (12 to 15 words per sentence). Use professional terminology associated with your industry when explaining your experiences. Avoid long blocklike paragraphs with a number of sentences tacked together. Rather, have each separate idea broken up into a unique paragraph.

9. Each post should include either a picture or video. Part of this assignment is to communicate your experiences visually. If there is no picture/video of your fieldwork, find a picture online that represents your experience for the week, and post it with correct citation. Each post should have a similar word count in order to create a visual consistency.

10. Submit 15 to 20 posts per semester (updated consistently – not just periodically). Also, embed links to source material.

11. For the final post(s), give an extended reflection on the entire experience and what you learned in the "big picture" sense. Reflect and articulate how this experience will shape your career goals.

    a. In order to write an effective self-reflection, students should look to answer questions such as: What did I learn; what am I most proud of; what will I do with the knowledge gained during the experiential class? These answers should be formulated by separating yourself from the work – (don't rely on "I" opinions or use clichés such as "I learned a lot . . .").

    b. Write your self-reflection as if you are talking about someone you observed, not about yourself (this helps eliminates excessive use of the first person. Readers who don't know you or where you did the experiential work, should be able to ascertain your placement and duties by reading your self-reflection. Use specific examples to document and highlight your learning experiences – don't assume the reader knows details about you or the industry.

c. To enhance your self-reflection, use an expert voice to develop and answer other such questions as: what communication/technical skills are needed for those in this industry; what are the ethical responsibilities of those in the industry; what recommendations would you make for those looking to enter this industry; what are the pros and cons of working in this industry; how would you rectify a mistake you made during the internship? This should be the longest post(s) of the semester in terms of word count.

Approximate time required

- Project runs over the course of the semester.
- At least two Tumblr posts every 10 days.
- At least eight to ten comments posted on other students' Tumblr portfolios.

Required resources

Students should familiarize themselves with Tumblr and its applications before making their online or e-portfolio. The site is similar but different in a number of ways compared to Facebook and Twitter. Several tutorials have been included in "Step-by-step directions". Here are some more:

http://howtousetumblr.com/
http://mashable.com/2011/11/14/tumblr-infographic/
http://mashable.com/2011/08/17/tumblr-marketing-guide/

Necessary technology includes:

- Internet access
- www.Tumblr.com
- Blackboard, WebCT, or other platform that connects students through a discussion board.

Variations on the basic theme

Tumblr is the best social media platform for this project because it provides for an effective combination of pictures and videos with the narratives. The layout of the site and the ability to put extended amounts of text alongside visuals is consistent with the appearance of an online portfolio. Tumblr enables students to create a developmental portfolio that could in the future be converted into a professional portfolio. During their experiential course, students can conveniently upload material to their Tumblr page making the project an ongoing formative, rather than a summative, activity.

Instead of the informal appearance of Facebook, Tumblr allows for modifications that help students create unique blogs that can also be used for professional branding purposes. Students can articulate their ideas with more support and analysis on Tumblr than they can on Twitter. Other sites such as WordPress and Blogger could be used for this assignment.

The Tumblr portfolio can also be used with Facebook or Twitter as those sites could be used to send out a message to the instructor and fellow students that the portfolio has been updated.

For disciplines or organizations where privacy is a requisite factor, pictures and video should be eliminated. This online portfolio can be used for any discipline since it allows students to conduct a narrative using both text and visuals to convey their meanings and ideas.

Observations and advice

This semester-long project assists in enhancing the academic experiences of internships and fieldwork placements. Prior to using the online or e-portfolio, I rarely encountered students actively making connections of ideas between their different courses. This lack of dialogue and synthesis was especially true between different disciplines. Students now exhibit greater self-assessment when they write how field experiences remind them of what they learned in other classes. Having students communicate about their experiences through the online portfolio fosters integrative learning and a sense of interdisciplinary connection. In order to nurture this thinking, the instructor needs to explicitly detail the assignment's expectations that students must critically analyze their experiences, not just log them.

The online or e-portfolio provides a valuable tool for students to communicate with their peers about their internship or fieldwork locations. Prior to using Tumblr, most of my students were unaware of the places their peers were doing similar work. Students now share information and insight about what businesses in the area provide the best (and worst) internships or field experiences. This shared information has helped increase the academic and professional rewards students are able to receive from their internships and field experiences.

An effective portfolio will be one that is updated regularly throughout the semester, uses proper grammar and a professional voice, but still follows best social media practices of direct and concise sentences and paragraphs. Also, each post will provide a deeper understanding of the student's learning by connecting it to learning in other courses or disciplines. The posts will also feature appropriate images or videos of the work. If students are unable to provide a picture of their work, they will use images (properly attributed) from the Web that best represents their experience. Finally the last few posts will be reflections or self-assessments of their experiences in the field, and students should articulate how this experience has shaped their future career goals. The reflective posts should be an overview of what the student learned about the industry and the expectations of those working in it.

From a social media standpoint, students will communicate more professionally than they were previously accustomed to when just used for informal matters. The instructor models the proper way of communicating (both text and visual) with his/her Tumblr page so students can see appropriate professional social media behavior. Students then do likewise, with the result that they have online portfolios that display their work and brand them as young professionals with field experience. The online portfolio is a way to transition students from just using social media for informal communication to professional outreach and development.

Recommended reading

Arum, R., and Roksa, J. (2011) *Academically Adrift: Limited Learning on College Campuses*. University of Chicago Press.

Benander, R. (2009, June) Experiential learning in the scholarship of teaching and learning. *Journal of the Scholarship of Learning and Teaching*, **9**(2), 36–41.

Challis, D. (2005, Autumn) Towards the mature ePortfolio: Some implications for higher education. *Canadian Journal of Learning and Technology*, **31**(3).

Cunnane, S. (2010, October) Don't be afraid to share. *Times Higher Education*. Available from *http://www.timeshighereducation.co.uk/story.asp?storycode=413795*

Ferriter, W. (2011, April) Digitally speaking. *Educational Leadership*, **68**(7), 92–3.

Gikandi, J. W., Morrow, D., and Davis, N. E. (2011, December) Online formative assessment in higher education: A review of the literature. *Computers and Education*, **57**(4), 2333–51.

Graff, G. (2009, January 13) It's time to end "Courseocentrism". *Inside Higher Ed*. Available from *http://www.insidehighered.com/views/2009/01/13/graff*

Kim, P., Ng., C. K., and Lim, G. (2010, November) When cloud computing meets with semantic web: A new design for e-portfolio systems in the social media era. *British Journal of Educational Technology*, **41**(6), 1018–28.

Mason, R., Pegler, C., and Weller, M. (2004, October) E-portfolios: An assessment tool for online courses. *British Journal of Educational Technology*, **35**(6), 717–27.

Matteson, A. (2011, February) Do you Tumble? Tumblr could change the way you blog. *School Library Monthly*, **27**(5), 54–6.

Minott, M. (2010, Spring) Portfolio development, reflection, personal instructional theory and the scholarship of teaching and learning. *College Quarterly*, **13**(2), 6–13.

Moores, A., and Parks, M. (2010, January) Twelve tips for introducing e-portfolios to undergraduates. *Medical Teacher*, **32**(1), 46–9.

O'Neil, L. (2011, May 21) A guide to happy and legal Tumbling. *Wall Street Journal*, **257**(118), D9.

Torras, M. E., and Mayordomo, R. (2011, November) Teaching presence and electronic regulation in online portfolios. *Computers in Human Behaviors*, **27**(6), 2284–91.

Yi-Li, L., and Chen, G. D. (2009, April) A coursework support system for offering challenges and assistance by analyzing students' web portfolios. *Journal of Education Technology & Society*, **12**(2), 205–21.

Young, J. (2002, February 21) Creating online portfolios can help students see "big picture," colleges say. *Chronicle of Higher Education*. Available from *http://chronicle.com/free/2002/02/2002022101t.htm*

Supplemental materials

Feedback and grade for internship e-portfolio

Since I do not want to post critical or evaluative comments on the portfolio which would then be available for public display, this rubric is presented to the students at the end of the semester. The criteria are based on the assignment and expectations presented to students at the beginning of the semester.

If there are issues with the quality of a student's portfolio during the beginning of the semester, I email him/her and have them come to the office for consultation rather than post them on Tumblr. Grading is based on a 1–5 point system with 5 being superior work that surpasses all expectations and 1 being inadequate work.

Table 16.1 E-portfolio grading

Criteria	Points (1–5)	Comments (if any)
Consistent/timely posts throughout the semester (total between 15 and 20)		
Proper attribution for outside Web content used in portfolio		
Professional presentation of material (spelling, formatting, tone, language, visual consistency)		
Appropriate use of visual material as support for written text		
Bio and resume		
Synthesis of experiential work with previous academic experience. Posts contain repeated connection with the fieldwork activities to ideas, theories and principles discussed in other classes		
Final post(s) are self-reflective and focus on what the student learned about him/herself during the experiential class. Posts demonstrate a growing awareness of the industry and the expectation of those within it. Effectively provides a self-reflection without excessive use of "I"		
Expert voice – over the semester, the student discussed topics such as ethical responsibilities, made recommendations about succeeding within the industry, and the pros and cons of working within the industry		
Made between 8 and 10 substantial comments on other students' Tumblr pages. Demonstrated a sense of communal learning		

17

The Biology Taboo Wiktionary: a tool for improving student comprehension of key terminology in introductory biology courses

Jeffrey T. Olimpo and Patricia A. Shields

Abstract: Knowledge of terminology and understanding of processes and concepts is a key foundational requirement in many disciplines. Learning a new disciplinary "language" is often a challenge for novice students, yet a strong foundation is essential for success in the major. This activity utilizes an in-class version of the commercial game Taboo©, in which students must define disciplinary terms in their own words, and without obvious terms. The in-class game is followed by a collaborative wiki, which provides students with an interactive opportunity to review and describe new terminology, and concepts. The goal of these activities is not only to develop a deeper appreciation for, and understanding of, the connections present between various biological processes, but to achieve a foundational understanding of the discipline. The wiki also serves as a resource to prepare for the final exam or to complete laboratory reports.

Key words: active learning, biology, collaborative learning, interactive learning, wiki, Wiktionary.

Discipline/Academic areas addressed

Biology, but applicable to any discipline where understanding of terminology concepts and processes is an important foundation to success.

Instructional purpose

Introductory courses, including those in the sciences, are rife with terminology. This demand presents a challenge for novice students, many of whom will go on to major in the sciences and whose success in the discipline is predicated on their understanding of such terminology, concepts, and processes. To address this concern, we developed and implemented a Biology Taboo Wiktionary activity that provided students with an interactive opportunity to review and describe concepts encountered during their first semester in an introductory biology course. We modified the traditional game of Taboo to include only relevant terminology, such as cellular respiration, glucose, ATP, and restriction enzymes, among others. Much like the traditional Taboo game, students could not use obvious terms to define the main term during gameplay. Following the game, students were asked to work collaboratively to upload a definition for an assigned word to the course Wiktionary page. Post-activity survey results suggest that >75% of the students found the activity engaging and that >80% of students utilized the Wiktionary page frequently to refresh their understanding of key concepts and to prepare for in-class assignments.

Student learning outcomes

After completion of these activities, students will have

1. Gained a richer understanding of key biological terminology, concepts, and processes.
2. Developed a deeper appreciation for, and understanding of, the connections present between various biological processes through active engagement in the Biology Taboo game and construction of the Wiktionary.
3. Achieved a foundational understanding of the discipline above and beyond the knowledge conveyed to them in lecture and in the text.
4. Made use of the Wiktionary in an engaging and resourceful manner, for instance, by using the Wiktionary to prepare for the final exam or to complete laboratory reports, etc.

Prerequisite skills and knowledge

No prerequisite skills or knowledge is necessary, though, from a technological standpoint, previous background in setting up and using

Wikis would certainly be helpful. In "Step-by-step directions" we provide a handout for using the wiki tool in LMS (pertinent to our setup) and Web resources for setting up and using a wiki space on Wikispaces.

Step-by-step directions

Prior to the activity

1. Prepare decks of playing cards. In the commercial game of Taboo (© 1989, Hasbro), one key word is placed at the top of the card, and several (~4) forbidden words are placed below the main term. One individual leads gameplay and the other team members attempt to guess the key word on the card. The individual leading gameplay may not use any of the forbidden words in describing the key term to their peers. If such a word is used, the game leader must discard the current term and move to the next one. One point is awarded for each term that is guessed correctly.
2. For the Biology Wiktionary activity, each deck may contain different sets of words depending on the amount of terminology you wish to include, etc. A diverse array of terms, concepts, and biological processes should be included in each deck.
3. Prepare a handout for students regarding how to upload their definition to the wiki page following gameplay and how they will be evaluated for this activity. We have included our version of this handout below (at the end of "Step-by-step directions").

Running the game (in class)

1. Organize students into groups of approximately 10–15 students each.
2. Distribute decks of playing cards to each student group, and select one individual to begin the game.
3. The remaining students in the group have 1 minute to guess as many terms as possible.
4. Graduate or undergraduate teaching assistants will monitor gameplay to ensure that the clue giver is not utilizing any forbidden words, and to enforce the 1-minute time limit. Alternatively, select one student in each group to monitor and maintain time for the group.

5. The clue giver may not immediately skip a term with which he or she is having difficulty. Terms may be skipped only after 20–30 seconds of gameplay has elapsed.

6. The role of game leader or clue giver is passed on to additional students as time permits.

Constructing the online Wiktionary

1. Immediately following gameplay, ensure that each student in the group has one card or term in their possession.

2. The instructor should inform students that they are to log on to the wiki space that you have established and upload a definition for the term that they possess. The time frame in which you allow them to complete this task is left to your discretion. Inform them also that they may use their textbooks and additional resources to complete this assignment and that forbidden words can now be used in defining their term. Specific instructions for students are provided below.

3. Inform students that you will be monitoring the wiki for accuracy and plagiarism. An accurate definition should resemble one that the student would find in a textbook, but it *must* be written in the student's own words. The Wiktionary page should be monitored biweekly as terms are uploaded, and inaccuracies/plagiarized entries should be flagged and reported to the responsible student(s) as appropriate. Note to instructors: If you are concerned about the volume of entries, you might also have students print their definition and submit it to you in class. We have found that this ensures a thorough review of all definitions and allows you [the instructor] to accurately attribute a particular definition to a particular student. This also facilitates the grading process by removing any ambiguity regarding who submitted what definition. Alternatively, if you utilize the LMS/Blackboard learning system, you can look at the revision history for each entry by clicking on the "history" link on the wiki main page (other wiki resources have this capability as well).

4. Once it is apparent that all students have contributed to the wiki page, remind students that they may access this page at any time during the course of the semester, and encourage them to use this as an online reference.

Instructions to students for completing the online Wiktionary assignment

1. Log on to

   http://www.elms.umd.edu

   [insert your Web page here], and click on the "Biology Wiktionary" link in the main menu.

2. Click on the "Add New Page" link on the right side of the main window.

3. You should input your term as the title of the page and create that page under the main wiki home page.

4. Once you have done this, you should (a) see a link to your page on the right-hand side of the home page and (b) currently be looking at the page you created.

5. To edit your page, click the "Edit" link immediately to the right of where your page title is posted. Please input only text. You may now use the taboo words in your definition, and you may reference any websites or textbooks necessary to help you construct the definition. However, *your definition must be in your own words!* Students found plagiarizing will be sent to the honor court!

6. Once you are finished entering your definition, click the "Save & Exit" button at the bottom of the page. Your definition should now be uploaded.

7. If, at any point, you need to edit your definition, you may return to your page and simply follow steps 6 and 7 above.

See "Supplemental materials" for more detail regarding student and faculty guidelines for self-evaluation (Appendix A) and monitoring and evaluating student posts (Appendix B).

Approximate time required

This activity requires approximately 20–30 minutes of in-class time. As students are tasked independently with creating their definitions on the online wiki space, the time it takes for entry into the system will vary.

Required resources

In previous iterations of this activity, we have made use of the university's online course delivery system (Blackboard) and would highly recommend the use of a similar system, if available at your institution. Furthermore, the use of these systems allows for the creation of a wiki in an already existent course space, which simplifies the process. However, we recommend the following sites in the event that you do not have such a system available to you:

1. Wikispaces (*http://www.wikispaces.com*)
2. PBworks (*http://www.pbworks.com*)
3. Google Docs (Note: This may be the least ideal of these options, but it still provides the collaborative workspace necessary to perform the activity.).

We have chosen to make these recommendations based on the ease with which the resources can be used.

Variations on the basic theme

The project, as described, can be modified in many ways. Several suggestions include modifying the activity to either encompass more or less class time, as appropriate; dividing students into smaller groups (perhaps in a discussion setting); and providing specific additional activities, such as worksheets, that could be used in conjunction with the online activity. In addition, the online Wiktionary can be established for virtually any course and can be maintained either for the immediate semester or made public for future semesters as well.

Observations and advice

Introductory courses in the sciences, much as is the case in other domains, are traditionally content and terminology dense. This caveat presents challenges for both students, who must master the vocabulary, and instructors, who must convey appropriate information to their students. The Biology Taboo Wiktionary provides a time-efficient, engaging, and cost-effective way to give students autonomy in mastering the language of science. We have personally found the activity to be highly rewarding for students, several of whom stated that constructing and utilizing the wiki "not only helped them do better in class but also made the concepts make sense." This observation was confirmed by survey data in which >75% of students self-reported that their understanding of the terminology was enhanced "above and beyond what they learned from lecture and the textbook alone", as well as monitoring of the wiki page, which indicated that students had defined more than 200 key terms and had collectively referenced these terms anywhere between 50 and 250 times.

With specific regard to the in-class portion of the activity, two things are noteworthy. The first is that it takes substantial time to design the playing decks for this activity. We had the distinct advantage of having several graduate teaching assistants who were willing to help in this regard. Certainly, running the activity in smaller classes would mitigate this concern. However, for situations in which this is not possible, we suggest limiting the amount of terms used during gameplay to reduce time spent constructing the playing decks. Second, though we organized groups of about ten students, not all students were seen to be engaged in the activity. To remedy this situation, we recommend either extending gameplay or having students present key words in pairs (i.e., have pairs of students lead the game).

Recommended reading

Cole, M. (2009) Using wiki technology to support student engagement: Lessons from the trenches. *Computers & Education*, **52**(1), 141–6.

Cress, U., and Kimmerle, J. (2008) A systemic and cognitive view on collaborative knowledge building with wikis. *International Journal of Computer-Supported Collaborative Learning*, **3**(2), 105–22.

Forte, A., and Bruckman, A. (2007) Constructing text: Wiki as a toolkit for (collaborative?) learning. *Proceedings of the 2007 International Symposium on Wikis* (pp. 31–41). Available from *http://www.andreaforte.net/ForteBruckmanConstructingText.pdf*.

Jacobson, A., and Kosinski-Collins, M. (2012) Using news and views articles, lab reports, and wiki entries to teach students how to read and write for diverse scientific audiences in an introductory biology laboratory course. *Journal of Studies in Education*, **2**(2), 1–9.

Karasavvidis, I. (2010) Wiki use in higher education: Exploring barriers to successful implementation. *Interactive Learning Environments*, **18**(3), 219–31.

Marintcheva, B. (2012) Motivating students to learn biology vocabulary with Wikipedia. *Journal of Microbiology & Biology Education*, **13**(1), 65–6.

Olimpo, J., Davis, S., Lagman, S., Parekh, R., and Shields, P. (2010) Learning can be all fun and games: Constructing and utilizing a biology Taboo Wiktionary to enhance student learning in an introductory biology course. *Journal of Microbiology & Biology Education*, **11**(2), 164–5.
Ortega-Valiente, J., Reinoso, A., and Muñoz-Mansilla, R. (2012) Analysis of the benefits of wiki platforms in university education. *International Association for Development of the Information Society International Conference e-Society*, pp. 447–50.
Parker, K., and Chao, J. (2007) Wiki as a teaching tool. *Interdisciplinary Journal of Knowledge and Learning Objects*, **3**, 57–72.
Wheeler, S., Yeomans, P., and Wheeler, D. (2008) The good, the bad, and the wiki: Evaluating student-generated content for collaborative learning. *British Journal of Educational Technology*, **39**(6), 987–95.

Supplemental materials

Students, note that your participation will be monitored by both GTAs and UTAs, as well as by your instructor as your group engages in gameplay. They will utilize the criteria in Appendices A and B to evaluate your performance during the in-class Taboo activity.

Appendix A

Table 17.1 Student rubric – monitoring and evaluating Wiktionary activity

Score	**4**	**3**	**2**	**1**
Group dynamics during gameplay	I respected all classroom norms and was *fully engaged* in the in-class Taboo game. In addition, I volunteered to be a game leader for at least one round	I respected most classroom norms and was *fully engaged* in the in-class Taboo game as evidenced by my active involvement in guessing terms	I respected *most* classroom norms, but was only *moderately engaged* in the in-class Taboo game (i.e., was distracted by computer, phone, etc.)	I did not respect my fellow teammates and/or did *not* take part in the in-class activity though I attended lecture
Content contribution to the Wiktionary	I was prepared for this activity, as reflected by my attendance in class as well as my contribution to the Wiktionary. My post was also free from content errors (*as evidenced from faculty monitoring of Wiki*)	I was prepared for this activity, as reflected by my attendance in class as well as my contribution to the Wiktionary. However, my post included some content errors (*as evidenced from faculty monitoring of Wiki*)	I attended class but did *not* complete the online Wiktionary assignment	I was not prepared for this activity because I did not show up to lecture on the day of the activity (**score of 0**). However, I attempted to contribute to *some* term based on my knowledge from the readings (**score of 1**)
Clarity and mechanics of response	My post is free of spelling errors, grammatically correct, and written in complete sentences	My post has one to two spelling or grammar errors and is written in complete sentences	My post has more than two spelling or grammar errors but is written in complete	I struggled with spelling and grammar, as well as writing my post in complete sentences

Appendix B Faculty guidelines for evaluating student posts

A grade of "A" is awarded to a student who ...

- Attended class on the day the in-class Taboo game was played and demonstrated a high level of engagement during gameplay, as evidenced by their willingness to guess terms, serve as team leader, etc. *and*
- Whose Wiktionary post demonstrated *mastery* in understanding the target term or phenomena assigned to them (see example in Figure 17.1) and contained few, if any, grammatical or content errors:

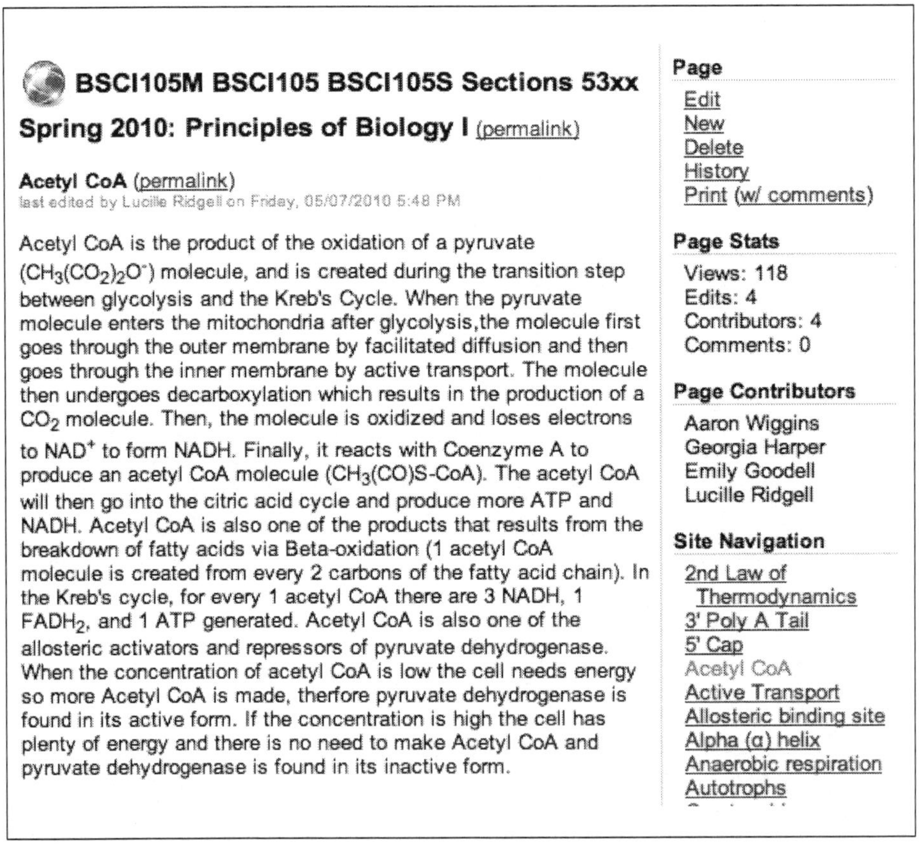

BSCI105M BSCI105 BSCI105S Sections 53xx Spring 2010: Principles of Biology I (permalink)

Acetyl CoA (permalink)
last edited by Lucille Ridgell on Friday, 05/07/2010 5:48 PM

Acetyl CoA is the product of the oxidation of a pyruvate ($CH_3(CO_2)_2O^-$) molecule, and is created during the transition step between glycolysis and the Kreb's Cycle. When the pyruvate molecule enters the mitochondria after glycolysis,the molecule first goes through the outer membrane by facilitated diffusion and then goes through the inner membrane by active transport. The molecule then undergoes decarboxylation which results in the production of a CO_2 molecule. Then, the molecule is oxidized and loses electrons to NAD^+ to form NADH. Finally, it reacts with Coenzyme A to produce an acetyl CoA molecule ($CH_3(CO)S$-CoA). The acetyl CoA will then go into the citric acid cycle and produce more ATP and NADH. Acetyl CoA is also one of the products that results from the breakdown of fatty acids via Beta-oxidation (1 acetyl CoA molecule is created from every 2 carbons of the fatty acid chain). In the Kreb's cycle, for every 1 acetyl CoA there are 3 NADH, 1 $FADH_2$, and 1 ATP generated. Acetyl CoA is also one of the allosteric activators and repressors of pyruvate dehydrogenase. When the concentration of acetyl CoA is low the cell needs energy so more Acetyl CoA is made, therfore pyruvate dehydrogenase is found in its active form. If the concentration is high the cell has plenty of energy and there is no need to make Acetyl CoA and pyruvate dehydrogenase is found in its inactive form.

Page
Edit
New
Delete
History
Print (w/ comments)

Page Stats
Views: 118
Edits: 4
Contributors: 4
Comments: 0

Page Contributors
Aaron Wiggins
Georgia Harper
Emily Goodell
Lucille Ridgell

Site Navigation
2nd Law of Thermodynamics
3' Poly A Tail
5' Cap
Acetyl CoA
Active Transport
Allosteric binding site
Alpha (α) helix
Anaerobic respiration
Autotrophs

Figure 17.1 **Screenshot of Biology Taboo Wiktionary page**

Source: Olimpo et al. (2010)

A grade of "B" is awarded to a student who . . .

- Attended class on the day the in-class Taboo game was played *and* demonstrated a *high level* of engagement during gameplay, as evidenced by their willingness to guess terms, serve as team leader, etc. *and*
- Whose Wiktionary post demonstrated *above average* understanding of the target term or phenomena assigned to them and contained few, if any, grammatical or content errors. In following with the example above, such a post might have concluded at the end of the sentence reading "The molecule then undergoes decarboxylation . . . production of a CO_2 molecule" and shown a diagram of the process but *without* much interpretation/description.

A grade of "C" is awarded to a student who . . .

- Attended class on the day the in-class Taboo game was played *and* demonstrated a *moderate* level of engagement during gameplay, as evidenced by their willingness to *occasionally* guess terms and follow classroom norms *and*
- Whose Wiktionary post demonstrated *adequate* understanding of the target term or phenomena assigned to them (i.e., a definition that is nearly equivalent to a textbook definition) *or*
- Whose Wiktionary post demonstrated *above average* comprehension of the target term or phenomena but which contained numerous grammatical errors, making it difficult for both other students and the instructor to understand.

A grade of "D" is awarded to a student who . . .

- Attended and participated in the Taboo in-class game, but *failed* to contribute to the Wiktionary page, as evidenced by their lack of a posting on the page *or*
- Attended and participated in the Taboo in-class game but was only weakly engaged in gameplay, as evidenced by lack of attentiveness to other team players and failure to comply with classroom norms *and/or* whose Wiktionary post demonstrated only a cursory understanding of the target term or phenomena. For instance, stating that "Acetyl CoA is

the product of the oxidation of a pyruvate molecule and is created during the transition step between glycolysis and the Kreb's Cycle" would be awarded a grade of "D".

A grade of "F" is awarded to a student who ...

- Failed to attend class during the Taboo game activity *or*
- Attended class but did not, in any way, participate in gameplay (as evidenced either by routine absences from the classroom during gameplay, preoccupation with laptop/phone, etc.) *or*
- Plagiarized their Wiktionary entry.

3B Creativity

Mobile digital storytelling in the second language classroom

Apostolos Koutropoulos, David Hattem, and Ronda Zelezny-Green

Abstract: This assignment facilitates the acquisition of etic perspectives of the target culture, as well as new vocabulary and new grammatical structures, through the use of mobile digital storytelling. Students are asked to explore a target culture through the lens of a nonnative of that culture, and then asked to put together a short narrated video on a given topic. Students can use a smartphone (or iPod Touch) to record video clips and then edit them together on their phone to create a longer video. Videos can then be uploaded to YouTube where fellow students will be able to view and comment on them. Although the original assignment was aimed at intermediate to advanced students in a language-learning classroom, the assignment can be utilized in other disciplines that deal with issues of group identity and self-identity.

Key words: digital storytelling, mobile video, language learning, smartphones, YouTube, video recording.

Discipline/Academic areas addressed

English as a Second Language, foreign language learning, classics, history, philosophy, economics, art history, Africana studies, American studies, African-American studies, LGBTQ studies, Asian-American studies, anthropology, Native-American studies, Hispanic studies, sociology, women's studies.

Instructional purpose

Many students are entering higher education these days with more computing power in their pockets than the average desktop computer had five to seven years ago. These smartphone devices afford students the possibility to audio or video record everyday encounters, thereby creating potential learning and teaching moments. This is a great asset to the language-learning classroom because the more exposure and practice students get engaging with the language, the more opportunities the students have to acquire the target language.

By using smartphone devices and digital storytelling methodologies, language instructors can enable students to break away from the prepackaged dialogues and traditional exercises that are available in language textbooks. These devices allow students to practice language by preparing and telling their own stories, in their own words, using audio and visuals of their choosing. Giving students this type of autonomy increases their motivation to learn more about the target language so that they can express their ideas more articulately and complexly.

This exercise can be used in other disciplines as well, particularly disciplines that explore self-identity, group identity, and how the two interact. Examples of this could be academic areas of study such as American studies, Asian-American studies, women's studies, LGBTQ studies, etc. where individual identities and personal histories, and group identities, their histories and relations to the dominant cultural discourse are connected, compared, and contrasted. Students can use digital storytelling as their medium to explore and share their own lived experiences, with the instructor serving as a guide to help students relate these experiences to the course objectives. For example, students could compare their experiences to what is considered the "group norm", and investigate how their lived experiences and group experiences weave into the overall dominant culture.

Academic areas such as history could also modify this exercise as a way of illustrating how historical events have influenced present day realities. Examples of historical events to be leveraged could be the Vietnam War, current events in foreign policy, immigration policy, and even the treatment of returned war veterans. By critically examining documentation, and using digital storytelling techniques, students could become amateur documentarians, using the digital storytelling exercise to illustrate how certain decisions or policies have manifested themselves and the effects they have had on present day society. Another potential application of digital storytelling would be to have students take on the persona of regular people in a historically significant period for a type of dramatic reenactment or have the students role-play and act as spectators to a significant historical event.

Student learning outcomes

1. Students will be able to shoot, edit, and upload a short video to YouTube, illustrating a given theme from a personal perspective.
2. Students will be able to demonstrate an etic understanding of the target culture through the creation of a personal video.
3. Students will review submissions of fellow learners on YouTube and provide reactions and constructive critique.
4. Students will augment their vocabulary by discovering and using words and phrases in their personal stories that they have not used, or seldom used.
5. Students will practice using grammatical constructions to talk about the past (e.g., the simple past tense, the past progressive, the perfect tenses, and "used to" phrases).
6. Students will demonstrate proficiency or intermediate proficiency, using American Council on the Teaching of Foreign Languages (1999a) standards

   http://www.actfl.org/i4a/pages/index.cfm?pageid=3392

Prerequisite skills and knowledge

Students ought to have some basic facility with mobile and computing devices in order to participate in this exercise. From our own experience using technology in education, we have observed two methods that are helpful for preparing students to use mobile phones, and other computing equipment, for this type of project. The first method is to arrange a training event at an Apple Store where the class can receive hands-on learning experience. These training events can also lead to end-of-semester gatherings in order to showcase the work created (Tang, 2011b).

The other method we have employed is utilizing existing campus resources for training on appropriate technology use. At the UMass Boston campus, for example, there is a Digital Learning Studio where faculty can arrange training sessions for their students with a technology and video specialist. Students can decide whether they want to participate in these instructor-led, hands-on learning opportunities after they have completed self-paced instructional videos for the software that they will use (see "Supplemental materials").

Step-by-step directions

The following are directions given to students. Citations and parentheticals are not part of the student handout, but are there for the benefit of fellow educators. See "Required resources" for links to tutorials on hardware, software, editing and video hosting, and "how-to" learning aids.

1. For this assignment the theme is national elections (e.g., Presidential elections in the U.S.A.).
2. View the YouTube tutorials on how to use the video editing software (see "Required resources"). You have a choice of iMovie or ReelDirector on the library-supplied iPod Touches.
   a. Assuming that you have your own iPod Touch or iPhone you can use iMovie, ReelDirector, Vimeo, or any other application that you feel comfortable with.
3. Create a draft script and a draft plan for your digital story and submit it to the instructor for review. I want to make sure that before you spend a lot of time and effort on your digital story you are not biting off more than you can chew.
4. While I am reviewing your scripts and plans, experiment with the iPod and the software so you can be ready to record your projects as soon as you get my feedback. As an exercise create a 1–2-minute video demonstrating that you can record and splice two segments together.
   a. I aim to give you feedback on your use of language within one class session, so you should have a couple of days to learn the software. [During this phase the instructor will give feedback to the students on their use of language, but not on their etic understanding. By doing this the instructor ensures that grammatically correct, clear

language is used, while avoiding the imposition of value judgments on the student. The etic perspective will be discussed following the presentation of the video to the class. Once the video is presented, the class will engage in discussions to analyze the short video's representation of the emic perspective, and through discussion create a more nuanced understanding of that perspective for the students.]

5. Once you have your story ready, choose your locations to film.

   a. Tip: Due to the limitations of the device, you need to choose a location that has enough light, and is not too noisy! A location that is too dark may work for your story, but a location that is too noisy means that we can't hear you!

   b. Tip: Don't record one long video, because this makes it hard to edit. Instead record many smaller clips (30–60 seconds in length) that you can stitch together with the video editing software.

   c. Tip: Be natural when you're speaking, but speak loudly so we can hear. Doing a few tests beforehand can really help you figure out how loudly you need to speak.

6. Once you have recorded all your video segments, it's time to put them all together.

   a. Tip: Once you put your video together, don't throw away the individual segments! They might still be useful, especially if your final video isn't what you thought it was.

   b. Tip: Feel free to experiment. Just because you gave me a plan, it doesn't mean that you need to stick to it exactly. If you have time, feel free to experiment with different ways of telling your story.

7. When you're done with the video editing, upload your video to YouTube (see "Required resources" for tutorials).

8. Once your video is on YouTube, send me a link by email. I will collect the video links for the entire class and email them out to your fellow students.

9. When I send you an email with all the video links from fellow students, take the time to view and comment on the videos before the next class session.

10. In the following class, once you've viewed all submissions, we will be discussing the videos submitted by your fellow classmates. Specifically, we will be examining and discussing why students selected the images that they did to show us, whose voice can be heard in the videos, and who is not represented (McLaughlin and DeVoogd, 2004). We will also be examining vocabulary that your fellow students used in their videos that you may not be familiar with.

Approximate time required

- One class session as a prep session (at the beginning of the semester)
  - 15–20 minutes to explain grammatical constructs required for this assignment;
  - 10–15 minutes to explain the cultural phenomenon to be explored by the students;
  - 30 minutes to explain the technology involved in this project (device basics, software required, links to any how-to guides).
- Two to three weeks for each cultural topic that is explored through digital storytelling.
- One class session to view and discuss videos as a group.

Required resources

- Required hardware
  - iPod Touch ($199) or iPhone ($199 + phone contract; prices as of January 4, 2012). These devices are often available at your university's library or media center or can be bought at Apple Stores or

    http://www.apple.com
  - A projection source for viewing mobile digital stories in a whole class setting.
- Software for iOS (iPhone, iPad, iPod Touch)
  - ReelDirector ($1.99) – video editing software

    http://itunes.apple.com/us/app/reeldirector/id334366844?mt=8

- iMovie ($4.99) – video editing software

  http://itunes.apple.com/us/app/imovie/id377298193?mt=8

- Vimeo (free) – basic video capture, video editing, and video uploading software.

  http://itunes.apple.com/us/app/vimeo/id425194759?mt=8

- Video hosting websites
  - YouTube – free video hosting

    http://www.youtube.com

  - Vimeo – free video hosting

    http://www.vimeo.com

- Examples of digital storytelling

  http://faculty.lagcc.cuny.edu/eiannotti/7.1/
  http://digitalstorytelling.coe.uh.edu/turkey/vacide/index.html
  http://www.prel.org/eslstrategies/moviemyculturepage.html
  http://www.prel.org/eslstrategies/moviediscriminationpage.html
  http://shirleystang.com/digitalstories/

- Free digital storytelling course on the Web

  http://ds106.us/

- How-to learning aids
  - how to use ReelDirector

    http://www.youtube.com/watch?v=yfj0dmTURSw

  - how to edit videos with ReelDirector

    http://www.youtube.com/watch?v=peg0L4ib9cU

  - how to use iMovie on the iPhone

    http://mashable.com/2010/06/24/imovie-for-iphone-how-to/

  - how to upload a video from an Apple iPhone to YouTube

    http://www.askdavetaylor.com/how_to_upload_video_apple_iphone_YouTube.html

- iPhone iMovie tutorial

  http://www.youtube.com/watch?v=PbyrBkn8bio
- YouTube in plain English

  http://www.youtube.com/watch?v=0klgLsSxGsU
- 1-in-8-Million or aha moment

  http://www.ahamoment.com/

Variations on the basic theme

With the use of mobile phones to complete this activity, students are empowered to use almost any location to shoot their digital story. Also, given that in most cases mobile phone technology is a commonplace item that students are likely to be comfortable using, any tension between the students and the use of the technology is likely to be minimal.

Camcorders could be another technology employed for the purposes of this activity, however their availability might be limited (if not already owned by the students), and the expense to replace the camcorder if lost or damaged are two strong factors in favor of using mobile phone technology. If camcorders are not available, a cheaper alternative is a webcam. While webcams do not provide the mobility of camcorders, they are cheap and simple to operate and don't entail a format conversion process as most camcorders do when transferring video from camcorder to computer.

A final alternative could be to have students create a digital photo montage using PowerPoint or a website like Prezi (*www.prezi.com*), which would primarily employ still images that are accompanied by voice narration. This technique would not encourage natural interaction by/between students when using the target language, and so would be practical even for learners who are at lower levels of English language speaking abilities.

With relatively few modifications, the assignment could easily be used in history classes for the making of personal historical accounts, English literature classes to produce student versions of literary classics, or even journalism classes for reporting purposes. Most disciplines are likely to find a use for mobile digital storytelling given that it is an engaging way for students to share their perspectives on class subject matter.

See "Supplemental materials" for alternate step-by-step directions for a Cultural aha moment assignment.

Observations and advice

"If we view the classroom as a springboard to the nonclassroom world and not a substitute for it, we can focus on the things that can be done well in classrooms and leave the rest to the outside world" (Lee and VanPatten, 2003, p. 5). Mobile digital storytelling benefits language learners in a variety of ways. First, it allows learners to untether themselves from the familiar location of the classroom, and bring their stories to life in more authentic cultural locations, using culturally authentic realia (Omaggio, 2001) and giving them more latitude in the creative process. Second, having students share their stories on a social-networking tool such as YouTube helps to create a sense of classroom community, which may lower students' affective filters (Krashen, 1988), which can positively affect the acquisition process. It also provides the students with an "audience" for their stories, thereby enhancing their motivation and their attention to form.

While digital story activities have been previously done in classroom settings, few have attempted to extend digital storytelling by making it mobile. Advances in technology, mainly miniaturization and cost reductions, have enabled us to help our students tell their story in authentic environments (i.e., not in a classroom) and have removed barriers by allowing capture, editing, and uploading to be done from a handheld device.

In our own experience, the main hurdle for a digital storytelling activity, which depends on students being in front of the camera, is student self-consciousness of their appearance or their video recording and editing skills. It is important to let the students know that they are in a safe environment and they will not be ridiculed. We stress that this is a learning experience where, with time, students can become more proficient with practice. Additionally, it is important that students know that they are being evaluated on their ability to think critically and communicate effectively, rather than being evaluated on their video production skills or their on-screen appearance. It might be helpful if the instructor creates his/her own digital storytelling video as an example for the students. This can help students feel less intimidated by the process of having their video posted on a public website like YouTube. It might also be useful for the instructor to tell the students that making mistakes is a beneficial part of the language-learning process. Sharing this knowledge at the start of the lesson may also encourage the students to decrease their use of avoidance strategies, such as the tendency to not to produce language constructions that require complex grammatical structures and lexicon.

Recommended reading

ACTFL [American Council on the Teaching of Foreign Languages] (1999a) *ACTFL Proficiency Guidelines – Speaking*. Available from: *http://www.actfl.org/files/public/guidelinesspeak.pdf*

ACTFL [American Council on the Teaching of Foreign Languages] (1999b) *National Standards for Foreign Language Education*. Available from: *http://www.actfl.org/i4a/pages/index.cfm?pageid=3392*

Adair-Hauck, B., and Donato, R. (2002, December) The PACE model: A story-based approach to meaning and form for standards-based language learning. *The French Review*, **76**(2), 265–76.

Burgess, J. (2006) Hearing ordinary voices: Cultural studies, vernacular creativity and digital storytelling. *Continuum: Journal of Media and Cultural Studies*, **20**(2), 201–14. Available from *http://eprints.qut.edu.au*

Burgess, J., Foth, M., and Klaebe, H. (2006) Everyday creativity as civic engagement: A cultural citizenship view of new media. *Proceedings Communications Policy & Research Forum, Sydney*. Available from *http://eprints.qut.edu.au*

Donato, R. (1994) Collective scaffolding in second language learning. In: J. P. Lantolf and G. Appel. (Eds.), *Vygotskian Approaches to Second Language Research* (pp. 33–56). Norwood, NJ: Ablex Publishing.

Freidus, N., and Hlubinka, M. (2002) Digital storytelling for reflective practice in communities of learners. *ACM SIGGROUP Bulletin Archive*, **23**(2), 24–6.

Kajder, S. B. (2004) Enter here: Personal narrative and digital storytelling. *English Journal*, **93**(3), 64–8.

Krashen, S. D. (1988) *Second Language Acquisition and Second Language Learning*. Upper Saddle River, NJ: Prentice Hall International.

Lambert, J. (2006) *Digital Storytelling Cookbook*. San Francisco, CA: Digital Diner Press.

Lee, J., and VanPatten, B. (2003) *Making Communicative Language Teaching Happen*. New York: McGraw-Hill.

Lowenthal, P. (2009) Digital storytelling: An emerging institutional technology? In: K. McWilliam and J. Hartley (Eds.), *Story Circle: Digital Storytelling around the World* (pp. 297–305). Hoboken, NJ: Wiley-Blackwell.

McLaughlin, M., and DeVoogd, G. (2004) Critical literacy as comprehension: Expanding reader response. Available from Colorado Language Arts Society at *http://www.clas.us/CriticalLiteracy.pdf*

Meadows, D. (2003) Digital storytelling: Research-based practice in new media. *Visual Communication*, **2**, 189–93, doi: 10.1177/1470357203002002004.

Mullen, R., and Wedwick, L. (2008) Avoiding the digital abyss: Getting started in the classroom with YouTube, digital stories, and blogs. *Clearing House*, **82**(2), 66–9.

Ohler, J. (2006) The world of digital storytelling. *Learning in the Digital Age*, **63**(4), 44–7.

Omaggio, A. C. (2001) *Teaching Language in Context: Proficiency-Oriented Instruction*. Boston, MA: Heinle & Heinle Publishers.

Rance-Roney, J. (2010) Jump-starting language and schema for English-language learners: Teacher-composed digital jumpstarts for academic reading. *Journal of Adolescent & Adult Literacy*, **5**(5), 386–95.

Reitmaier, T., Bidwell, N. J., and Marsden, G. (2010) Situating digital storytelling within African communities. *International Journal of Human-Computer Studies*, **69**(10), 658–68, doi: 10.1016/j.ijhcs.2010.12.008

Robin, B. R. (2006) The educational uses of digital storytelling. Available from *http://www.coe.uh.edu/digitalstorytelling/evaluation.htm*

Robin, B. R. (2008). Digital storytelling: A powerful technology tool for the 21st century classroom. *Theory into Practice*, **47**, 220–8, doi: 10.1080/00405840802153916

Tang, S. (2011a) What is digital storytelling in Asian American studies? Available from *http://shirleystang.com/digitalstories/*

Tang, S. (2011b) Asian American digital storytelling event and reception. Available from *http://shirleystang.com/2011/05/asian-american-digital-storytelling-event-and-reception/*

Wlodkowski, R. J. (1999) *Enhancing Adult Motivation to Learn: A Comprehensive Guide to Teaching All Adults*. San Francisco, CA: Jossey-Bass.

Supplemental materials

Directions are given to students. Citations are not part of the student handout, but are there for the benefit of fellow educators.

Cultural aha moment

Pre-task orientation and planning

Class 1, time: 30 minutes

1. The instructor explains to students that they will be working together to create a mobile digital story that reports on a cultural aha moment the student has experienced since living in the target culture. The instructor provides a definition of an aha moment, what may constitute a cultural aha moment, and shows the students a few examples of aha moment videos from

   http://www.ahamoment.com/

2. The instructor provides students with links to YouTube tutorials on how to use the video editing software on the library-supplied iPod Touch, and explains to them they have the choice of iMovie or ReelDirector.

3. The students are then instructed to create a draft for their digital story for homework. They are encouraged to view some aha moment videos for homework with a focus on collecting lexical phrases that they can use in their own stories.

Class 2, time: 80 minutes

4. Students work in small groups, peer-editing each others' drafts, spending no longer than 25 minutes on one draft. They are instructed to supply their partners with corrective feedback, as well as negotiate meaning, share the lexical phrases they have accumulated, and discuss whether any of them are appropriate for their stories.

5. The instructor provides a handout to the students that gives them tips for their video production. Students then have 1 week to shoot, edit, and post their videos onto YouTube.

    a. Tip: Due to the limitations of the device, you need to choose a location that has enough light, and is not too noisy! A location that is too dark *may* work for your story, *but* a location that is too noisy means that we can't hear you!

    b. Tip: Don't record one long video, because this makes it hard to edit. Instead record many smaller clips (30–60 seconds in length) that you can stitch together with the video editing software.

    c. Tip: Be natural when you're speaking, but speak loudly so we can hear. Doing a few tests beforehand can really help you figure out how loudly you need to speak.

    d. Tip: Once you put your video together, don't throw away the individual segments! They might still be useful, especially if your final video isn't what you thought it was.

    e. Tip: Feel free to experiment. Just because you gave me a plan, it doesn't mean that you need to stick to it exactly. If you have time, feel free to experiment with different ways of telling *your* story.

Task, time: 1 week

6. Students work together to shoot, edit, and post their videos onto YouTube. The teacher provides them with technological support as necessary

Post-task activities homework

7. After everyone has posted their videos successfully onto YouTube, students are instructed to view three videos that they did not participate in making. After the students view the videos, they are to leave a constructive critique of the video that includes at least one positive comment about the use of language in the video, and 1–3 comments about the learner's use of oral language, including any grammatical or phonological mistakes. Should students wish to reshoot their video, they would be free to do so. However, it is not required for this exercise since more than one video will be made during the course, and students could also use older videos such as ePortfolio items to demonstrate evidence of steady academic progression.

19

Creating a video dialogue with streaming video clips

Sandra L. Miller

Abstract: Teaching with film has been around for quite a while. We can all remember when the instructor took class time to show a movie. Often, we discussed it afterwards – that is, if there was time. However, today, methods of instructional delivery have changed – largely due to the Internet. Now, with streaming video, we can take advantage of the Internet's ability to deliver anytime, anyplace without taking up class time, thus leaving more class time available for discussion. Moreover, with today's video teaching tools, discussion has evolved as well. Discussion can now be conducted electronically with annotated clips punctuating key points in debates engendered by reviewing a film or set of film clips (playlist). Because more and more students use high-bandwidth Internet service providers (ISPs), the question is not whether to teach with interactive streaming video, but rather how to access, create annotations and playlists, and share with others in the class. Using these tools and building interactivity into the experience removes the passivity of watching, making active learners of today's students. Points addressed in this chapter include where the resources are, how teachers can use them to the highest advantage of students, how students can use them to their highest advantage, and, ultimately, what that means in terms of student learning outcomes.

Key words: digital video, media literacy, streaming video, video annotations, playlists, visual literacy.

Discipline/Academic areas addressed

Instructional technology and a variety of academic disciplines served by visual content such as humanities and social sciences, science and health, business, education, arts, and communication.

Instructional purpose

Streaming video is a powerful tool to introduce new concepts, reinforce learned concepts, and inspire class discussion whether it is face-to-face (f2f) or virtual. Digital video can convey concepts and ideas in a way that the book or lecture simply doesn't. For instance, video "can bring the past 'to life' creating an emotional impact" (Daley, 2003). Using short clips to create a visual language of expression annotated by analytical text empowers students to understand the message more completely and cocreate a common base of knowledge amongst them. This leads to a more engaged and motivated student and an actively engaged student in his/her own learning can lead to greater retention (Davis and Murrell, 1994).

Using streaming video can motivate and engage students in their learning process, enabling them to better retain what they have learned (Choi and Johnson, 2005). However, as with all educational technology tools, the devil is in the details of how streaming video is used (Karppinen, 2005). Using the three I's (image, interaction, and integration – Thornhill et al., 2002), streaming media takes video to new levels of learning. Today the ability to bookmark and customize clips with personal comments in significant areas is available either through an educational vendor-supported or video-sharing website. Different vendors/video-sharing websites refer to it as annotations, clips, or bookmarks. That is what the instructor should look for when researching which video content to use.

Using annotations and playlists (the ability to string a series of annotations or customized clips together creating one link with which to access) gives students a locus of control, positively affecting the learner's self-efficacy (Constantinou et al., 2009). Situating the clips within a student–teacher–student conversation (Vygotsky, 1978) enables students to use streaming video within a constructivist framework. When students are able to choose specific clips, they are visualizing the construction of knowledge and being able to add commentary aids their reflection (Kukulska-Hulme et al., 2004). Using these new tools with streaming video augments student learning.

Student learning outcomes

1. Students understand how different sensory experiences can assist or detract from their grasp of disciplinary concepts.

2. Students comprehend the meaning of visual literacy in the context of information literacy as they research and critique through the usage of video.
3. Students create graphic representations of data, information, knowledge, and wisdom via videos, video clips, and/or playlists.
4. Students provide classmates with constructive f2f and online feedback for their video-enhanced commentaries and analyses.
5. Students demonstrate critical thinking through their clip choices, commentaries, and analyses of video playlists.
6. Students demonstrate visual and media literacy.

Prerequisite skills and knowledge

Internet searching skills, including browsing of video-sharing websites, are necessary. The ability to create annotations and playlists can be learned (or honed) via educational vendor or video-sharing website–supplied annotation tools. When selecting these sites, the instructor should ensure that the sites should provide instructions as to how to create clips, playlists, etc. as each site may be slightly different. Also necessary is the ability (possessed by most students) to copy and paste links of video clips/playlists into shared class course websites.

Step-by-step directions

There are three current methods of teaching and learning with streaming video although many more uses are being discovered all the time. The first, and the one discussed most fully in this chapter, is audiovisual content to accommodate multiple intelligences (Gardner, 1983) and different learning styles (Kolb, 1984). The video content is used to present a problem and start a discussion around the problem whose subject is related to the course's content learning objectives. Media librarians are a great resource for faculty to find content related to their specific curriculum. Educational video vendors also can supply video content directly correlated with curriculum. Educational video-sharing websites also can supply pertinent video content. The important tool to look for from any source is the ability for both faculty and students to create annotated video clips and/or playlists. It is important to note that educational video vendors charge for their usage. Without licensing payment, access is denied. Again, check with your media librarian to see which educational video vendors your school has access to and whether they offer the more advanced tools.

The steps involved in this method are simple:

1. Search for appropriate and relevant video content that will stimulate a healthy discussion or dialogue surrounding the video's content.

2. Stream video in class or require students to view video outside of class by posting the persistent URL in the course's website.

3. Discuss in class or through the discussion forum in the course website. Use open-ended questions about the subject being discussed.

4. Use annotated video clips and/or playlists to enhance the discussion (model for your students what you want them to do).

5. Have students develop clips and/or playlists with their own annotations to respond to your question(s). The instructor may need to demonstrate how to develop playlists and/or clips. Annotations or clips are developed by bookmarking the video timeline with the start and end points for the clip to be saved – usually done by clicking on the timeline while in annotation mode. It does not alter the original video in any way. It merely points to the particular section of the video that the student wishes to play without having to play the entire video again to get to that portion. There is often a text box that accompanies the clip so the student can type in information they wish to share about the clip. A playlist is created by sequencing clips in the order in which the student would like them played. A single URL is formed that links to all the ordered clips the student has saved on the vendor or video-sharing website. This URL can be embedded in any HTML method of communication (i.e., discussion forum posting, email, Web page, etc.).

6. Have students respond to the other student's clips/playlist arguments.

7. Use the Center for Media Literacy's

   http://www.medialit.org/

   guidelines to discuss what makes these clips so meaningful both in terms of content and construction of content.

8. Use the ACRL's guidelines

   http://www.ala.org/acrl/standards/informationliteracycompetency

   to discuss the pros and cons of using these clips from an information literacy perspective.
9. Use an evaluation rubric to determine student perspicacity in clip choice, understanding of the issues, reliability of information presented, and student's ability to analyze the issue(s) discussed (see rubric in "Supplemental materials").
10. Present a summation of lessons learned either f2f or virtually through a compilation of relevant clips presented by all students.

Approximate time required

The time required depends on the curriculum and the number of class sessions that are being enhanced by streaming video. Planning in advance is necessary as the content is to be picked out or created in advance of usage. Selecting relevant content can be shortened with the help of your media librarian or through intelligent use of the search tool available on the educational vendor/video-sharing website.

Allow 20–30 minutes for viewing via the Web. Lengthier viewing times are much less desirable so chunking the content into these time lengths is advised. Discussion times can be anywhere from 15 to 45 minutes depending on the complexity of the subject. More time can be allotted in the virtual discussion forum as it is not restricted by class time.

Required resources

A wide range of tutorials is available, some of which are listed here:

http://ed.ted.com
http://YouTube.com
http://www.teachertube.com/
http://njvid.net http://www.ohiolink.edu/
http://www.teachwithmovies.org/
http://mediapede.org/filmhistory/
http://www.teachersdomain.org/
http://www.filmsmediagroup.com/
www.intelecomonline.net/
http://collegeanywhere.org/

The technology needed includes

- Course website or HTML-enabled sharing medium (email could be used, but discussion forums in course websites are preferable).
- Broadband access.
- Access to streaming digital video repository(ies) of educational video with authenticated access as needed, advanced search, annotation, and playlist capabilities.

Variations on the basic theme

An alternative method is using recorded video of the student him/herself during an applied session of lessons learned in the curriculum (e.g., student teaching, analyzing a patient's medical condition, etc.) for self-critique and reflection. The steps include the following:

1. Record a student demonstration.
2. Upload the video to a shared video website.
3. Critique and annotate with noted comments. Create a playlist if necessary of those video segments that are indicative.
3. Share with the professor and/or students for further comments and reflections.

A final variation is the "flipped classroom" (Bergmann and Sams, 2010):

1. Faculty record their lectures, demonstrations, etc. and publish to a video-sharing website.
2. Faculty require students to view the videos prior to the class.
3. Students do their homework in the class with the faculty member providing guidance and tutorial assistance.

Observations and advice

Today's students are learning via distance education more so than ever. The Sloan Consortium indicates that online education is part of the mainstream of higher education and is continuing to grow at a phenomenal rate (Allen and Seaman, 2010). On-demand delivery needs for video with which to teach and learn will continue to grow alongside the growth in online education (Hartsell and Yuen, 2006).

Net Generation students rely much more on visual literacy than text to acquire their knowledge (Oblinger, 2005). Digital video increases motivation and engagement (Larkin-Hein and Zollman, 2000). Digital video can diversify types of resources, provide a match between content and need, and aid in instructional differentiation (Mardis, 2009). So, whether students are online or simply learning in a hybrid or traditional environment, using streaming video over the Internet can strengthen rather than replace the campus experience (Creighton and Buchanan, 2001).

It is critical, however, that the video clips are not used simply as supplemental materials for students to passively view at their leisure. They must be thoroughly integrated into the class curriculum (either through f2f discussion, graded virtual discussion, or graded multimedia presentations. The clips provide the foundation for interactive discussion. Often, with educational videos from educational vendors, there are supplemental materials that can also be integrated into class activities. These supplemental materials assist in further explanation. However, again it must be noted that there are licensing costs for these types of videos. Discussion with your media librarian can be very helpful concerning which videos would have the most impact and are, therefore, worth the investment.

Excellent examples of using videos to start a discussion are some of the YouTube video clips of the Occupy Wall Street movement. Beginning with these clips and throwing in questions that stimulate further discussion, have your students search for new clips that add meaning, and create annotations of those clips bringing in more of the complex issues around why these movements are occurring, how might they end, and so forth. Another example could be getting clips of the "Arab Spring" and using that as a jumping-off point for a thorough discussion of democracy and the preparation for democracy. What are these countries fighting for? What caused it to happen now? The bottom line is that video clips help to make it real for students who can't really visit the places or see for themselves what is happening.

Recommended reading

Allen, E. I., and Seaman, J. (2010, November) Class differences: Online education in the United States, 2010. The Sloan Consortium. Available from *http://sloanconsortium.org/sites/default/files/class_differences.pdf*

Bergmann, J., and Sams, A. (2010, December) The flipped classroom. Available from *http://www.youtube.com/watch?v=2H4RkudFzlc*

Boster, F. J., Meyer, G. S., Roberto, A. J., Lindsey, L., Smith, R. et al. (2004) A report on the effect of the unitedstreaming® application on educational performance. *The 2004 Los Angeles Unified School District Mathematics Evaluation.* Mason, MI: Cometrika; Milwaukee, WI: Baseline Research; and Farmville,VA: Longwood University.

Branigan, C. (2005, April 1) Technological, societal factors are driving the video trend. *eSchool News*, pp. 12–16. Available from: *http://eschoolnews.eschoolnetwork.com/?p=10551*

Calandra, B., Brantley-Dias, L., and Dias, M. (2006) Using digital video for professional development in urban schools: A preservice teacher's experience with reflection. *Journal of Computing in Teacher Education*, **22**(4), 137–45.

Choi, H. J., and Johnson, S. D.(2005) The effect of context-based video instruction on learning and motivation in online courses. *American Journal of Distance Education*, **19**(4), 215–27.

Copyright Clearance Center, Intelligent Television, and New York University (2009) Video use and higher education: Options for the future. Available from *http://library.nyu.edu/about/Video_Use_in_Higher_Education.pdf*

Constantinou, C., Retalis, S., Papadopoulos, G., and Charalambos, V. (2009) Combining streaming media and collaborative elements to support lifelong learning. In: T. Daradumis et al. (Eds.), *Intelligent Collaborative e-Learning Systems and Applications* (pp. 19–36). Berlin, Germany: Springer-Verlag.

Creighton, J. V., and Buchanan, P. (2001) Toward the E-campus: Using the Internet to strengthen, rather than replace, the campus experience. *EDUCAUSE Review*, **36**(2), 12–14.

Daley, E. (2003) Expanding the concept of literacy. *EDUCAUSE Review*, **38**(2), 32–40.

Davis, T. M., and Murrell, P. H. (1994) *Turning Teaching into Learning: The Role of Student Responsibility in the Collegiate Experience* (ASHE-ERIC Higher Education Report No. 8). Washington, D.C.: George Washington University.

Gardner, H. (1983) *Frames of Mind: The Theory of Multiple Intelligences.* New York, NY: Basic Books.

Hartsell, T., and Yuen, S. C. (2006) Video streaming in online learning. *AACE Journal*, **14**(1), 31–43.

Karppinen, P. (2005) Meaningful learning with digital and online videos: Theoretical perspectives. *AACE Journal*, **13**(3), 233–50.

Kolb, D. A. (1984) *Experiential Learning: Experience as the Source of Learning and Development.* Upper Saddle River, NJ: Prentice Hall.

Kukulska-Hulme, A., Foster-Jones, J., Jelfs, A., Mallett, E., and Holland, D. (2004). Investigating digital video applications in distance learning. *Journal of Educational Media*, **29**(2), 125–37.

Larkin-Hein, T., and Zollman, D. A. (2000) Digital video, learning styles and student understanding of kinematic graphs. *Journal of SMET Education*, (May/August). Available from *http://web.phys.ksu.edu/papers/2000/dig-video-learning-styles.pdf*

Mardis, M. A. (2009) Viewing Michigan's digital future: Results of a survey of educator use of digital video in the USA. *Learning, Media and Technology*, **34**(3), 243–57.

Moore, K. (2011) *71% of Online Adults Now Use Video-sharing Sites* (Pew Internet Project). Washington, D.C.: Pew Research Center. Available from *http://pewinternet.org/Reports/2011/Video-sharing-sites.aspx*

Oblinger, D. G. (2005) Learners, learning, and technology: The EDUCAUSE Learning Initiative. *EDUCAUSE Review*, **40**(5), 66–75.

PBS/Grunwald Associates (2010) Deepening connections: Teachers increasingly rely on media and technology. Available from *http://www.pbs.org/about/media/about/cms_page_media/182/PBS-Grunwald-2011e.pdf*

Sausner, R. (2005) Hot technologies. *District Administration*, **41**(1), 17.

Shephard, K. (2003) Questioning, promoting and evaluating the use of streaming video to support student learning. *British Journal of Educational Technology*, **34**(3), 295–308.

Teaching and Learning Editors (2008) We all stream for video. *Tech & Learning*. Available from *http://www.techlearning.com/article/We-All-Stream-For-Video/45423*

Thornhill, S., Asensio, M., and Young, C. (Eds.) (2002) Video streaming: A guide for educational development. *The JISC Click and Go Video Project*. Manchester, U.K.: Joint Information Systems Committee. Available from *http://www.cinted.ufrgs.br/videoeduc/streaming.pdf*

Vygotsky, L. (1978) *Mind in Society*. Cambridge, MA: Harvard University Press.

Young, C., and Asensio, M. (2002) Looking through the three "I's": The pedagogic use of streaming video. In: S. Banks, P. Goodyear, V. Hodgson, and D. McConnell (Eds.), *Third International Conference of Networked Learning, Sheffield, England* (pp. 628–35).

Supplemental materials

Table 19.1 Evaluation rubric

Category	Rating		
	3	**2**	**1**
Clips are relevant to the main concept	In a visual manner, clips clearly express an important aspect of the main concept	Clips chosen are sometimes on target, but some have no bearing on the main concept	Clips are rather pointless concerning the main concept and veer away from the main concept
Clips added greater complexity to the issues involved around the main concept	In a visual manner, clips revealed more deeply the variance and intricacy involved with the main theme	Clips chosen are sometimes on target, but some digress to irrelevant issues	Clips chosen are random and unrelated to the issues
Annotations for the clips were founded on reliable information and/or data	Annotation resources demonstrate the student's ability to identify and document appropriate resources	Student identifies some resources appropriate to the topic and cites them correctly	The information gathered lacks relevance, quality, and balance. The citations are incomplete
Student's analysis was insightful and thought provoking	Student was able to make connections between video clips/annotations and to integrate information from multiple sources	Student summarizes information in an organized manner in support of a position, but does not provide further synthesis	Student is unable to integrate the information in a coherent manner

Category	Rating		
	3	**2**	**1**
Student's choice of clips and resulting annotations showed an awareness of their audience	Strong awareness of audience in the design of their playlists. Students can clearly explain why they felt the chosen clips fit the target audience	Some awareness of audience in the design. Students can partially explain why they felt the chosen clips fit the target audience	Limited awareness of the needs and interests of the target audience
Images chosen within the clips enhance the impact upon the audience	Images create a distinct atmosphere or tone that matches different parts of the annotations or commentaries. The images may communicate symbolism and/or metaphors	An attempt was made to use images to create an atmosphere/ tone but it needed more work. However, image choice was logical	Little or no attempt to use images to create an appropriate atmosphere/tone
Analyses and commentaries provided constructive feedback to other students	Student monitors the effectiveness of another student's playlists/ annotations, and makes constructive suggestions to make it more effective	Student monitors the effectiveness of another student's playlists/ annotations and responds cursorily	Student monitors the effectiveness of another student's playlists/ annotations and does not work to make it more effective

20

Remix as an educational activity

Christopher Shamburg, Kate Mazzetti-Shamburg, and John Shamburg

Abstract: This chapter will introduce and develop the concept of remix as a tool for understanding and developing literary and communication skills. Students are encouraged to understand the creative process by understanding that "creativity" does not have to be limited to creating new material from scratch, but can be about reorganizing and recombining existing work. With this philosophy in mind, this chapter gives a rationale using remix practices for teacher education with a variety of technological tools. The focus is on two projects from the humanities, which can easily be adapted for any curriculum or source material, to help teachers understand the educational applications of remix.

Key words: appropriation, audio editing, multimedia, podcasting, remix, video editing, YouTube.

Discipline/Academic areas addressed

While appropriate for teacher education, humanities and communication, the activities can be adapted to any discipline.

Instructional purpose

Remix is a problem, a process, an opportunity, the folk art of the twenty-first century, and a fundamental part of the information economy. It can also be a useful framework for education. The concept of remix, although often thought of in terms of the modern day recording industry, is actually as old as the creative process itself, and is applicable to a growing set of media creation and social media tools. Today remix is a part of both commercial and user-created media – from presidential campaigns to popular music to fan-created videos on YouTube. At its core, remix is the process of taking cultural artifacts and rearranging them into new kinds of creative blends (Knobel and Lankshear, 2008). Though it is strongly associated today with digital technologies, remix has corollaries in culture, science, art, and cognition. Remix happens when people make video montages of their favorite TV, movie, and videogame characters, set them to music, and post them on YouTube for other fans to enjoy.

Remix happens when Jay-Z produces the award-winning song *Hard Knock Life* with inspiration and clips from the Broadway musical *Annie*. Remix happens when Shepard Fairey takes an Associated Press photo of then presidential candidate Barack Obama, colorizes it, and typesets the word HOPE at the bottom.

The process of appropriating and repurposing existing works to create something original can be a framework for educators. Appropriation and remix has been used as a framework to examine literature (Shamburg, 2008), science and invention (Johnson, 2010), and culture (Jenkins, 2006). It has also been proposed as a model for literacy education (Knobel and Lankshear, 2008). Indeed, journalist and author Thomas Friedman makes a compelling case for remix and mashups in higher education because of its value for the twenty-first century economy (Pink, 2008). Finally, because they are critical to so many twenty-first century activities, students and teachers need to know that appropriation and repurposing are legitimate, worthwhile, and legal. An excellent starting point for the discussion on the legal and ethical considerations is the *Fair Use Guidelines* that are part of U.S. Copyright Law (U.S. Copyright Office, 2009).

Remix is happening outside of schools, but this process has value for cognition, research, and the economy. This chapter discusses projects that can be adapted to a variety of students to teach and capitalize on remix.

Student learning outcomes

Although each remix project below has specific parameters (e.g., one-minute audio, a specific number of primary sources or media items) that should be a part of a grade, the heart of the assessment is on the student's ability to

1. Synthesize a variety of material in original ways.
2. Demonstrate creativity in applying remix practices in meaningful educational projects.
3. Use the material of others legally and ethically.

Prerequisite skills and knowledge

Computer literacy and familiarity with Internet search engines.

Step-by-step directions

The following are two projects – "Six Sounds in Search of an Author" and "Movie Trailer" – which we've done with students enrolled in a teacher education program. The premise is "reflective modeling" in which we do projects teachers do with students, but with added rationales and reflections.

At the beginning of a class's first remix project, you should review the ethical and legal ramifications of remix. Keep in mind that there are no specific legal guidelines (e.g., two minutes of movie) that mandate fair use. A teacher should begin with an overview of the law on fair use (U.S. Copyright Office, 2009) and the principles behind the law which balance an individual's right to own intellectual property and the public's right to disseminate knowledge and information. Renee Hobbs' book *Copyright Clarity* (2010) is an excellent resource for this conversation. It is not crucial for the first project, but it becomes important for the second.

Six Sounds in Search of an Author

An idea that uses technology, language, and remix is the "Six Sounds in Search of an Author" project. This project introduces students to the creativity of remix by emphasizing the protean nature of same material. This project has been used as an introduction to audio editing as well as an introduction to remix practices. It has been done by graduate students with their students from New Jersey to the Ivory Coast. This was originally a tutorial on remix and audio editing used for graduate education students, but became the basis for an intention contest sponsored by ISTE as well as a recurring state-wide contest by the New Jersey Association for Educational Technology.

Students are given six mp3 sound files, each 5 seconds long, and must mix the sounds into a one-minute story. The sound effects are

- a striking match
- an engine roar
- a heartbeat
- a cricket chirping
- a ringing phone
- a splash.

While some technical knowledge is required to operate Audacity, the freeware sound-editing program used with this project, the program itself is simple and intuitive. All of the resources and a tutorial for this project can be found at

https://sites.google.com/site/sixsoundsproject/

a permanent site designed and maintained by the authors.

Each sound must be used at least once, and no other sound effects may be used. However, the sounds may be altered for length, pitch, volume, etc., and sounds may be used more than once during a story.

The "Six Sounds in Search of an Author" project is an excellent way for students to get creative with a set of resources. It is also illuminating for them to see the different directions other students take with the same rules and sounds – from horror to comedy to romance. It also lays the groundwork for more sophisticated applications for the appropriation and synthesis of other people's material – as in research.

Movie Trailer

The purpose of a movie trailer is to concisely summarize the most important parts of a movie in order to generate the greatest amount of interest from the audience. The "Movie Trailer" project applies the same methods and same goal to either classic works of literature or key events in history. This project has been done in various ways and the main concern for teachers should be to make instructions clear enough for students to follow successfully, but still permit a variety of topics, allowing the student to be creative.

This project has been shown to be most effective with a focus on material with challenging language, especially language of primary sources. Teachers should begin this project by showing students a variety of trailers (Shamburg, n.d.)

http://www.youtube.com/playlist?list=PLD41EDDA0908BB486

in order to engage in a discussion on the functions and conventions of them.

The simplified instructions are based on the mixing narration, original content developed by the students, and primary sources – for example, Shakespeare's lines, facts, or quotes from a primary source.

For this project, students must

- Create a video trailer approximately 2–3 minutes in length.
- Recreate key scenes from the primary source for use in the trailer.
- Include a balanced mix of "original content" (plot descriptions, analysis, crucial background information) with research from the primary source.
- Include appropriate dramatic effects (background music, sound effects, etc.) to generate interest from their target audience.

This has been done successfully for *The History of Pi* for a math class

http://youtu.be/ADhUXbctsek

Shakespeare's *King Lear* for an English class

http://youtu.be/A7hDoOECsSE

and the Dred Scott Decision for social studies

http://is.gd/trailermedia

For social studies, the trailer project is a great way to breathe life into primary sources and to focus on important but undertaught and difficult-to-teach topics. Many primary historical texts have very interesting concepts to offer students, but they often seem overwhelming as a wall of unfamiliar language. As it is the nature of a trailer to highlight compelling or important scenes from a movie, students will have to select important lines from their source material, thus controlling their content as well as applying critical thinking skills. This is a powerful process applied to crucial but undertaught pieces of history – examples such as the Magna Carta, the Whiskey Rebellion, unsung years such as 1799 or 1880, or the Dred Scott Decision work well.

Based on students, objectives, and time, a teacher can offer a spectrum of starting material – from simple instructions to raw content. Even when the teacher provides all the raw content, student projects will vary greatly, as evidenced in the "Six Sounds in Search of an Author" project. Even when given the same materials, students can use their creative imaginations to produce widely varied results.

This project has already been done in teacher workshops and in graduate classes, where the students were given the choice of doing a trailer for a work of their own choice, or doing one on the Dred Scott Decision where the media pieces and primary source had already been selected. At this site

http://is.gd/trailermedia

the authors have provided instructions, related media (e.g., images of Dred Scott, James Buchanan, a city from the mid-nineteenth century, the MGM Lion), and instructions with quotes from a primary source. The primary source in this case was an editorial on the decision from the *Albany Evening Journal*, March 9, 1857 (Furman University, n.d.) and the lines for the trailer were

- The legislation of the republic is in the hands of this handful of slaveholders!
- The conspiracy is nearly completed. The American Congress has no power to prevent the enslavement of men?
- Compact yourselves together for the struggle which threatens your liberty and will test your manhood!

As students use these lines and the material from the hypothetical movie, they are adding context, explanation, analysis, and importance with their original trailer narration.

Approximate time required

Either of these projects can be completed in two to three class sessions. Allow five to six sessions if both projects are done together.

Required resources

- Basic computer resources.
- Tutorials mentioned in the article:

  https://sites.google.com/site/sixsoundsproject/ and
  https://sites.google.com/site/sixsoundsproject/

  All material relating to this article can be found at

  https://sites.google.com/site/educationalremixing/

- Audacity audio-editing software downloadable at

  http://audacity.sourceforge.net/

- Windows Movie Maker video-editing software downloadable at

  http://www.microsoft.com/download/en/details.aspx?id=34

Variations on the basic theme

The concept of remix and appropriation can be introduced with limited or no technology. For example, the remixing text assignment can be done with index cards, if need be – each line of each work written on a single card, which are then literally "remixed". More advanced tools can be introduced with each subsequent project – introducing students not only to the concepts of remix and appropriation, but to the tools of educational technology themselves.

Observations and advice

Looking at the larger picture, however, the appropriation of the ideas and material of others that occurs with remix can be a lens to consider art, history, and cognition. For example, Shakespeare's major plays come from source material, and he lifted lines verbatim from other works (Pettitt, 2007). Michelangelo's Sistine Chapel is a reworking of Biblical figures into the style of Renaissance humanism. And the influence of Locke and Rousseau on the Declaration of Independence and U.S. Constitution is appropriation at its highest. Whenever messages, genres, and materials from separate sources are combined in new and creative ways, remix happens.

Technology from the printing press to the iPad can be seen through the lens of appropriating–combining existing elements and ideas. As Steven Johnson says, the history of many major technological innovations is "more bricolage than breakthrough" (Johnson, 2010, p. 152).

The remix lens can help to spur creativity and research skills. It can help students create transformational and original work as they learn to use the material of others effectively and ethically.

Recommended readings and resources

Furman University (n.d.) *Nineteen Century Documents Project*. Available from *http://history.furman.edu/benson/docs/nyajds57309a.htm*

Gaylor, B. (2008) *RIP: A Remix Manifesto* (film). Available from *http://www.ripremix.com/*

Hobbs, R. (2010) *Copyright Clarity: How Fair Use Contributes to Digital Learning*. Thousand Oaks, CA: Corwin.

Jenkins, H. (2006) *Convergence Culture: Where Old and New Media Collide*. New York: New York University Press.

Johnson, S. (2010) *Where Good Ideas Come From*. New York: Penguin.

Knobel, M., and Lankshear, C. (2010) *DIY Media: Creating, Sharing, and Learning with New Technologies*. New York: Peter Lang.

Knobel, M., and Lankshear, C. (2008, September) Remix: The art and craft of endless hybridization. *Journal of Adolescent & Adult Literacy*, **52**(1).

Lessig, L. (2008) *Remix: Making Art and Commerce Thrive in the Hybrid Economy*. New York: Penguin Press. Available from *http://www.archive.org/details/LawrenceLessigRemix*

New Jersey Association for Educational Technology (2011) *2011–2012 Six Sounds Contest*. Available from *http://njaet.org/njaet/Grants & Contests/2011-2012 Six SoundsContest/*

Pettitt, T. (2007). Before the Gutenberg Parenthesis: Elizabethan-American compatibilities. Available from *http://web.mit.edu/comm-forum/mit5/papers/pettitt_plenary_gutenberg.pdf*

Pink, D. (2008). Tom Friedman on education in the "flat world". *The School Administrator*, **65**(2). Available from *http://www.aasa.org/SchoolAdministratorArticle.aspx?id=5996*

Shamburg, C. (2008) *National Educational Technology Standards for Students: English Language Arts Units for Grades 9–12*. Washington, D.C.: International Society for Technology in Education.

Shamburg, C. (n.d.) *Trailers* (YouTube playlist). Available from *http://www.youtube.com/playlist?list=PLD41EDDA0908BB486*

U.S. Copyright Office (2009) *Fair Use Guidelines*. Washington, D.C.: U.S. Copyright Office.

Supplemental materials

Table 20.1 Rubric for remix evaluation

	Exemplary	**Satisfactory**	**Unacceptable**
Rules of the project (e.g., time limit, number of items)	Followed all parameters	Generally followed most parameters	Did not follow majority of parameters
Synthesis	Individual items transformed into a clearly new production	Individual item generally transformed, but some derivative elements are apparent	New product is derivative of source material, lacking clear distinction from the original items
Creativity	New creation is engaging, informative, and/or provocative for a real audience	New creation is generally informative and engaging	Audience experience and expectations are inadequately addressed
Legal and ethical	Student can clearly articulate how project correlates to all four fair use factors	Student can connect project to fair use in a general way	Student can articulate little or no consideration of fair use

21

Using Twitter to assist students in writing a concise nut graph

Tia C. M. Tyree

Abstract: One of the foundational writing, pitching, and reporting skills students learn in the communication field is how to encapsulate information using the "5Ws", which are Who, What, When, Where, and Why. This assignment provides students with a sample formula to use that will allow them to concisely provide information to an audience and challenge them to do so, both with and without time constraints. Many students are being hired to use social media, including Twitter, as a channel to communicate with a company's stakeholders. This assignment gives students a chance to sharpen their ability to write a concise nut graph (a journalistic paragraph that summarizes the news value of the story) as well as participate in live microblogging with classmates in an effort to sharpen their summarization and audience engagement skills.

Key words: 5Ws, communications, effective writing, microblogging, nut graph, strategic thinking, Twitter, writing.

Discipline/Academic areas addressed

This activity is applicable across many communication disciplines, including journalism, public relations, and marketing. It can also be adapted to any discipline in which concise writing is desirable.

Instructional purpose

The nut graph is an important paragraph for it helps the reader understand the significance or "point" of an article. It offers the "so what" for those reading and provides the reader with the reasons to care about the topic. When constructing a proper nutgraph, it is important to clearly and concisely write the 5W's – Who, What, When, Where, and Why. When journalism students are taught to write inverted pyramid articles for newspapers, they are taught the importance of writing a strong nut graph. For students entering the public relations field, it, too, is important, because students must be able to provide readers with the compelling reason – the "so what"; they should care about a topic and heed a call to action offered on behalf of a client. PR students may also be taught to write summary leads, which contain the same type of information as the nut graph. Therefore, it is important for students to learn to create a well-written nut graph that can summarize, pitch, or describe what will happen, is happening, or has happened.

Student learning outcomes

1. Students will improve their ability to clearly and concisely write a nut graph.
2. Students will learn to engage audiences during a live event.
3. Students will improve their ability to summarize information.

Prerequisite skills and knowledge

Basic computer skills and access to the Internet, which most students possess.

Step-by-step directions

First class

1. Students should bring three newspaper articles written in inverted pyramid style to class.
2. In class, they will be introduced to the Nutgraph Twitter Formula (see below).

3. Each student will be asked to locate the nut graph in the articles. Once done, they should critically think about how to summarize the information and use the formula to develop a concise tweet.

4. Students should share their tweets with one another in small groups.

Second class

1. Students should be reminded of the formula and asked to watch a video screened by the professor in class.

2. Each student should write sample tweets using the Nutgraph Twitter Formula during the screening. The first should provide a preview of the video. The second should be constructed at the midway point and offer a compelling idea within the video, and the last should summarize the video.

3. Tweets should not be sent live. Instead, at the end of the class, the professor should ask students to get into small groups and share their potential tweets, which will provide them with a chance to obtain feedback and constructive criticism about how the information was structured and learn which tweets were the most successful in summarizing information and answering the "so what" question.

Third class

1. The professor should identify one television program students will watch and liveblog.

2. Students should receive a hashtag to use as a means to track tweets.

3. Using the formula, students should again be asked to develop three tweets – one in the beginning, middle, and end of the program. However, the second (middle) tweet should contain a question or a call to action designed to engage the audience and get individuals to respond in some behavioral way on the Internet (e.g., sign a petition, log onto a blog, "like" a Facebook page, retweet a message).

Fourth class

1. The professor should take a few moments in the beginning of class to engage students in a discussion about the liveblogging session.

2. While searching Twitter for the hashtag, students should review tweets to note which ones provided proper summaries and information with the 5W's.

3. Students should also note how many retweets, responses to questions, and other types of audience engagement occurred.

Nutgraph Twitter Formula

- *Who:* Use the handle of the person or entity at the center of the topic (e.g., @PRSA, @HowardU), or shorten the topic to a hashtag (e.g., #Olympics, #Starbucks).
- *What:* This should be five to seven words that summarize what is happening (e.g., releasing a book, holding a fund-raiser for autism, having a grand opening ceremony).
- *When:* This should include the day and time. To simplify the time, the number of the hour and first letter of the time period should be used. For example, 7 p.m. becomes 7p. There are several options for the date. Whenever possible, students should use "today", "tonight", or "tomorrow" as the date. However, if the event is farther away, only the number of the day and month should be used (e.g., 3/12).
- *Where:* Students should note the exact street location or use the Twitter handle of the location (e.g., @STAPLESCenterLA, @TimesSquareNYC).
- *Why:* This is probably the most important aspect of the formula, students should work to summarize the "point" here. Students should work to answer the "so what" question in five to seven words. Here is the optimal chance for public relations students to place the call for action. When structuring tweets designed to engage feedback or behavioral change, this section should include a question or directions on what to do, such as vote, press the "like" sign, comment, or call.
- *Link:* Students are encouraged to use a site, such as

  www.bitly.com

  to shorten links and provide more information.
- *Hashtags:* If possible, hashtags should be used to increase visibility in the "Twittersphere".

- *Examples* (the examples below are fictitious and used for illustrative purposes)
  - @Frontsteps rallying @TheNationalMall on 4/1(9a) to increase awareness + raise money. Support us. Come march. *www.bit.ly./GA6im*
  - @BarackObama speaking at @Frontsteps rally now. He says "any one of us could be homeless one day." Do you agree? #homelessness #poll.
  - 50,000 attend @Frontsteps rally @TheNationalMall today. $100K raised to fight homelessness. See pics/Get recap. *www.bit.ly./GA6im*

How do you know you are meeting your student learning objectives

Students should be able to write a tweet that has all 5W's. This is the foundational principal of the assignment, and it is what is needed to convey basic information. To ensure tweets are clear and concise, they must be readable and free from unnecessary jargon and abbreviations. Ultimately, tweets must provide the essence of the event being captured. They should not allude to points, but be able to stand alone and be understood, regardless of whether a person has seen or been a part of an event being discussed. Finally, engagement on Twitter can be measured by a retweet, answer to a question or a general comment to a tweet. It shows the tweet has grabbed the attention of someone enough in the Twittersphere to prompt a response. What is also critical to engagement is continuing to answer significant tweets from respondents until a mutually agreed-upon end to the conversation or official end to the program, event, or discussion. Students must not send tweets and then ignore those who respond.

Approximate time required

Four class sessions are needed.

Required resources

- *www.Twitter.com*
- *www.bitly.com*
- Television to view program to liveblog.
- Computer or smartphone to access Twitter and Internet.
- Access to a newspaper either hard copy or online.
- Camera or smartphone with a camera, if the student wants to provide photographs.
- *http://support.twitter.com/groups/31-twitter-basics*

Variations on the basic theme

Twitter's 140-character tweet limitations help push students to think critically about exactly what is needed to best explain the important information about an idea, issue, or event. By challenging students in this manner, students are forced to carefully select their words and only use what is essential to convey basic, yet necessary, information. In addition, since Twitter is a social medium, it is an ideal training ground for students to engage audiences, which is a critical aspect of public relations. Live microblogging is becoming a more common way to engage audiences, and it will help students begin to understand and develop the skill.

Developing a concise nut graph using the formula can also be utilized on Facebook. In fact, with the many features that allow students to add rich media, such as videos and audio, Facebook provides another social media platform for students to share ideas and exercise their ability to summarize information in the form of a post.

Observations and advice

When I have asked students to write a tweet that includes the 5W's, they think it is easy. However, when it is time to structure the actual tweet, they run out of space, forget to include one of the essential components, or simply fall short of the goal of summarizing the key information. Further, students do not understand the importance of providing a link for the audience to obtain more information at their leisure, nor do they understand the need to use hashtags or proper Twitter handles for those entities currently using the medium. Once introduced to the formula, students quickly and easily developed "nut graph tweets" without hesitation, because each of the components was readily available to simply "plug in". Further, they could now focus more on how to strategically select the proper words needed to summarize the information, instead of whether they were including all of the required components.

Recommended reading

Botha, D, and Botha, C. (2007) *Public Relations: Fresh Perspectives* (pp. 137–40). Cape Town, South Africa: Pearson.

Ehrlich, K., and Shami, N. S. (2010) Microblogging inside and outside the workplace. *Fourth International Conference on Weblogs and Social Media, Washington, D.C.* Association for the Advancement of Artificial Intelligence.

Honeycutt, C., and Herring, S. C. (2009) Beyond microblogging: Conversation and collaboration via Twitter. *HICSS 2009: Proceedings of the 42nd Hawaii International Conference on System Sciences* (pp. 1–10). Washington, D.C.: IEEE Computer Society.

Huberman, B. A., Romero, D. M., and Wu, F. (2008) Social networks that matter: Twitter under the microscope. *First Monday*, **14**(1).

Jansen, B., Zhang, M., and Chowdury, A. (2009) Twitter power: Tweets as electronic word of mouth. *Journal of the American Society for Information Science*, **60**(11), 2169–88.

Java, A., Song, X., Finin, T., and Tseng, B. (2007) Why we twitter: Understanding microblogging usage and communities. *Proceedings of the Knowledge Discovery and Data Mining (KDD) Workshop, San Jose, CA.* (pp. 56–65).

Kwak, H., Lee, C., Park, H., and Moon, S. (2010) What is Twitter, a social network or a news media? *Proceedings of the 19th International World Wide Web (WWW) Conference, Raleigh, NC.*

Naaman, M., Boase, J., and Lai, C. (2010) Is it really about me? Message content in social awareness streams. *Proceedings of the ACM Conference on Computer Supported Cooperative Work*, pp. 189–92.

Lenhert, A., and Fox, S. (2009) *Twitter and Status Updating* (Pew Internet & American Life Project). Washington, D.C.: Pew Research Center.

Rolnicki, T. E., Tate, C. D., and Taylor, T. (2007) *Scholastic Journalism*. Malden, MA: Blackwell Publishing.

Rich, C. (2010) *Writing and Reporting News: A Coaching Method* (p. 132). Boston, MA: Wadsworth.

Wilcox, D. (2009) *Public Relations Writing and Media Techniques* (Sixth Edition). Boston, MA: Pearson Education.

Part 4
Integrative learning

22

Using simulation, video sharing, and discussion threads for practice-based skills

Lindsay B. Curtin and Laura A. Finn

Abstract: This instructional technique is used to improve the student's ability to demonstrate practice-based skills and use critical thinking to apply complex practices to real-life scenarios. This may be extrapolated to complex skill sets in a variety of disciplines. First, students command an electronic caregiver in a computer-based simulation to practice treating patients. Students receive immediate electronic feedback from the program. Then students are video-recorded completing a live simulation where they demonstrate the complex skill set with a high-fidelity mannequin. Lastly, students view uploaded recordings of their peer teams and assess their peers in an online discussion board. Live simulation after practice with computer simulation improves the teams' ability to achieve the learning objectives in live simulation when compared to live simulation alone. Students report greater satisfaction and increased levels of confidence in their skills compared to the one-step approach. Peer assessment enhances student learning by repetitive review of the complex skill set to evaluate peer teams. The use of technology to support this activity encourages a real-world experience in simulation and provides a convenient and efficient medium to facilitate constructive student feedback.

Key words: critical thinking, clinical practice, demonstration of skills, online discussion board, simulation, video-sharing website.

Discipline/Academic areas addressed

This activity is applicable to disciplines that require hands-on, complex skill sets performed by individuals or teams. It may be especially beneficial in communications and clinical practices.

Instructional purpose

Active learning in a student-centered environment produces superior results to traditional didactic methods. Simulation is an active learning technique placing the student in control of the scenario and offering the ability to truly demonstrate knowledge and skills. Additionally, simulation is beneficial when teaching skills for high-stress, high-risk situations because it offers the safety of being able to make a mistake without the threat of serious consequences, a risk of on-the-job or real-world training.

Students are challenged to use critical thinking skills in a comprehensive activity that assesses their abilities globally, rather than assessing the individual components of skill sets and knowledge. The addition of a computer-based simulation prior to live simulation improves the quality of the live simulation experience, thus improving the efficiency of delivering education, the value of live simulation, and the student experience.

Following the simulations, use of electronic discussion boards allows students time to review skill demonstrations of their peers and reflect on their own problem-solving strategies. Discussion threads can initiate reflection and queries into decision making by peer teams. By observing alternative paths to successful scenarios, critical thinking can be reinforced. Feedback from peers may reinforce skills in applying theoretical knowledge to actual patient scenarios.

Student learning outcomes

1. Diagnose the problem during live simulation scenarios by analyzing data.
2. Select appropriate interventions for each diagnosed problem in the scenario.
3. Perform appropriate interventions at appropriate times using an algorithm.
4. Demonstrate patient care skills by performing them in a live scenario.
5. Improve critical thinking skills during high-stress, high-risk scenarios.
6. Identify best practice scenario outcomes through online peer review.
7. Identify best practice scenario outcomes through self-reflection.

Prerequisite skills and knowledge

Participant skills

- The basic or foundational skills of the complex task and access to actual or simulated tools and environment are required to complete a skill simulation. For example, basic life support skills, a high-fidelity mannequin, and a simulated patient-care setting are required if simulating Advanced Cardiac Life Support (ACLS).
- Access an online video-sharing website, view simulations, and participate in an online discussion board via the learning management system. For example, utilize peer review and feedback to the discussion board thread.

Facilitator skills

- Record simulations using a digital or film recording device.
- Upload recorded simulations to a video-sharing website.
- Establish a discussion board in the learning management system (or other venue).
- Moderate discussion threads in an online discussion board.

Step-by-step directions

These directions are for simulation of an Advanced Cardiac Life Support (ACLS) system. They can be adapted for different disciplines.

1. Students receive a schedule of the class period with learning objectives, a rubric for the live simulation (see Appendix A in "Supplemental materials"), and guidelines for providing written feedback to their peers via discussion threads (Appendix B). This information is uploaded to the learning management system (LMS) and is accessible to students at least until the due date of the peer feedback.
2. Students receive required readings one week in advance of the simulation session. Readings include the *Cardiopulmonary Resuscitation (CPR) Guidelines* and *Advanced Cardiac Life Support (ACLS) Guidelines* published and endorsed by the American Heart Association. The readings are due prior to the class period where computer simulation

and live simulation are performed. This pre-class assignment reviews the prerequisite knowledge that students must have prior to simulation, including medication properties and clinical care algorithms (Swor et. al., 2010; Davis et. al., 2010). Students are encouraged to review the learning objectives before the reading assignments so they may pay special attention to learning diagnoses, properties and therapeutic use of skills and medications, and learning the proper sequence of interventions within the complex skill set. Algorithms and charts from the guidelines may be used during the computer-based and live simulation scenarios since this is a typical practice in real-life clinical situations.

3. Students attend class on the simulation day. Students may complete a ten-question graded quiz immediately before computer simulation to assess baseline knowledge of CPR and ACLS. Competency in these basic principles may contribute to successful completion of learning objectives because complex skill sets will require a strong foundation of basic skills and knowledge. The quiz is optional and may be omitted if the instructor feels that the students will complete pre-class assignments or the students have established competency through other means. Alternatively, a graded pre-activity quiz may be used as an incentive to complete pre-class assignments. Algorithms and charts cannot be used during the quiz.

4. Student teams (four to six students) complete three ten-minute computer-based simulations of increasing difficulty. Computer simulations are similar to the planned live simulation and are completed independently without facilitator assistance. Practicing with computer-based simulation allows additional opportunities to decide medical diagnoses, select appropriate medical interventions and medication, and review the appropriate sequence for delivering patient care. This practice also provides opportunities to practice critical thinking skills by problem solving during a fast-paced, lifelike scenario. Without application in simulation, students only read about CPR and ACLS sequences with little opportunity to practice data analysis and decision making. Live simulation tends to be a high-stress, fast-paced scenario relative to computer-based simulation and didactic lessons. Computer simulation prior to live simulation may improve performance during live simulation by providing opportunities to practice complex skills and by increasing student confidence in the live simulation (Curtin et. al., 2011).

5. Students receive immediate summative feedback about their performance after each computer-based simulation. The computer program includes this feature and provides a summary of all therapeutic decisions made by the team and the reasons they were correct or incorrect. Student teams review the feedback and discuss their performance with their teammates. In this way, the team pinpoints areas for improvement, clarifies confusing points, and uses the feedback to improve performance during the next simulation.

6. After the computer-based simulation, student teams complete one, ten-minute live simulation under the supervision of a facilitator. The facilitator programs the medical condition on the high-fidelity mannequin, controls the sequence of medical conditions, video-records the simulation session for each team, records interventions on the rubric, and provides feedback to the teams once the scenario is completed. After ten minutes have elapsed or the student team feel that they have completed all necessary steps (whichever is first), the facilitator closes the scenario and tells the team if the patient survived.

    a. Live simulation sequence: The student team wait to be called into the session by the facilitator announcing "Code Blue", which is a term used to announce patient distress in many medical facilities. Students assess the patient by employing necessary basic life support skills (the facilitator has programmed the mannequin to be unresponsive). Students diagnose the heart rhythm, select medical interventions and medications, and work together as a team to provide patient care. Appendix A in "Supplemental materials" provides an outline of the sequence of events in an ACLS scenario specific for the medical condition "ventricular tachycardia/fibrillation".

    b. Video recording: The facilitator will set up the video recording device on a tripod or platform ensuring that the recording device will capture all students' actions and voices. The facilitator should begin recording prior to student entry to the simulation room and stop recording before feedback is given to the group. This recommendation reduces the amount of editing required prior to uploading the videos to the video-sharing site, and allows peer groups to provide unique feedback. The facilitator should not hold the recording device unless he/she has a second facilitator recording interventions on the rubric.

c. Evaluation (see Appendix A in "Supplemental materials"). The facilitator will record each intervention, the time of intervention, and provide notes if necessary on a standardized rubric. The rubric provides a fast and easy way to assess the scenario and provide feedback to the team. Additionally, it offers a standardized approach to the simulation scenario and provides the teams guidance prior to the simulation activity. The facilitator scores the scenario and reports the patient outcome to the team once the simulation is complete. Detailed feedback is reserved for online discussion threads, and student teams are encouraged to meet afterward to reflect on their simulation. This self-reflection as a team is similar to Group Teach where groups problem-solve, analyze, review, and self-correct as they work through decision making.

7. After all teams have performed the live simulation, the facilitator uploads each team's video recording of their simulation to a video-sharing website such as YouTube®. Students have access to the videos via this website only, and are not responsible for uploading videos. The facilitator provides hyperlinks or directions to the students to access the video recordings.

    a. Preparing recording for upload

        i. Use appropriate equipment and software to convert recording to an electronic file. This may be easily accomplished if the video recording device uses memory cards instead of cassette tapes or disks.

        ii. Separate the videos to individual files, ensuring that each file is less than 15 minutes in length.

        iii. Title each video file with the name of the group and date of simulation for easy identification.

    b. Uploading to YouTube

        i. Go to *www.youtube.com*

        ii. Sign up for a free YouTube account to enable video sharing.

        iii. Select "Upload", and "select files from your computer". Browse your computer for the first video to share, click upload.

        iv. Title the video when prompted.

v. Select privacy settings. It is recommended to use the most private settings to ensure that only students in the class will receive the links to the videos.

vi. Copy the hyperlink to a document and label the hyperlink with the team name and date of simulation. Save the document with the hyperlink so you can provide links to teams.

vii. Details on uploading videos for specific video-sharing websites can be found by searching "how to upload videos" in the most common Internet search engines. The steps are usually quite easy to follow.

8. The facilitator establishes a discussion board in the LMS. This program will be different depending on the system used at the institution. Most LMSs have tutorials or support staff to assist in setting up a discussion board. It is recommended that students' comments are identifiable and not anonymous to encourage respectful, honest, and constructive critiques. Ensure that the settings of the discussion board are programmed to the specific needs of the class. The facilitator will select the first video to critique and provide the private hyperlink to the first video by typing it in the body of the initiating message of the first discussion thread.

9. Students click on the hyperlink to access the first video from the video-sharing website (they will leave the LMS and be directed to the video-sharing website). Students watch the video in full, noting the appropriateness of the interventions. Students use the guidelines for providing written feedback to form their assessment of peer groups (see Appendix B in "Supplemental materials"). By reviewing peer groups, students analyze peer decisions and work to identify the best practices of the complex skill set. If students review videos as a team, they are able to reflect upon their own scenario while assessing their peers to arrive at a group consensus about how to appropriately and skillfully perform ACLS.

10. Teams (or individuals) write their assessment as a message or response in the discussion thread. Each assessment should follow the guidelines for providing written feedback and should focus on providing objective assessments of skills. When providing subjective feedback, statements should be supported with evidence. Professionalism and respect is mandatory; the facilitator should establish and maintain

professionalism at all times and address unprofessional behavior promptly.

11. Steps 8–10 should be performed to upload and establish a unique discussion thread for each team's video. Students should be able to access videos and provide feedback at any time prior to the due date of feedback. Teams are encouraged to check the discussion thread that includes their video and discuss feedback within their team.

12. Once all simulation and assessment is complete teams may be scored. Reserve scores until all assessment is complete to encourage unbiased feedback from peers. Teams receive full credit by participating in all assigned simulation and providing a team critique for each assigned video that complies with the provided guidelines (Appendix B). Individuals are scored by their performance on the ten-question quiz.

13. After reading the assessments of their peer groups, teams are encouraged to discuss what they did well and where they can improve. If time permits, students may complete another live simulation to incorporate peer feedback and practice the skill set one more time. Through reading, quizzes, and repeated computer simulation students build their foundation of knowledge about CPR and ACLS. Through live practice in mannequin-based simulation, students apply knowledge and gain tactile experience that is very similar to a real-world scenario. Peer review and feedback helps teams improve themselves by a repeated review of the algorithms, medications, and skill sets.

Approximate time required

- Pre-reading and student preparation: 1–3 hours (out of class).
- Quiz: 10–20 minutes (in class).
- Part 1: computer simulations are approximately 10 minutes per simulation – three simulations recommended (30 minutes total, in class).
- Part 2: live simulations are approximately 10 minutes per simulation – one to two simulations recommended – time will vary depending upon the number of facilitators available to lead simulations and the number of simulations that can occur simultaneously (in class).

- Part 3: each critique should be 15–30 minutes which includes viewing the 10-minute simulation – time will vary depending upon the number of critiques required for each team (out of class).
- Total in-class time: one 2-hour class period to complete all simulations.
- Total out-of-class time for participants (assuming 12 groups with 12 critiques completed individually): 4–10 hours.

Required resources

- Computers and appropriate software to support the skill set: MicroSim™ software used for computer simulation (Laerdal Medical AS, Stavanger, Norway).
- Mannequin or live simulation equipment: MegaCodeKelly™ mannequin with VitalSim™ (Laerdal Medical AS, Stavanger, Norway).
- Video recording equipment.
- Internet access.
- Online video-sharing account (YouTube preferred due to ease of use, free access, and limited access to the public).
- Learning management system or access to a discussion board.

Variations on the basic theme

This technology originally was used to teach clinical interventions in the case of cardiac arrest in a simulated intensive care unit; however, this concept is appropriate in situations where students need to learn real-life skills and practice them in a low-risk situation. The underlying theme is a three-step sequential practice where the first step is performed on the computer, the second step is performed live, and the third step involves participation in the evaluation of peers.

Quizzes are included as a student incentive to complete the out-of-class preparation and encourage mastery of the basic skills prior to completing the simulations. Quizzes may be omitted if necessary.

If computer simulation software is not available, moderators could develop multimedia slide presentations that walk the student through the scenario. Tools with multiple endings are favored over a simple stepwise process. For example, if the student selects option A the student is taken to slide #1, or if the student selects option B he/she is taken to slide #2. In this way, there are different consequences for each decision. Feedback may be programmed into the slide presentation to discuss final results of each pathway. Computer simulations add value to the live simulations, but may be omitted if necessary.

If high-fidelity mannequins are not available for live clinical simulations, patient actors could be used instead. Live simulations may be conducted with the equipment that would normally be used for that particular skill set. For example, if simulating a collection of field samples, collection equipment may be very similar to, if not the true, equipment used in the field. Live simulations are the most valuable exercise in this learning activity.

If video sharing via Internet-based video-sharing or social media websites is not preferred due to privacy or other sensitive issues, videos may be uploaded to a learning management system with password-protected access. Alternatively, videos may be made into hard copies to distribute or shown in a large group setting from one recording. Video recording is highly recommended in order to facilitate critique of performances.

Discussion boards may take place in a learning management system venue for password-protected access; however, if all students are members of the same social media website, videos could be uploaded to the social media website. In this way, students would be able to provide comments that are linked directly to the uploaded video. Extra measures should be taken to ensure privacy of information and social media profiles prior to participation.

Learning objectives will vary based upon the skill set that is simulated; however, the general learning objective is successful completion of the entire skill set, in the appropriate manner and sequence which will lead to the favored outcome. For example, the patient survives when the live ACLS simulation is completed successfully. A generic activity template is listed below:

Live simulation and student critique

1. Students receive preparatory materials in advance of simulation.

2. Students receive learning objectives for the activity, rubrics for the activity, and guidelines for providing critique of video recordings.
3. A quiz is administered immediately before simulation sessions (optional).
4. Student teams complete three ten-minute computer simulations (optional).
5. Student teams complete one ten-minute live simulation under the supervision of the facilitator. The facilitator records with an audio/video recording device and documents interventions.
6. The facilitator uploads team recordings to the video-sharing website after all teams have completed the simulation.
7. The facilitator establishes a discussion board and begins discussion threads for each of the recordings.
8. All participants provide feedback on assigned recordings.
9. After all recordings are viewed and critiqued, teams may repeat the simulation (optional).
10. Teams are scored according to pre-established team objectives.
11. Participants are scored according to pre-established individual objectives.

Observations and advice

Simulation engages students while providing "hands-on" or tactile stimulation to make complex decisions. Students work as a team to practice skills with a program that provides immediate feedback. Subsequent opportunities with the computer simulation allow the team to improve skills based on this feedback in advance of working in the more stressful environment of the live simulation. Live simulation allows the team an opportunity to make decisions in a real-life scenario beyond a paper medical record or case study, and students see first hand the value and impact of their skill sets.

The majority of students reported enjoying the simulation. Students are more confident when performing the live simulation after computer-based simulation and prefer to complete the computer session before completing the live simulation. Pre-reading alone was not as effective as pre-reading and computer simulation prior to live simulation in achieving learning outcomes. Instructors often expect that reading alone, or foundational knowledge, will ensure that students may successfully apply knowledge and skills. From this technology we realize that practice with computer scenarios can greatly improve success when performing live simulation. Computer simulation increases the value of live simulation by encouraging repeated practice and conserving facilitator time and live simulation equipment.

Engaging students in peer critique encourages peer-to-peer teaching while providing additional learning opportunities each time an individual provides feedback. By providing strengths and weaknesses of each recording, students review, dissect, and summarize the complex skill multiple times. Students receive the added benefit of learning constructive feedback and peer-to-peer coaching.

Video-sharing technology allows each student to view the recordings on his or her time and encourages pausing, rewinding, and replaying. Students may critique anytime and anyplace with Internet access which increases the student-friendliness of the activity. Using online discussion boards has similar benefits in that students can provide feedback when it is convenient for them. Furthermore, students have immediate access to the comments of their peers and may review feedback an unlimited number of times to improve their skills.

Using video sharing, social media, and discussion boards increases the convenience, efficiency, and conservation of resources and facilitator time. Students are often skilled in using these technologies and may prefer operating in the electronic arena.

Recommended reading

Cooper, J. B., and Taqueti, V. R. (2004) A brief history of the development of mannequin simulators for clinical education and training. *Qual Saf Health Care*, **13**(Suppl. 1), i11–i18.

Curtin, L. B., Finn, L. A., Czosnowski, Q. A., Whitman, C. B., and Cawley, M. J. (2011) Computer-based simulation training to improve learning outcomes in mannequin-based simulation exercises. *American Journal of Pharmaceutical Education*, **75**(6), 113.

Davis, D., Sinz, E., Morrison, L. J., Silvers, S. M., Passman, R. S. et al. (2010) Adult basic life support: 2010 American Heart Association Guidelines for Cardiopulmonary Resuscitation and Emergency Cardiovascular Care. *Circulation*, 122, 729–67.

Lee, J., Sobieraj, D., and Kuti, E. (2010) Student measurement of blood pressure using a simulator arm compared with a live subject's arm. *American Journal of Pharmaceutical Education*, **74**(5).

Mieure, K. D., Vincent, W. R., Cox, M. R., and Jones, M. D. (2010) A high-fidelity simulation mannequin to introduce pharmacy students to advanced cardiovascular life support. *American Journal of Pharmaceutical Education*, **74**(2).

Orr, K. (2007) Integrating virtual patients into a self-care course. *American Journal of Pharmaceutical Education*, **71**(2).

Resnik, D. (2005) Using electronic discussion boards to teach responsible conduct of research science and engineering. *Ethics*, **11**, 617–30.

Scalese, R. J., Obeso, V. T., and Issenberg, B. (2007) Simulation technology for skills training and competency assessment in medical education. *Journal of General Internal Medicine*, **23**(Suppl. 1), 46–9.

Seybert, A., Laughlin, K., Benedict, N., Barton, C., and Rea, R. (2006) Pharmacy student response to patient-simulation mannequins to teach performance-based pharmacotherapeutics. *American Journal of Pharmaceutical Education*, **70**(3).

Steadman, R. H., Coates, W. C., Huang, Y. M., Matevosian, R., Larmon, B. R. et al. (2006). Simulation-based training is superior to problem-based learning for the acquisition of critical assessment and management skills. *Critical Care Medicine*, **34**(1), 151–7.

Swor, R. A., Cave, M., Hazinski, E., Lerner, B., Rea, T. D. et al. (2010) Adult basic life support: 2010 American Heart Association Guidelines for Cardiopulmonary Resuscitation and Emergency Cardiovascular Care. *Circulation*, **122**, S685–705.

Wayne, D. B., Didwania, A., Feinglass, J., Fadulu, M. J., Barsuk, J.H. et al. (2008) Simulation-based education improves quality of care during cardiac arrest team responses at an academic teaching hospital: A case-control study. *CHEST*, **133**, 56–61.

Wiecha, J. M., Gramling, R., Joachim, P., and Vanderschmidt, H. (2003) Collaborative e-learning using streaming video and asynchronous discussion boards to teach the cognitive foundation of medical interviewing: A case study. *Journal of Medical Internet Research*, **5**(2).

Supplemental materials

Appendix A

Table 22.1 Rubric for mannequin-based simulation

Mannequin-Based Simulation Collection Sheet and Rubric (to be completed by facilitator during live simulation)					*(for pulseless ventricular tachycardia/ fibrillation – according to 2010 American Heart Association Guidelines)*
Group code:	Time				NOTES
Task			Correct	Designation	
Checked responsiveness			Y/N	minor	
Called for help			Y/N	minor	
Checked pulse			Y/N	MAJOR	
		Rate of compressions/ breath (30:2)	Correct	Designation	
Started compressions			Y/N	MAJOR	Must start CPR by 2 min and cannot interrupt compressions by more than 30 s at a time
Administered breaths			Y/N	MAJOR	
Resumed compressions (second round)			Y/N	MAJOR	
Administered breaths (second round)			Y/N	MAJOR	
Resumed compressions (third round)			Y/N	MAJOR	

Mannequin-Based Simulation Collection Sheet and Rubric (to be completed by facilitator during live simulation)					*(for pulseless ventricular tachycardia/ fibrillation – according to 2010 American Heart Association Guidelines)*
Group code:	Time				NOTES
Administered breaths (third round)			Y/N	MAJOR	
		Rhythm	Correct	Designation	
Identified rhythm			Y/N	MAJOR	
Shocked (if appropriate)			Y/N	MAJOR	
Identified rhythm (second round)			Y/N	MAJOR	
Shocked (2nd round)			Y/N	MAJOR	
Identified rhythm (third round)			Y/N	MAJOR	
Shocked (third round)			Y/N	MAJOR	
		Medication and dose	Correct	Designation	
Administered vasopressor		1)	Y/N	MAJOR (first dose)	Must give epinephrine 1 mg IV/IO or vasopressin 40 units IV/IO after first shock
Administered vasopressor or antiarrhythmic		2)	Y/N	minor	Must state that 3 min have elapsed from last vasopressor if giving second dose of vasopressor

Appendix B Guidelines for providing written assessment (of peer videos)

Successful completion of each critique includes answering the required questions and following the set rules

Objectives of peer review

By assessing peer videos for appropriate interventions and sequencing of skills, students have an additional opportunity after live simulation to learn and review the complex skill set of Advanced Cardiac Life Support. After live simulation students have their own experience to reference as they view peer performance. Students can compare and contrast each video to their understanding of the process. This is another way of student-to-student teaching because the videos are essentially a demonstration of those skill sets. Students can learn from visualizing both appropriate treatment sequences and from seeing the consequences of inappropriate treatment. Increasing the number of videos for each student to review increases the opportunity for students to review ACLS skills in this low-risk environment.

Learning objectives specific to the peer critique

1. Diagnose the problem during the live simulation scenario by analyzing data – performed by verifying if the group appropriately identified the ACLS heart rhythm.

2. Select appropriate interventions for each diagnosed problem in the scenario – performed by verifying if the group appropriately administered non-medication and medication-related interventions during the scenario.

3. Perform appropriate interventions at appropriate times using an algorithm – performed by verifying if the group intervened in the appropriate sequence.

4. Improve critical thinking skills during high-stress, high-risk scenarios – possible through the repeated review of peer groups and the repeated learning and critique of how other groups intervened.

5. Identify best practice scenario outcomes through online peer review – performed by submitting an assessment for each assigned video.

6. Identify best practice scenario outcomes through self-reflection –

performed by reviewing peer feedback and discussing outcomes with peer group.

Answer at least one of the following questions (set 2): 40%

(1) Did the group diagnose the patient's problem correctly and efficiently? What was done well? What could be improved?

(2) Did the group select appropriate interventions for each problem and intervene at appropriate times? What was well done? What could be improved?

And answer at least one of the following questions (set 2): 40%

(3) What were your observations on how the team performed in this scenario?

(4) Overall what did the team do well? What are your concerns? What suggestions do you have for improvement?

Rules: 20%

- Use appropriate medical terminology.
- Use respectful and professional language.
- When presenting a concern, make a suggestion to address your concern.
- When presenting a subjective assessment, include at least one piece of evidence to tell the group why you assessed them in that particular way.

23

Using Facebook Mobile as a tool to create a virtual learning community for pre-service teachers

Erkkie Haipinge

Abstract: This teaching strategy focuses on students' use and integration of different information and communication technologies (ICTs) in teaching and learning. Facebook is utilized as a Web 2.0 tool available via mobile phone to create and facilitate a virtual learning environment for pre-service teachers. Facebook is used to connect pre-service teachers with practicing teachers in the field. Through online discussions and postings, pre-service teachers reflect on their learning while observing practicing teachers who reflect on their teaching. The interaction between the groups facilitates an interface between educational technology theory and practice. This enriches both groups by improving both learning and practice. This activity was used in a teacher education course called "Integrated Media and Technology Education" (IMTE) at the Windhoek College of Education in Namibia, Africa.

Key words: community of practice, Facebook, Facebook Groups, mobile/cell phones, online social networks, virtual learning community.

Discipline/Academic areas addressed

Education, educational technology, and other disciplines utilizing clinical work.

Instructional purpose

Due to the digital divide, access to computers and Internet in Namibia is highly limited. Similarly, the digital divide within the country is just as prominent with huge disparities in access to technology and connectivity between urban and rural, as well as between the wealthy and the poor. However, as elsewhere in Africa, there is tremendous growth in ownership of mobile phones and the expansion of mobile telecommunication networks. As a result many students and teachers own mobile phones with Internet connectivity or, at minimum, text messaging. The most popular social network tool used is Facebook; however, little has been done from a pedagogical perspective to harness the potential of both access to and use of Facebook by students and especially young teachers. Most of the teaching of technology integration courses has focused on teaching about, and the use of, technology. Little or no attention has been paid to using technology for teaching and learning. This project gives students and teachers an opportunity to do exactly that.

Using the Group facility on Facebook, a learning community is created which serves as a discussion platform for students to interact with each other as well as with teachers. The goal is to promote the construction and sharing of knowledge through reflection and discussion, to connect theory and practice, and to teach students and teachers the potential of Facebook as a learning tool. Facebook was chosen on the basis that it was the most popular amongst the learning group, was easily accessible through mobile phones, and was most convenient due to familiarity with its interface.

Student learning outcomes

1. Students will connect educational technology theory to practice through their online discussions with practicing teachers.

2. Students will explore educational and professional development uses of social networking tools such as Facebook through hands-on experience.

3. Students will become familiar with codes of conduct in online discussion contexts.

4. Students will engage in an online learning community and share ideas and skills with colleagues.

5. Students will learn the skills and value of reflection by observing practicing teachers engaged in these activities.

6. Students will analyze and synthesize online discussion threads and produce a report on current educational technology beliefs and practices in their learning community.

Prerequisite skills and knowledge

- Basic computer and Internet skills
- Word-processing skills
- Mobile phone texting skills
- Facebook use skills.

Step-by-step directions

1. Create a Facebook Group on the Facebook social network and add students as friends as well as to the Group (ask students to add fellow education students).
2. Have students participate in a "practice" Facebook Group discussion via their mobile phones or computers, to ensure that they all have the skills and technology access to complete the assignment.
3. Use college records to add previous students (who are now practicing or in-service teachers) to the Group (in my case, many of the former students were already friends on my Facebook network).
4. Create a student online engagement continuous monitoring sheet (using spreadsheet software or any other suitable application) containing a list of all students and the key student learning outcomes. The instructor can then use the sheet to monitor students' activities online. This is particularly suitable for SLOs 1, 3, and 4 (as listed earlier). The spreadsheet can simply indicate whether a learning outcome has been fulfilled or not. (Note that the assessment rubric in "Supplemental materials" focuses on selected key aspects of the online engagement, whether they have been carried out, and to what degree.)
5. Simultaneously, students are paired (by the instructor) with teachers teaching the same subjects as their majors (e.g., a secondary-grade

math education student will be paired with a secondary-grade math teacher). Each pair will have a minimum of three critical discussions, including at least one discussion on an educational technology theory, a student's post, and a teacher's post on technology integration in the particular subject. This will be done throughout the three weeks and into the fourth and final week of the online interaction:

(a) the instructor suggests a reasonable range of educational technology theory issues as discussed in the course. From the suggested or related issues, the student and teacher pairs choose one to discuss by relating it to their subject area;

(b) the teacher writes a post on the link between the theory and the integration made which the student then comments on.

6. For three weeks, practicing teachers are requested to share a weekly post on the Facebook Group critically reflecting on their teaching of their specific subject content and how they integrate (or not) particular technologies. They will be encouraged to interact with students once a week and answer any questions that students may post:

   (a) teachers reflect on a lesson/lessons taught in the course of a week and make a post on the Facebook Group (this may be done on a Wednesday or Thursday afternoon or evening) using the following as a guide:

      - they briefly state what the lesson was about and how technology was integrated *or* why technology was *not* integrated;

      - they explain briefly how the technology used was an advantage and what pedagogical or learning challenges it created *or* explain what technology could have been useful as well as the challenges it could have posed you.

   (b) Teachers read the comments made on the post by the student teacher they are mentoring and engage in a discussion. They can also comment and have a discussion on the student's own post.

7. For the same three weeks, students post weekly reflections on what they are learning in the IMTE course (theory, practical skills, or ideas on how to integrate technology in teaching) that they share on the

Facebook Group. The reflection can be done either through starting a discussion or commenting on an existing discussion thread:

(a) students choose the most interesting learning concept for themselves during the week (this could be a theoretical concept, a skill, or an idea discussed in or outside class);

(b) while reflecting individually or discussing with a friend, students consider the relevance of the learning aspect to their future teaching and continued professional learning; the advantages it may have for the facilitation of student learning; economical/social/cultural or ideological bias the learning aspect may be showing, implying, or perpetuating; and/or what ethical issues the students may be grappling with in their roles as teachers with regard to the learning aspect in question;

(c) students post their thoughts on the Facebook Group page; and/or

(d) comment on the post made by their mentor teacher on the Group page by relating what has been said with the course materials and by thinking about alternative ways of using the technology described or using alternative technologies to the one used. They engage with the teacher in a discussion on either of the postings.

8. In the fifth week students will be paired with each other, again on the basis of their subject majors, to evaluate their online interaction and identify main issues and themes:

   (a) in pairs, students scan through each other's discussion threads on the Group and identify the following: technologies teachers used and/or did not use and reasons given; issues addressed in student–teacher discussions; learning aspects students shared;

   (b) students discuss their findings and suggest what they could have done differently.

9. In the same pairs, the students will compile an academic essay or report focusing on the following essay-writing guidelines for students:

   (a) their personal learning experiences as they explored the theory, ideas, and skills of technology integration;

   (b) the teachers' practical use or nonuse of technology in their teaching;

(c) the relationship between theory and practice of technology integration in their subjects;

(d) recommendations on the technology integration course's curriculum;

(e) reflection on their use of Facebook as a tool for facilitating interactive learning and creating learning communities (similarly, teachers, though not for assessment purposes, were requested to share a reflection on the process and activities);

(f) an abstract (80–120 words) to be posted on the Facebook Group to share with teachers and fellow students.

Note: Just as in points 8(a) and 8(b) above, 9(a)–9(e) make reference to and integrate the online discussions and engagement to support arguments made in the essay. The guidelines in 9 above serve as criteria for grading the essay. The essay is graded as simply Pass or Fail. It must meet all criteria to be graded as a Pass.

10. The essay is either printed out or emailed for assessment.

Approximate time required

- The weekly postings will take 5–10 minutes (students will be encouraged to first organize their ideas on paper).
- The whole project runs over 6 weeks (the final 2 weeks focusing on analysis of discussion posts and formulating the essay).
- Editing and completion/printing of the essays takes 2–4 classes, depending on the size of class and technical issues encountered.
- Final posting of abstracts takes 10–15 minutes.

Required resources

- *http://www.facebook.com/* or *http://m.facebook.com/*
- Mobile phone with Internet or texting capabilities *or* smartphone with Facebook app *or* Internet-connected computer.
- Word-processing program.

- Printer.
- How to create Facebook Groups tutorial:

  https://www.facebook.com/groups

Variations on the basic theme

Facebook was chosen for its easy access through mobile phones due to the limited access to computers or Internet-connected computers in Namibia. Similarly, Twitter can be used for reflections and discussions although this would not display as effectively as a threaded discussion. Depending on the main goal of the project or exercise, blogs and Google+ can also fulfill the same purpose. The goal is to use a platform that enables people to connect to each other as a community, and to enable easy access to posted materials.

In the future, teachers will rely more and more on online technologies for their professional development and engagement in professional learning communities. It is important that these opportunities are accessible to educators around the world, particularly as mobile technologies allow those from previously disadvantaged locations and communities to join the global conversation.

Observations and advice

When doing this kind of assignment with my classes I have found that it can be very successful in a developing country like Namibia, and in other countries in Africa where access to computers and the Internet is still limited, but where the growth in mobile telephony is very strong. Through my observations, many students in Namibia with Internet-enabled mobile phones use Facebook for social and amusement purposes, but little has been done to explore and investigate possibilities for its educational value. I think that it can be a powerful tool not just for carrying out learning projects but also for creating long-term learning communities for knowledge creation and sharing.

Challenges in carrying out this project may initially be in convincing students to take seriously, as an implement for learning, a tool that they have long used for triviality. Many students do not have Internet-enabled mobile phones. In such cases they borrow friends' or family members' phones, or simply use the college computer lab for Internet access. It was also difficult to convince the college administration to unblock Facebook, which was deemed disruptive and was blocked on the college local network.

It is advisable to create a new Facebook profile/account specifically for educational purposes. The same may be recommended for students. In most cases it is not a good idea to "friend" one's students; however, the good part is that as a teacher educator one does not need to befriend all students to enable them to join a Facebook Group as they can invite each other in a chain reaction manner. Simply ensure that the Group settings are suitable for that.

Overall it takes time to plan and requires negotiation skills in persuading teachers to share their reflection ideas online. It was not particularly difficult in the Namibian context as most teachers are involved in pre-service teacher training, with many acting as support teachers (mentors) when student teachers carry out school-based studies (practice teaching). Thus the sharing of ideas for teachers was simply an online extension of the mentoring responsibilities they were already engaged in.

Recommended reading

Anderson, P. (2007, February) What is web 2.0? Ideas, technologies and implications for education. *JISC Technology and Standards Watch*. Available from *http://www.scribd.com/doc/300024/*

Brady, K.P., Holcomb, L.B, and Smith, B.V. (2010) The use of alternative social networking sites in higher educational settings: A case study of the e-learning benefits of Ning in education. *Journal of Interactive Online Learning*, **9**(2), 151–70. Available from *http://www.ncolr.org/jiol/issues/viewarticle.cfm?volID=9&IssueID=29&ArticleID=149*

Burt, R. (2011, May 11) The why and how of using Facebook for educators—No need to be friends at all! Available from *http://theedublogger.com/2011/05/11/the-why-and-how-of-using-facebook-for-educators-no-need-to-be-friends-at-all/*

Hendricks, N. (2012) An E-Learning collaborative environment: Learning within a masters in education. *International Journal on E-Learning*, **11**(1), 39–53. Available from *http://www.editlib.org/p/33297*

Hodes, C., Pritz, S., Kelley, P., and Foster, J. (2011) Developing an online community of in-service teachers. *Contemporary Issues in Technology and Teacher Education*, **11**(3), 313–23. Available from *http://www.editlib.org/f/36082*

Kale, U., Brush, T., Bryant, A., and Saye, J. (2011) Online communication patterns of teachers. *Journal of Interactive Learning Research*, **22**(4), 491–522. Available from *http://www.editlib.org/p/33247*

Morgaine, W. (2008) Drive belonging and engagement in the classroom using Facebook. Available from *http://openedpractices.org/resource/drive-belonging-and-engagement-classroom-using-facebook*

Schunk, D. H. (2009) *Learning Theories: An Educational Perspective* (Fifth Edition). Upper Saddle River, NJ: Pearson Education International.

Ryberg, T., and Christiansen, E. (2008) Community and social network sites as technology enhanced learning environments. *Technology, Pedagogy and Education*, **17**(3), 207–19, doi: 10.1080/14759390802383801.

Vaughan, N., Nickle, T., Silovs, J., and Zimmer, J. (2011) Moving to their own beat: Exploring how students use web 2.0 technologies to support group work outside of class time. *Journal of Interactive Online Learning*, **10**(3), 113–27. Available from *http://www.ncolr.org/jiol/issues/viewarticle.cfm?volID=10&IssueID=33&ArticleID=162*

Yang, S.-H. (2009) Using blogs to enhance critical reflection and community of practice. *Educational Technology & Society*, **12**(2), 11–21. Available from *http://ifets.info/journals/12_2/2.pdf*

Supplemental materials

Appendix A

Table 23.1 Assessment rubric: student Facebook discussion engagement

Criteria	**Exemplary**	**Accomplished**	**Developing**	**Beginning**
Possible points: 18	**4**	**3**	**2**	**1**
Timeline/ posting	Both posting and interaction with the mentor were done on the deadline and timeline set	Both posting and interaction with mentor were done within the deadline set	Posting and interaction occurred 1–2 days after the set deadline	Posting and interaction occurred 3–4 days after the suggested deadline
Participation	A posting made at length and expanded on with a different line of thought; comments on mentor post show variance in ideas	A posting made and expanded on with additional comment; two comments made on mentor's post	A posting made as well as comment on the mentor teacher's post; little depth or variance in ideas	Only one posting or comment made
Content	More than one learning aspect discussed and related to the mentor's topic; mentor's topic strongly related to student learning experience	A particular learning aspect discussed and related to the teacher's topic; mentor's topic is discussed with limited relation to own learning	A particular learning aspect (theory, skill, or pedagogical approach) discussed but not related to mentor's topic	A vague learning aspect identified with little discussion; no engagement with mentor's topic

Criteria	Exemplary	Accomplished	Developing	Beginning
Possible points: 18	**4**	**3**	**2**	**1**
Critical engagement	Evidence of critical reflection of student's role in application of technology, theory in teaching; ethical, cultural/ ideological issues discussed; mentor's ideas questioned and alternatives suggested and defended with reference to theory or own experience	There is evidence of critical evaluation of learning aspect in terms of both future application, critical issues or questions; mentor's ideas are challenged or alternatives suggested	Discussion of learning aspect addressed at least one critical issue – bias or ethical concern; discussion on mentor's post questions or suggests an alternative	Learning aspect discussed with no reflection on its implications for teaching/ professional career

24

Using social software tools to facilitate peer e-mentoring and self-reflection among students on practicum

Mark J. W. Lee and Catherine McLoughlin

Abstract: In this activity, students from a single cohort undertaking practicum placement at geographically dispersed locations form online, peer-to-peer mentoring relationships in which they assist and support one another with the help of Web-based social software tools. They undertake structured tasks requiring them to create weekly blog entries and voice recordings of critical incidents, and to invite comment on their responses and reactions from peers. Through dialogue, students learn not only about the profession they are entering, but also about themselves as practitioners. By pooling expertise and tuning in to one another's experiences, they become active members of a community while simultaneously reflecting on and refining their own professional knowledge and skills in preparation for future employment. Although the activity was originally conceived for use with student teachers, it can easily be adapted and applied to industry or field practicums for noneducation majors.

Key words: blogging, community of practice, e-mentoring, fieldwork, online learning community, professional learning, peer mentoring, podcasting, practicum, Wimba Voice Board.

Discipline/Academic areas addressed

The activity may be customized to suit the needs of any academic program that contains field practicum or work placements, in any discipline.

Instructional purpose

Many pre-service academic programs in disciplines such as teacher education, nursing, and social work require students to complete a series of field practicum experiences before they become qualified to work in their chosen profession. When on practicum, for the first time in their program the students are separated from their instructors and classmates and expected to work independently. It is at this time that they are most in need of emotional support and encouragement as well as access to timely advice and feedback on their professional competencies. For many students the sense of isolation experienced while on practicum contrasts sharply with the supportive environment they have become accustomed to at university. During this critical period, time and place constraints often act as an impediment to the maintenance of successful mentoring relationships. Online or e-mentoring between the students using Web-based social software tools can help overcome these constraints while fostering the growth of open, supportive relationships and friendships that transcend the walls of the institution. The dialogue that emerges from these peer-mentoring relationships can develop participants' self-awareness, reflective and collaborative/communicative skills, while at the same time requiring command of a range of cyber or e-literacies. This is reflective of the increased importance of personal and professional digital connectivity, as evident in the human resource development and recruitment strategies being adopted by many organizations worldwide.

Student learning outcomes

1. Students will demonstrate an ability to reflect critically on their own professional practice and experiences, and to articulate their reflections in both written and oral form.

2. Students will display an awareness of the importance of accessing and drawing upon professional learning networks and resources to support their practice.

3. Students will become active participants in an online community, networking and forming relationships with their peers and learning both with and from one another.

4. Students will develop a range of interpersonal communication skills,

including the ability to apply active listening techniques, to show empathy with and respect for differing points of view, and to solicit and accept constructive feedback from others.

5. Students will attain competence in using Web-based social software tools to communicate with and assist one another through different modalities (e.g., text and voice).

Prerequisite skills and knowledge

Before commencing the activity, students should possess basic computer and Internet proficiency. Ideally, if the social software tools that will be used are situated within a learning management system (LMS), as they were in our case, students will have prior experience using that system to access course materials and resources. If students are inexperienced in the use of the software, the instructor should spend some time before the activity assisting them in becoming comfortable with the relevant software tools.

Step-by-step directions

1. At the beginning of the semester, a training session should be conducted in an on-campus classroom or computer lab to ensure all students are familiar with the procedure required to set up their headsets and microphones for use on the computers they will be using while on practicum (e.g., their home computers or personal laptops), as well as to acquaint them with the Web-based tools to be used for the activity. In our case, students used two social software tools embedded within the Blackboard LMS, namely a multiuser blogging tool and a tool called the "Wimba Voice Board" that allows for the creation of threaded, asynchronous audio discussions. At this time, the requirements of the activity should be explained in detail, and students should be given opportunities to seek clarification as needed.

2. Throughout the practicum period, each student should be required to reflect and report on critical incidents he/she encounters, using the nominated social software tools. Our students, who were aspiring primary and secondary school teachers pursuing a Graduate

Diploma of Education with the Australian Catholic University in Canberra, were expected to do this on a weekly basis during the course of their four-week school-based practicum. Each week, they had to write a 200 to 300-word report in the form of a post on the blog, as well as to produce a 90-second Wimba Voice Board recording containing different content to the written report, about a significant incident, issue, or problem that occurred during that week. The report was to include a description of the context of the incident as well as an account of both their actions and those of their students. (A simple handout on critical incident analysis for student teachers is included in Appendix A in "Supplemental materials". It should be straightforward to modify for use in other disciplines.)

3. In addition, students should be encouraged to identify aspects of their practice in which they need advice or assistance, inviting their peers to respond. We asked our students to respond to at least one of their classmates each week, orally as well as in writing, commenting constructively on his/her postings and providing helpful support and suggestions. The author of the original posting in each case was also expected to respond to the feedback received. This aspect of the activity may call for some monitoring and input on the part of the instructors, particularly during the early stages, to encourage productive dialogue and avoid the reinforcement of inappropriate suggestions/comments. The instructors may need to employ strategic questioning to ensure students' reflective processes, and to take steps to stimulate their critical thinking through cueing, prompting, and the provision of appropriate examples. To aid students in evaluating their own performance and in formulating useful, knowledgeable feedback to their peers, it may be useful to devise for their use a concise list of guidelines that directs them back to key principles learned in their classes. When moderating the online discussion, instructors may like to refer students to specific items within these guidelines as a means of gently "steering" and refocusing the dialogue where necessary.

4. At the conclusion of the practicum, students should complete a capstone task in the form of a live presentation or an artifact that can be shared with the entire cohort. Our students each created a two-minute podcast reflecting on the highlights and challenges of their practicum experience. These podcasts were shared with the class at a post-practicum debriefing session. They were also assessed for evidence of critical thinking and reflection, and, in conjunction with

the weekly blog and Voice Board postings, contributed to students' grades for the practicum course. (A sample assessment rubric for the peer-e-mentoring activity appears in Appendix B in "Supplemental materials").

Approximate time required

- Approximately 1 hour is required for the pre-practicum briefing and training session.
- It is estimated that each student needs to devote 90 minutes each week during the practicum period to fulfilling the requirements of the core part of the activity (weekly reflective and e-mentoring tasks), plus a further 2 hours at the end of the practicum period to complete the capstone task.
- 2–3 hours should be allowed for the post-practicum debriefing and sharing of experiences, though this may vary depending on the size of the cohort and the presentation mode that is chosen.

Required resources

- Technological requirements include access to an Internet-connected desktop or laptop computer along with a compatible headset with a built-in microphone for the duration of the practicum.
- Students may optionally also use their mobile devices (e.g., iPods, smartphones, PDAs) to create their podcasts/voice recordings, and may download others' recordings to these devices for listening to on the move.
- Given that one of the goals of the activity is to assist students in reflecting on and evaluating their own practice, it may be beneficial for them to have access to texts and/or readings on reflective practice and professional learning. For example, an excellent resource for student teachers is the book *Reflective Teaching* by Pollard (2008). The author of this book has also compiled a companion volume of readings (Pollard, 2002) and maintains a website at

  http://www.rtweb.info/

containing supplementary material to support his texts, including additional activities, free downloads, and links to further reading. Another book, *Field Experience: A Guide to Reflective Teaching* by Posner and Vivian (2010), is written specifically with teaching practicums in mind.

Variations on the basic theme

The way in which social software tools are used in this activity encourages students to reflect on the professional growth they undergo while on practicum. It also offers a solution to help alleviate the loneliness and feelings of isolation these students experience as a consequence of being assigned to distributed sites. It is the constructive, communicative, and collaborative affordances of the tools, combined with their ease of use and the incorporation of appropriate pedagogical scaffolding, that hold the key to this activity's success.

While the activity could quite conceivably be carried out solely using text-based media, we believe that part of the power of our e-mentoring approach lies in the psychoacoustic benefits arising from the use of audio as a communication medium. Durbridge (1984) argues that "As compared with a written text, the spoken word can influence both cognition (adding clarity and meaning) and motivation (by conveying directly a sense of the person creating those words)" (p. 100). Power (1990) concurs: "The ability to adjust or modulate [the] frequencies [of our voice] allows us to communicate in a correct and artistic way with words and sounds ... the ability to adjust intonation, inflexion, phrasing, pacing, volume, loudness and timbre distinguishes a spoken text from a written one" (p. 44). He goes on to state that "spoken words through heightened intonations or subtle nuances can communicate ... emotions and create a sense of intimacy at the same time" (p. 44). In our context, we believe the use of voice recordings led to a greater sense of immediacy and social presence than would have arisen from the use of the blog alone, although this has yet to be validated empirically.

The university's LMS was chosen as the platform for hosting the social software tools in our case as it provided students with easy access to the tools within an online environment that was safe and familiar to them. Nevertheless, there are myriad open, Web 2.0–based social software tools available on the Internet that may also be appropriated for the purposes of the activity. For example, many popular social networking sites like Facebook and Ning that many students already use for social and entertainment purposes can be used to create the type of online community and facilitate the types of peer-to-peer dialogue, exchange, and sharing that this activity seeks to promote (English and Duncan-Howell, 2008). Alternatively, dedicated blogging platforms (e.g., WordPress, MovableType, TypePad) could be used for the text-based aspects of the activity, and tools like Voxopop and Audioboo could be employed for the voice recordings. Voxopop

http://www.voxopop.com/

provides voice-based discussion boards similar to the Wimba Voice Board, and, like the Wimba Voice Board, does not require the installation of specialized software as it runs in a standard Web browser. Audioboo

http://audioboo.fm/

allows digital recordings of up to five minutes long, called "boos", to be recorded via a smartphone (iPhone or Android) application, which can then be posted on the Audioboo website, where users have their own pages or channels similar to those seen on YouTube and Twitter. Users without compatible smartphones can upload their boos directly through the website or via email.

While student-generated video clips or video blogs (vlogs) may be added to the technology framework for the activity, the extra technical overhead and resource requirements this would impose need to be weighed up against the anticipated pedagogical benefits that would or could accrue as a result. Importantly, students would also need to be thoroughly informed and educated about the legal considerations involved in filming video material within workplaces. They might face difficulty in obtaining consent from those being filmed (and parental consent in the case of minors); this alone could make it prohibitive to produce anything other than one-person, talking head videos.

Finally, a variation on this activity might involve complementing and augmenting the asynchronous communication modes and tools with synchronous facilities that give students real-time access to their peers and instructors. Audio and videoconferencing applications such as Skype and FaceTime as well as instant messaging programs such as Google Talk, iChat, AOL Instant Messenger, Windows Live Messenger, and Yahoo! Messenger are among those that immediately come to mind as being suitable for this purpose; all have desktop as well as mobile versions. A more recent service from Google called Google+ Hangouts

http://plus.google.com/hangouts/

allows users to set up ad hoc virtual spaces in which a maximum of ten people can concurrently participate in a voice and video chat.

Observations and advice

Both formal evaluation data we have gathered through questionnaires and focus groups as well as informal feedback we have received attest strongly to the effectiveness of our adopted approach to supporting our students' development through opportunities for peer-to-peer learning and reflection. Student comments focused on the benefits of sharing their practicum experiences through the social software tools; the majority of these comments were related to aspects of establishment of common ground, engagement with others, and building of rapport. During the project, Web-based resources and communication tools were seen by the student teachers as a way to meet the variety of their needs, and proved to be both a catalyst and a support for the development of an online community. More specifically, the provision of the Voice Board and blog enabled students to communicate while on practicum, to exchange ideas, reflect on experience, and develop a sense of professional identity. Evidence from the student podcasts also demonstrates that the participants understood this transformation of identity, and became increasingly aware of their professional roles as teachers during the course of the practicum. Furthermore, throughout the activity, they engaged in roles in which they mentored and supported one another and took responsibility for furthering their collective expertise.

In retrospect, our students found the sharing of voice-recorded episodes of classroom incidents while on teaching practicum to be highly motivating, reassuring, and supportive. They were less excited, however, about the use of the blog, on which they were also required to produce written accounts of the critical incidents. In this sense, they felt there was overlap in the activities, and some did not fully understand the distinction between the blogging and Voice Board components. In future iterations of the exercise, we would consider a similar structure for describing the teaching incidents in the audio recordings, but focus on critical reflection in the blog postings, together with links to relevant literature on pedagogy and classroom management. The main issue of concern here is how to stimulate students to reflect deeply on their experiences and to comment constructively on the postings and contributions of others.

Our students additionally had to identify areas in which they required advice or assistance, inviting their peers to respond. Not all of them asked questions of others, but some did so using the blog. We initially paired our students up in dyads and asked them to provide feedback primarily to their allocated partners, but they often chose to reply to more than one person according to their level of interest in the matter. This situation was, in fact, more productive than the paired responses that had originally been planned, and generated a larger volume of postings and comments. The participants appeared to be quite open and ready to respond to one another in this way, particularly when they had had similar experiences. For this reason, we are likely to consider omitting the set pairing of students in future iterations. In "real-world" communities of practice, choices are available to participants in terms of who they relate to; similarly, there may be value in allowing a degree of flexibility and autonomy within an online community designed to support the transition of students from formal learning environments into the workplace and industry.

We had also hoped that our students would provide helpful comments and support to one another in ways that connected theory to practice. This posed a major challenge, as it called for them to consider theoretical aspects of pedagogy and classroom management prior to coming up with informed advice. Many of them had limited success in achieving this goal. They admitted that they were not always able to provide useful practical advice, although most displayed empathy in their postings. In order to ensure better outcomes in this area the next time the activity is run, greater levels of instructor intervention may need to be introduced to ensure the quality of feedback goes beyond expressions of sympathy to the critical application of theory to practice. This would entail monitoring the discussion more frequently and providing better, perhaps fading levels of scaffolding in the form of hints and prompts. While the difficulty here is finding the "ideal" balance between providing the necessary instructional support and encouraging students to be independent and self-directed learners, it is arguable that an element of control and structure is necessary when using a community-of-practice pedagogy with a group of novices.

In closing, for tertiary educators wishing to implement this or a similar type of exercise, it is recommended that participants are trained well in advance in the use of the technology, and that the purpose and goals of the activity are made explicit to them at the outset. At the same time, it is essential to have realistic expectations of what these students, as novice professionals, understand and are able to maturely deal with. An environment must also be created where peer learning, mutual support, and interdependence are encouraged and enabled though authentic tasks and appropriate technological support. In such contexts, students can engage in active roles as experts, co-learners, and protégés, in a dynamic endeavor that leads to professional learning. The psycho-social dimensions support individuals, and, by providing critical feedback, can lead to the generation of innovative ideas, while adding value to students' professional and interpersonal skills.

Recommended reading

Atkinson, T., and Claxton, G. (Eds.) (2000) *The Intuitive Practitioner: On the Value of Not Always Knowing What One Is Doing*. Buckingham, U.K.: Open University Press.

Bierema, L. L., and Merriam, S. B. (2002) E-mentoring: Using computer-mediated communication to enhance the mentoring process. *Innovative Higher Education*, **26**(3), 211–27.

Boud, D., Keogh, R., and Walker, D. (1985) *Reflection: Turning Experience into Learning*. London: Kogan Page.

Boyd, E. M., and Fales, A. W. (1983) Reflective learning: Key to learning from experience. *Journal of Humanistic Psychology*, **23**(2), 99–117.

Bright, B. (1996) Reflecting on "reflective practice". *Studies in the Education of Adults*, **28**(2), 162–84.

Cavallaro, F., and Tan, K. (2006) Computer-mediated peer-to-peer mentoring. *AACE Journal*, **14**(2), 129–38.

Colvin, J. (2007) Peer tutoring and social dynamics in higher education. *Mentoring & Tutoring*, **15**(2), 165–81.

Dewey, J. (1933) *How We Think: A Restatement of the Relation of Reflective Thinking to the Educative Process* (Revised Edition). Boston: D.C. Heath.

Durbridge, N. (1984) Audio-cassettes. In: A. W. Bates (Ed.), *The Role of Technology in Distance Education*. Beckenham, U.K.: Croom Helm.

English, R., and Duncan-Howell, J. (2008) Facebook goes to college: Using social networking tools to support students undertaking teaching practicum. *MERLOT Journal of Online Learning and Teaching*, **4**(4), 596–601.

Ensher, E., Heun, C., and Blanchard, A. (2003) Online mentoring and computer-mediated support: New directions in research. *Journal of Vocational Behavior*, **63**(2), 264–88.

Eraut, M. (1994) *Developing Professional Knowledge and Competence*. London: Falmer.

Feinman-Nemser, S. (2001) From preparation to practice: Designing a continuum to strengthen and sustain teaching. *Teachers College Record*, **103**(6), 1013–55.

Gutke, H., and Albion, P. (2008) Exploring the worth of online communities and e-mentoring programs for beginning teachers. In: K. McFerrin, R. Weber, R. Carlsen, and D. A. Willis (Eds.), *Proceedings of the Society for Information Technology and Teacher Education (SITE) International*

Conference 2008 (pp. 1416–23). Chesapeake, VA: Association for the Advancement of Computing in Education.

Kennet, K. (2010) Professionalism and reflective practice. In: S. Wallace (Ed.), *The Lifelong Learning Sector Reflective Reader*. Exeter, U.K.: Learning Matters.

Kilburg, G., and Hockett, E. (2007) E-mentoring: Providing support for teacher education graduates in their first year of teaching. In: C. Crawford, D. A. Willis, R. Carlsen, I. Gibson, K. McFerrin et al. (Eds.), *Proceedings of the Society for Information Technology and Teacher Education Conference 2007* (pp. 2021–5). Chesapeake, VA: Association for the Advancement of Computing in Education.

Kolb, D. (1984) *Experiential Learning*. Englewood Cliffs, NJ: Prentice Hall.

Moon, J. A. (2004) *A Handbook of Reflective and Experiential Learning: Theory and Practice*. London: Routledge Falmer.

Osterman, K. F., and Kottkamp, R. B. (1993) *Reflective Practice for Educators: Improving Schooling through Professional Development*. Thousand Oaks, CA: Corwin.

Paulus, T., and Scherff, L. (2008) "Can anyone offer any words of encouragement?": Online dialogue as a support mechanism for preservice teachers. *Journal of Technology and Teacher Education*, **16**(1), 113–36.

Pollard, A. (Ed.) (2002) *Readings for Reflective Teaching*. London: Continuum.

Pollard, A. (2008) *Reflective Teaching* (Third Edition). London: Continuum.

Posner, G. J., and Vivian, C. (2010) *Field Experience: A Guide to Reflective Teaching* (Seventh Edition). Boston: Allyn & Bacon.

Power, D. J. (1990) The use of audio in distance education. In: S. Timmers (Ed.), *Training Needs in the Use of Media for Distance Education* (pp. 43–60). Singapore: Asian Mass Communication Research and Information Centre.

Schön, D. A. (1983) *The Reflective Practitioner: How Professionals Think in Action*. London: Temple Smith.

Schön, D. A. (1987) *Educating the Reflective Practitioner: Toward a New Design for Teaching and Learning in the Professions*. San Francisco: Jossey-Bass.

Thomas, M. (2005) Opportunities and challenges of online mentoring in teacher education. In: P. Kommers and G. Richards (Eds.), *Proceedings of the World Conference on Educational Multimedia, Hypermedia, and Telecommunications 2005* (pp. 848–53). Chesapeake, VA: Association for the Advancement of Computing in Education.

Topping, K. J. (2005) Trends in peer learning. *Educational Psychology*, **25**(6), 631–45.

Tripp, D. (1993) *Critical Incidents in Teaching: Developing Professional Judgment*. London: Routledge.

Yang, S.-H. (2009) Using blogs to enhance critical reflection and community of practice. *Educational Technology & Society*, **12**(2), 11–21.

Supplemental materials

Appendix A Critical incident analysis

(adapted from the guide developed by the ProDAIT project at the University of Birmingham, available at

http://www.prodait.org/approaches/cia/)

A critical incident is something we interpret as a problem or a challenge in a particular context. For example, students may constantly arrive late to class, or talk among themselves when other students are presenting their ideas. Critical incident analysis is an approach to dealing with challenges in everyday practice. As reflective practitioners we need to pose problems about our practice, refusing to accept "what is". We need to explore incidents that occur in day-to-day work in order to understand them better and find alternative ways of reacting and responding to them. Critical incident analysis can help us to know more about how we operate, to question our own practice, allow us to develop understanding, and increase control of professional judgment. It can enable us to reflect on our practice and to explain and justify it.

David Tripp (1993), in his book *Critical Incidents in Teaching*, puts it simply: when something goes wrong we need to ask what happened and what caused it to happen. The guiding principle is to frame incidents as questions. Thus "students always come late to my class" changes to "why do students always come late to my class?" In this way, critical incidents can become turning points and lead to changes to our understanding. By asking "why did I do that?" or "why did I let them do that?" we are working on the values in our practice.

The following is one method for analyzing critical incidents (these steps have been adapted from Coventry University (2001) Critical incident analysis. Retrieved February 15, 2012, from

http://web.archive.org/web/20051216020630/
http://legacywww.coventry.ac.uk/legacy/ched/research/critical.htm):

1. Select a critical episode: for example, students continually arriving late, or students talking during class discussions. Note that very often a critical incident is personal to an individual. Incidents only become critical – that is, problematic – if the individual sees them in this way. It is after the event occurs that it is defined as critical (i.e., in retrospect).

2. Describe the incident, including
    - When and where it happened (time of day, location, social context)
    - What actually happened (who said and/or did what)
    - What you were thinking and feeling at the time and immediately after the incident.
3. Interrogate your description by asking the following questions:
    - Why did this incident stand out?
    - What was going on?
    - Were there different levels of "behavior" or activity?
    - Did I bring personal bias or a particular mindset to the event?
    - Could I have interpreted this event differently from another point of view?
    - What can I learn from this episode?
    - What can I do to progress toward a resolution of the problem(s) it suggests?
4. Invite a friend or colleague *not involved in the episode* to share your account of the episode and discuss your interpretation. Then, modify your analysis, where necessary, in the light of his/her perspective and suggestions/advice.
5. Where appropriate, you may want to compare your analysis with the views of other key people involved in the episode (e.g., colleagues, supervisors).
6. Briefly write up your report. Remember to take the necessary steps to protect the confidentiality of all those involved (e.g., by referring to them using pseudonyms), particularly if your report will be publicly shared or distributed.

Appendix B

Table 24.1 Assessment rubric for peer e-mentoring activity

Criteria	Excellent	Good	Fair	Poor
Selection of critical incidents	Identification of appropriate incidents for reporting that are highly significant, interesting, and challenging	Identification of appropriate incidents for reporting that are significant, interesting, and at least mildly challenging	Identification of incidents for reporting that are somewhat interesting and significant	Poor choice of incidents for reporting
Critical reflection upon experiences and learning	Consistent and coherent critical reflection that is deeply insightful and well articulated	Consistent and coherent critical reflection that is clearly articulated	Satisfactory critical reflection, demonstrating some ability to move beyond the recounting and describing of incidents	Solely descriptive postings, with little or no evidence of critical reflection
Engagement with and application of literature	Evidence of deep engagement with, and extensive application of, practicum course readings. Several references to relevant wider literature	Evidence of engagement with practicum course readings, with attempts to apply them to the activity. Few references to relevant wider literature	Evidence of limited, surface-level engagement with and application of practicum course readings. No references to wider literature, or references bearing little relevance	Little or no evidence of engagement with and application of practicum course readings. No references to wider literature
Connection of prior learning to practical experiences	Highly robust and profound connections made to course content from previously studied courses	Reasonably strong and sensible connections made to course content from previously studied courses	Cursory connections made to course content from previously studied courses	No connections made to course content from previously studied courses

Criteria	Excellent	Good	Fair	Poor
Participation in and contribution to the online community	Postings exceed the stipulated requirements in terms of number and frequency. Successful networking, relationship building, and collaborative problem solving carried out over the entire duration of the activity. Reciprocity shown, as seen in the quantity and quality of postings, with others' postings analyzed and built upon to generate meaningful discussion	Postings meet the stipulated requirements in terms of number and frequency. Networking, relationship-building, and collaborative problem-solving efforts sustained over most of the duration of the activity. Reciprocity shown, as seen in the quantity and quality of postings, with existing postings elaborated upon through further observations and comments	Postings meet the stipulated requirements in terms of number and average frequency, but are not done consistently and regularly throughout the duration of the activity. Shallow contributions made that do not enrich the discussion (e.g., merely stating agreement or disagreement in response to others' postings)	Postings do not meet the minimum requirements of the activity in terms of number and frequency. Few or no follow-up responses to others' postings
Offering of feedback and assistance to peers	Feedback and emotional support provided both preemptively and in a timely fashion in response to others' requests for help. Constructive suggestions offered that are clearly explained and supported by	Feedback and emotional support given in a timely fashion in response to others' requests, with some constructive suggestions offered, but room for improvement exists in the clarity of the explanation and/	Feedback given to others primarily empathetic or sympathetic in nature, with little or no constructive suggestions included, or simplistic and not accompanied by any useful explanation	Feedback either off topic, too late to be of use, or rudely/ harshly stated with no constructive suggestions offered. No attempt made to justify the (purely critical) stance adopted

(continued)

Appendix B (*continued*)

Table 23.1 Assessment rubric for peer-ementoring activity (*continued*)

Criteria	Excellent	Good	Fair	Poor
Offering of feedback and assistance to peers (cont.)	a well-argued rationale that draws on specific examples from own experiences and/or the literature	or the strength of the underpinning rationale.		
Reception and use of feedback from peers	Feedback and critique from others actively solicited, discussed in detail, and where appropriate adopted and operationalized, with a view to improving long-term practice	Feedback from others sought largely to address immediate needs and difficulties, then accepted and applied following some thoughtful discussion	Feedback from others rarely requested but accepted when offered, though this is often done unquestioningly, in the absence of thoughtful discussion	Feedback from others constantly refused or rejected without clear reasoning
Mediation of responses and respect for contrasting viewpoints	Participation by others welcomed and encouraged. Own ideas and beliefs assertively defended while having the flexibility needed to engage in a balanced debate. Genuine receptiveness and open-mindedness displayed, including a serious desire to listen to, consider, and where applicable accommodate and assimilate differing points of view	Own ideas and beliefs openly expressed while allowing others to do the same, but others' perspectives treated superficially and not actually considered as plausible alternatives	Own ideas and beliefs stated while displaying tolerance for those of others, but others' perspectives generally ignored, passed over, or quickly dismissed	Refusal to give others an opportunity to voice their opinions, marked by continual dominance of the discussion and deliberate blocking or stymieing of others' attempts to contribute

Criteria	Excellent	Good	Fair	Poor
Questioning of key topics and issues	Varied, strategic, and creative questioning used effectively and consistently to reflect deeply on key topics and issues, as well as to challenge own assumptions and those held by others about those issues	Varied and strategic questioning used effectively and consistently to reflect further on key topics and issues	Some basic questioning used to reflect further on key topics and issues	Inadequate use of questioning as a reflective tool
Examination of changes in own knowledge, skills, and beliefs	Extensive connections made between old and new learning, with explicit links made to own beliefs about pedagogy, classroom management, and the teaching profession	Several connections made between old and new learning that are related to own beliefs about pedagogy, classroom management, and the teaching profession	Few connections made between old and new learning, with some mention of own beliefs about pedagogy, classroom management, and the teaching profession	No connections made between old and new learning, and little or no reference made to own beliefs about pedagogy, classroom management, and the teaching profession
Clarity of expression and mechanics	Precise and highly engaging language used in oral and written components of the activity. Written components free or almost free of grammar, spelling, and punctuation errors	Fluent and creative language used in oral and written components of the activity. Written components contain few grammar, spelling, and punctuation errors	Appropriate language used in oral and written components of the activity. Written components contain some grammatical, spelling, and punctuation errors	Basic language used in oral and written components of the activity. Written components contain many grammatical, spelling, and punctuation errors

25

Using opinion leaders on Twitter to amplify PR and marketing messages

Sarah H. VanSlette

Abstract: This project is a component of a larger social media campaign assignment for a client (usually a nonprofit). Students are tasked with using the microblogging tool, Twitter, to amplify the reach of their campaign via a retweet (RT) by an opinion leader or "celebrity." Over the course of the semester, students build a Twitter campaign, sending messages about their client to their personal followers. Along the way, students will try to appropriately engage a "celebrity" Twitter account by @ing them in messages about their cause (putting the celebrity's Twitter handle within the message), perhaps even directly requesting a RT by that celebrity. If the opinion leader is persuaded to tweet about the client or RTs the student's tweet to their many followers, this could be a game changer for the campaign. A RT to that many followers would be a huge coup to any PR or marketing campaign because of the large new audience that will be viewing the message. That new audience may, in turn, RT the message again (further amplifying the message), and also may start following the student for more news about the campaign and/or the client.

Key words: anywhere/anytime technologies, microblogging, mobile phone, multimedia sharing sites, tablet apps, Twitter, TwitPic, YouTube.

Discipline/Academic areas addressed

Public relations, marketing, and strategic communication.

Instructional purpose

Students need to understand the power of opinion leaders within any public relations or marketing campaign. While it may take work to compel an opinion leader to endorse your client or cause by tweeting about it or simply retweeting (RTing) your message to them about your client, this publicity can be immensely valuable. Additionally, PR and marketing students need to understand how to use Twitter with consideration and propriety, how to write short (within the 140-character Twitter limit), compelling messages and to think of ways to creatively engage their audiences (celebrity, or otherwise).

Student learning outcomes

1. Students will understand how to use Twitter to send strategic messages, to link to websites, photos, and videos using their Twitter account, and to identify opinion leaders on Twitter.
2. Students will demonstrate creativity and perseverance through tweets that engage their followers and that develop new followers.
3. Students will be able to strategically craft messages about their campaign/client that attract opinion leaders and will promote both RTs and unique tweets about their campaign/client by their Twitter followers.
4. Students will learn how to evaluate their campaign by assessing their Twitter RTs, their direct messages (DMs) from followers about the campaign, and tweets to them from followers (@s) about the campaign.

Prerequisite skills and knowledge

This assignment requires access to the Internet via computer, smartphone, or other device. Some knowledge of flip cameras, smartphones, or other digital recording devices is helpful, but not essential, as students can learn how to create videos using online tutorials such as

http://www.youtube.com/watch?v=3zFePU1uvtc

or

www.wondershare.com/.../video-slideshow-maker.html

Step-by-step directions

1. Prior to the start of the semester, select a client (nonprofits from the local community make a good choice). Decide what PR/marketing needs the client has that can be addressed in a three month long social media campaign. An example from my class is an awareness campaign about the local community's problem with sex trafficking and what can be done to stop it.

2. At the start of the semester, have the client come to class to discuss the campaign goals and objectives. Make it clear that it is a social media campaign and the use of Twitter, YouTube, TwitPic (and any other SM tools you prefer) is a requirement. Students should set up their accounts on these websites immediately if they haven't already done so, for a required discussion on ethically appropriate uses of Twitter and other social media to promote a cause, but at the same time, not create spam (or Twitter equivalent), and to also respectfully link the cause or client to a celebrity without cyberstalking or abusing that person's status.

3. Students work on the campaign tweeting regularly about their client and/or their cause/industry. Each week they must send at least five campaign-related tweets per student (all must include the client's Twitter handle) with at least three tweets per week that include a link to a website (usually the client's website), and can include student-made videos, student photos, related news stories on the Web, and videos/photos created by the client.

4. As a class, the students need to create at least two videos about the campaign over the course of the semester, and post them to YouTube:

   http://www.youtube.com/watch?v=NlCQrSVMzfM

   As individuals, students need to post at least two photos related to the campaign over the course of the semester, and post them to TwitPic.
5. Early on, students must identify opinion leaders that will be relevant to their client and campaign. These opinion leaders must have many followers (thousands or even millions), a reputation that is in line with the mission of the client and the campaign goals, and tweet regularly. An example from my class: For the campaign to stop local sex trafficking, students targeted the Polaris Project, which is a leading nonprofit organization committed to ending human trafficking

(@Polaris_Project); the actors and anti-trafficking advocates, Demi Moore (@mrskutcher) and Ashton Kutcher (@aplusk), along with their foundation (@dnafoundation) that works to end sex slavery around the world.

6. Students are encouraged to @ the opinion-leaders with messages about their client or campaign. Students may want to consider coordinating the class's tweets to the opinion leaders in the hopes of getting a RT or a unique tweet from them about the campaign/client.

7. At the end of the campaign, students evaluate the campaign by reviewing how many tweets they each sent out with the client's Twitter handle in the message, how many RTs they each got (and how many people were reached by counting the followers of all who retweeted the client-related messages), how many @s they each got about the campaign (tweets from followers that included the student's and client's Twitter handle), any DMs they each got about the campaign, and how many new followers the client gained overall. This evaluation, along with recommendations for future social media campaigns that the client may undertake, should be written in a business-style report and submitted to the client and the professor at the end of the semester.

Approximate time required

- First week spent on introduction to the client and the client's goals/objectives, along with familiarizing the students with Twitter, YouTube, TwitPic, and any other social media tools.
- Campaign runs 12 weeks, with students tweeting five times per week outside of classroom time.
- Final campaign evaluation and report compilation takes 2 weeks.

Required resources

Required websites

www.twitter.com *www.twitpic.com* *www.youtube.com*

- Twitter tips

  http://support.twitter.com/groups/31-twitter-basics

- How to upload a video to YouTube

  http://support.google.com/youtube/bin/answer.py?hl=en&answer=57924

Technical requirements

- A computer and access to the Internet *or* a smartphone with Twitter, TwitPic, and YouTube apps.
- Flip cameras and digital cameras *or* smartphones with camera functions and video recording device.
- Flip camera support

  http://support.theflip.com/en-us/home

- Inspiration for making viral videos that are actually advertisements

  http://mashable.com/2011/05/31/viral-video-advertising/

Variations on the basic theme

The opinion leaders who students identify on Twitter may also have Facebook pages and/or a blog. While it may lead to a more difficult evaluation at the end, students could attempt to engage general followers as well as opinion leaders using a myriad of social media tools: tweeting about the campaign on Twitter; posting comments on their Facebook walls and by posting comments on the walls of opinion leaders; blogging about the campaign while leaving comments on the opinion leaders' blogs, etc. This broader approach to the campaign could utilize Twitter, Facebook, YouTube, TwitPic, Flickr, WordPress, Tumblr, Blogspot, etc. The students could use as many social media tools as they can manage.

Observations and advice

Many students had never used Twitter before my class, so a considerable amount of time was spent in class the first week discussing what Twitter is and how it functions as a PR/marketing tool. I tracked students' progress by following all of them on Twitter for the duration of the semester. As a result, I saw both personal and class-related tweets. This led to a number of class discussions about how to appropriately present ourselves to the world using social media. I also learned that many students don't use Twitter to its fullest potential, instead using it more as a free texting service between them and their friends. That led to more class discussions about finding good content on Twitter and following people or organizations that offer helpful or interesting tweets. When the class first started "Twitter bombing" our opinion leaders, we got no response, and it was frustrating. But students saw an opportunity to piggyback on a new campaign being launched by @dnafoundation (called "The Real Men" campaign) and saw that Demi and Ashton were constantly tweeting about the "Real Men" campaign. Students used the key words "Real Men" in tweets about our client, and started creating videos and photos about the "Real Men" in our class who were fighting to end sex trafficking, linked those videos and pictures to tweets @mrskutcher, @dnafoundation, and @aplusk. This was the tipping point of our campaign. Once Demi Moore and the DNA Foundation saw the tweets sent by our students, linking to videos and photos created by our students, they not only RTd them but they also sent unique tweets encouraging their followers to watch our videos and view our photos. Our client gained a lot of new Twitter followers that semester, mainly due to the opinion leaders who lent us credibility and visibility. The class was ecstatic when they started getting RTs and tweets from Demi and the DNA Foundation, and started to immediately see the power of an opinion leader in a PR campaign.

Recommended reading

Ankeny, J. (2009) How Twitter is revolutionizing business. *Entrepreneur*, **37**(12), 26–32.

Evans, L. (2010) *Social Media Marketing*. Indianapolis, IN: Que Publishing.

Fathi, S. (2009) Avoiding hashtag hijacking and other Twitter fouls. *Public Relations Tactics*, **16**(11), 13–22.

Gillette, F. (2010, July 15) Twitter, Twitter, little stars. *Bloomberg Businessweek*, 64–7.

Jansen, B. J., Zhang, M., Sobel, K., and Chowdury, A. (2009) Twitter power: Tweets as electronic word of mouth. *Journal of the American Society for Information Science and Technology*, **60**(11), 2169–88.

Lowe, B., and Laffey, D. (2011) Is Twitter for the birds?: Using Twitter to enhance student learning in a marketing course. *Journal of Marketing Education*, **33**(2), 183–92.

Moody, M. (2010) Teaching Twitter and beyond: Tips for incorporating social media in traditional courses. *Journal of Magazine & New Media Research*, **11**(2), 1–9.

O'Reilly, T., and Milstein, S. (2009) *The Twitter Book*. Sebastopol, CA: O'Reilly Media.

Qualman, E. (2011) *Socialnomics*. Hoboken, NJ: Wiley.

Rinaldo, S. B., Tapp, S., and Laverie, D. A. (2011) Learning by Tweeting: Using Twitter as a pedagogical tool. *Journal of Marketing Education*, **33**(2), 193–203.

Rybalko, S., and Seltzer, T. (2010) Dialogic communication in 140 characters or less: How Fortune 500 companies engage stakeholders using Twitter. *Public Relations Review*, **36**(4), 336–41.

Scott, D. M. (2010) *The New Rules of Marketing and PR: How to Use Social Media, Blogs, News Releases, Online Video, and Viral Marketing to Reach Buyers Directly*. Hoboken, NJ: Wiley.

Solis, B., and Breakenridge, D. (2009) *Putting the Public Back in Public Relations: How Social Media Is Reinventing the Aging Business of PR*. Upper Saddle River, NJ: FT Press.

Warren, M. (2011) Why should Twitter matter to marketers? *Marketing Magazine*, **116**(14), 54.

Index